Iceland
The First New Society

Iceland

The First New Society

Richard F. Tomasson

Department of Sociology
The University of New Mexico

UNIVERSITY OF MINNESOTA PRESS □ MINNEAPOLIS

949.12
TÓM

Publication of this book was assisted by a grant
from the publications program of the National Endowment
for the Humanities, an independent federal agency.

Published by the University of Minnesota Press,
2037 University Avenue Southeast,
Minneapolis, Minnesota 55455
Printed in the United States of America

Library of Congress Cataloging in Publication Data

Tomasson, Richard F   1928-
      Iceland, the first new society.

      Bibliography: p.
      Includes index.
      1. Iceland--Civilization. I. Title.
DL326.T65   949.1'2   79-19080
ISBN 0-8166-0913-6

Foreword

For the author of a work called *The First New Nation*, a book entitled *Iceland: The First New Society* is intriguing. Richard F. Tomasson well demonstrates that Iceland deserves this description. Once a completely uninhabited land, the island was settled by the Norse between 870 and 930, fully six centuries before Columbus landed in the West Indies.

Iceland appears to be truly a fragment culture of medieval Europe. Lacking an aboriginal population to conquer or exploit, and never recruiting from a non-Nordic immigrant population, Iceland has remained, culturally, the purest Scandinavian nation. Modern Icelandic is much closer to the language spoken during the Middle Ages than any other living European tongue. Icelandic kinship terminology is close to the ancient forms of the Teutonic tribes. The relations between the sexes, which are surprisingly egalitarian, do not represent an adjustment to modern values but rather are continuations of the old pre-Christian northern customs, as are the Icelandic betrothal patterns. The rate of illegitimate births is remarkably high, an apparent reflection of the continuity between the modern Icelandic society and the medieval pre-Christian society that held a "tolerant and accepting view of [premarital] sexual behavior and its fruits." Unlike much of continental Scandinavia, Iceland "has been little affected by any form of evangelical Protestantism" and has had a generally permissive attitude toward many forms of behavior that are defined as immoral by pietistic Christians.

As a new society, Iceland, like frontier America, was and remains committed to egalitarianism in class relationships. Income differentiation is relatively low, the rate of social mobility is high, and social interaction and marriage across occupational class lines are easy and common. Literacy has been nearly universal for centuries. The num-

v

ber of books sold each year to the 225,000 Icelanders is fantastic by American and European standards.

Tomasson is to be congratulated for introducing the culture of Iceland to the international world of social science scholarship. He demonstrates that the importance of a nation for comparative analysis is not related to its size; in fact, the very opposite may be true. By intensively studying a distinct national culture—which, because of its limited size, can be looked at in terms of all its characteristics—it is possible to discover more about the potential for cultural variation in all societies than it is from examining large, complex, regional, and ethnically and religiously heterogeneous societies in which it is difficult to separate out distinct analytical elements.

This study of Icelandic culture may well prove to be but the first major study of this society. It is clear from the data reported in this book that many of our assumptions about the necessary interrelations among social variables may be oversimplified. Thus, sexual and familial egalitarianism, raising children in a nondiscriminatory fashion appears to be compatible with a highly differentiated occupational structure in which very few women hold high-level positions within the economy or polity. Although "a low degree of class consciousness combined with a radical egalitarian ethic" stemming from its origin as a new society continue to characterize Iceland, "there has been a tendency for leading political figures to come from a few high status families."

Economic and social egalitarianism and one of the highest standards of living in the world go hand in hand with a political system in which a communist party secures a larger percentage of the vote (23 percent in 1978) than in any Western nation except Italy and in which political conflict between factions is bitter. An easygoing, permissive religious culture in which almost no one attends church services has been congruent with strong support for temperance. In 1915, Iceland was "the first country to enact total prohibition, seven years before the United States," and the island nation continues to outlaw "beer with an alcoholic content in excess of 2.25 percent" in the belief that discouraging the consumption of strong beer will affect the legal use of strong liquor. In contradiction to the generally accepted sociological principle that all societies "have a norm that every child should have a social 'father,'" Tomasson reports that there are many unwed mothers in Iceland without functional fathers for their children.

Iceland, as described by Tomasson, has a fascinating, often contradictory culture. Tomasson's book not only informs us about the Icelandic culture, but also should encourage a stream of sociological tourists, scholars who may want to look intensively at the way this "new society" has managed to incorporate such diverse behavioral patterns into a stable culture.

Seymour Martin Lipset
Stanford University

Preface

*Iceland is a rock in the ocean surrounded by fish—take
away the fish and what have you got left?*
                                    Hans G. Andersen (1976)

*Iceland is a country of quite exceptional interest, not only
in its physical but also in its historical aspects. The Icelanders
are the smallest in number of the civilized nations of the
world. . . . The island . . . is a Nation, with a language,
a national character, a body of traditions that are all its
own. . . . Nowhere else, except in Greece, was so much
produced that attained . . . so high a level of excellence.*
                                    James Bryce (1916)

Some years ago the *Iceland Review* (1968), an English-language
quarterly published in Reykjavík, asked several Icelandic writers an
open-ended question: what is Iceland? The writers' answers were
diverse. One pointed out that Iceland is "a sort of national park of
Nordic culture"; another, that the country "is a hard, cold land, and
barely habitable"; another, with the most weighty answer of all, that
Iceland is "the third peak in the medieval history of European civilization after Greece and Rome"; still another, that it is the "remembered and continuing land of frontiersmen." Add to these the
observations of Andersen and Bryce and we have a good array of
starting points for a macrosociological comprehension of Icelandic
society.

All of these observations make up the foundations of this book.
And I have added two more: First, a structural and cultural continuity has characterized this island society during the eleven centuries
of its existence. Throughout this examination of the Icelandic society
there is a persistent concern with these continuities—the results of

the society's isolation, small size, homogeneity, and unique national literary tradition. I have tried to be aware of what discontinuity there is, too, and it is clear that it has been rapidly increasing from the effects of the internationalization of Icelandic culture and the pressures of advanced modernization..A second observation, one that is reflected in the title of the book, is that Iceland can be seen as a fragment new society (Hartz, 1964), which, like the other New World societies, is an offshoot of a European mother country — Viking Norway. The similarity of the title to that of Seymour Martin Lipset's book — *The First New Nation: The United States in Comparative and Historical Perspective* (1963) — is fully intended. Iceland is the first new society founded *prior* to the modern period (Lipset's frame of reference) and whose origins are known to history.

I have made use of a variety of Icelandic sources in this undertaking, together with the extensive travel literature that exists for Iceland. I also have the kind of familiarity that comes from having lived in a country for some time (a total of more than twelve months between 1964 and 1973). In addition, I interviewed a representative sample of 100 Icelandic adults in 1971. The details of this project are to be found in chapter 5, and my interview schedule is reproduced in appendix A. Until recent years, there has been almost no social research in Iceland, but this has changed since the recent institution of a sociology department at the University of Iceland. My interview study was, as a matter of fact, the first systematic attempt to gather information on the beliefs, behavior, and knowledge of the Icelanders in a number of areas.

A small but continual problem in writing about Iceland is the spelling of proper and place names. My solution, I am sure, is as unsatisfactory as all of the others. Icelandic has four letters that do not appear in English:

Ð,ð   pronounced as *th* in *the*
Þ, þ   pronounced as *th* in *think*
Æ, æ   pronounced as *i* in *like*
Ö, ö   pronounced as *i* in *bird*

These letters are used in the spelling of names except for the þ (thorn), which can be exactly transliterated into English as unvoiced *th*; hence, I write Thorsteinn, not Þorsteinn, but Sigurður, not Sigurdur. An accent over a vowel never means stress — Icelandic words invariably put the stress on the first syllable — but that it has a different sound from the usual. Icelandic names are inflected, and I use the nominative form, for example, Haraldur, not Harald. The careful reader may think I have made a number of mistakes in the spelling of Icelandic names, but I do not think this is the case; at least I have been careful about spelling. In the bibliography, for example, one will note there is a Stefánsson, two Stefanssons, a Steffensen, and a Stephensen; the first is the conventional spelling of the Icelandic patronymic meaning son of Stefán, the second is the spelling of the names of two Icelanders outside of the country writing in English, and the remaining two are Danified family names. Incidentally, the spelling of my name is purely and almost uniquely Icelandic, but I am not an Icelander, nor am I of Icelandic descent. Indeed, I barely knew more than where the country was before my first visit there in 1964.

I would like to express my appreciation to the late Fru Catherine Djurklou, past Director of the Swedish Fulbright Commission for giving me the opportunity to visit Iceland for ten days in 1964, and to John Berg (now in Copenhagen) who was then Director of the Icelandic Fulbright Commission and a good host. For financial support I wish to express my gratitude to the National Endowment for the Humanities which made me a Senior Fellow enabling me to spend the whole academic year 1970-71 in Iceland. The Research Allocations Committee of the University of New Mexico paid for my transportation and helped support me in Iceland for the summer of 1973, and later supplied a grant for typing the manuscript of this book. Among the individuals I would like to acknowledge for diverse sorts of help are Robert and Thórunn Boulter, Björn Björnsson, Jesse Byock, Pétur Guðjónsson, Jóhann S. Hannesson, Andri Ísaksson, Sigurður A. Magnússon, Ólafur Ragnar Grímsson, Sveinn Hauksson, the late Sigurður Nordal, the late Stefán Einarsson, Thora Tanner (of Albuquerque), Thor Vilhjálmsson, Bragi Jósepsson, Ottar Thorgilsson (of Massachusetts), and Franklin D. Scott. I would like to note my appreciation to William J. Goode, who vigorously criticized an early draft of part of Chapter 4. Berglind Ásgeirsdottír, Chief of the Information Division of the Icelandic Foreign Ministry, obtained for me most of the pictures in this book. Gregory C. Zimmerman competently prepared the maps. Above all, I would like to thank Tamara Holzapfel who didn't know much about Iceland when I began this book, but learned a lot in the process and helped me in countless ways, and last, but not least, Jule Ensminger Gargoura for her continual good humor while typing the manuscript, and always.

Contents

LIST OF TABLES

xiv   Contents

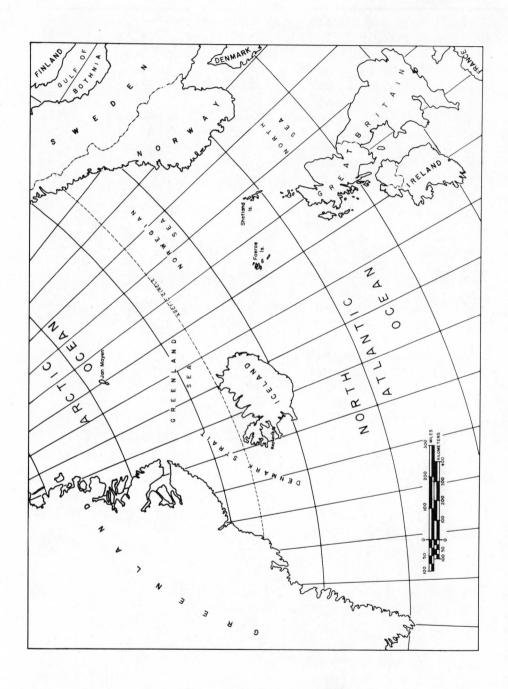

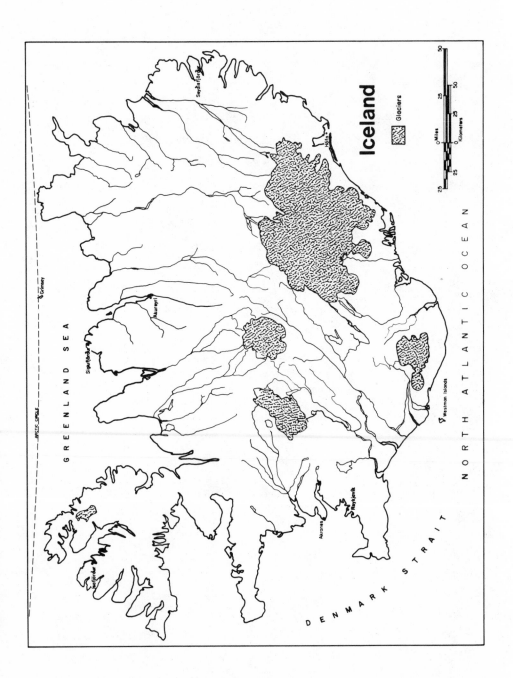

It is true that it is a sunny island.

Charles Edmond (1857)

Iceland
The First New Society

CHAPTER 1

The First
New Society

*Much of the story of Iceland is repeated in that of the early
white settlers in America.*

Ellsworth Huntington (1924)

*Europe develops many teleologies but because it intertwines
them with one another, because it locks them together in a
seething whole, it gives none of them the freedom to evolve.
The fragments provide that freedom. . . . A part detaches
itself from the whole . . . and the part develops without
inhibition. The process is as simple, as intelligible as any historical process we take for granted.*

Louis Hartz (1964)

Iceland can be spoken of as a "new nation" and a "new society" in the
same way these concepts are used by Seymour Martin Lipset (1963)
and Louis Hartz (1964). There are also some parallels between the Icelandic and the American experiences as new nations. I do not mean to
challenge Lipset's view of America as "the first new nation." He sees
America as first only in the modern period, a world that was postfeudal,
post-Protestant, and postcapitalist. Iceland, by contrast, was founded
centuries earlier in a different historical epoch, in the middle of the
period of the great expansion of the Scandinavian peoples (A.D. 800-
1050). And there are numerous other differences, but there remain
some noteworthy similarities in their dynamics of development, too.

What is significant is that new nations are confronted by similar
challenges and experiences. This is particularly true of those that have
come into being through distant overseas migration. In addition to
being new nations, they are "fragment societies," a species of society
with different dynamics than "whole societies." In the words of Louis
Hartz (1964, pp. 3-4), whose terms these are:

3

When a part of a European nation is detached from the whole of it, and hurled outward onto new soil, it loses the stimulus toward change that the whole provides. It lapses into a kind of immobility. Nor does it matter what stage of European history the part embodies, whether it is feudal, as in Latin America and French Canada, bourgeois, as in the United States, Dutch South Africa, and English Canada, or actually radical, charged with the proletarian turmoil of the Industrial Revolution, as in Australia and British South Africa. The fragments reflect every phase of the European revolution, but they evince alike the immobilities of fragmentation. . . . When a fragment of Europe becomes the whole of a new nation, it becomes unrecognizable in European terms.

Iceland, then, can properly be placed in that category of fragment new societies like America or Australia, New Zealand or Argentina that are offshoots of a European mother country, transmuted by transmarine migration and faced with similar challenges of establishing national autonomy and nation building. Indeed, Iceland is the first "new nation" to have come into being in the full light of history, and it is the only European society whose origins are known. Perhaps, though, we should not even regard Iceland as a European nation, but rather we should consider it, as Vilhjalmur Stefansson (1939) does, as "the first American republic." After all, the line dividing the Eastern and Western hemispheres cuts east of the center of Iceland.

THE ORIGINS OF THE ICELANDERS

Iceland was settled in the six decades between 870 and 930. (See Brøndsted, 1965; Foote and Wilson, 1970; Jón Jóhannesson, 1974.) Before the middle of the tenth century, all of the pastureland in Iceland had been taken. According to Ari the Learned (1067-1148), who wrote the *Book of the Icelanders*, the earliest history of Iceland: "Wise men have said . . . that in the space of sixty years Iceland was fully occupied, so that after that there was no further taking of land" (translated by Gwyn Jones, 1964, p. 103). At this time, the population of the country was probably between 20,000 and 30,000 (Steffensen, 1968).

It is clear from the *Book of Settlements* (1972), first completed early in the twelfth century, that most of the settlers were Norwegians, with a minority of Irish and Scots. Most of the Norwegian settlers did not migrate directly from Norway but came to Iceland indirectly after spending some years in Britain and Ireland, the Hebrides and Orkney. Many brought Celtic wives and slaves. Of those who came directly from Norway, most came from the southwest, particularly from Sogn and Hordaland. Some also came from north Norway, but few came from the eastern part of the country. There were also a handful of Danes and Swedes, and a few from other places.

The settlement of Iceland was a part of the dispersion of the Nordic peoples, a movement that occupied the Scandinavians from the late eighth century into the eleventh. The defeat of the invading Harald the Ruthless at Stamford Bridge in 1066 marked the end of the Viking era, at least for the Norwegians. During this period, the Vikings traveled westward to Britain, Ireland, France, the islands in the North Atlantic, and the coast of North America. To the east, they settled around the Baltic, went into Russia, and traveled south to Constantinople. They even made sojourns into Spain, Italy, and North Africa. Scholars emphasize different reasons for this outpouring from the north. Some stress the shortage of land and the pressure of a growing population; others emphasize the desire for adventure, plunder, and honor—values so strong among the ancient Scandinavians. Of importance for the specific migration out of Norway was the desire to escape the rule of Harald Fairhair, who had succeeded in unifying Norway during the second half of the ninth century and was trying to force all of the petty chieftains to submit to his rule, which many refused to do. What made the fantastic exploits of the Norsemen possible—and this is beyond question—were their extraordinary advancements in the art of shipbuilding (Brøndsted, 1965, pp. 139-47). Other Europeans did not begin to catch up with the Vikings' achievements in shipbuilding until after Columbus's time, and the Viking longships traveled faster than any vessels built before the invention of the steamship, a millennium later. When the weather was good, the Icelanders could make it to Norway in four days, but seven or eight days was more typical.

Things were not going at all well for the Vikings in the British Isles at the end of the ninth century, and Iceland must have appeared a welcome refuge with its abundance of pastureland and hot springs. This appeal accounts for the rapid settlement of Iceland at that time. The Vikings were defeated in Wessex and Mercia by Alfred the Great at the end of the ninth century, they were thrown out of Dublin in 901 or 902, and at about the same time they became insecure in Scotland and the Hebrides.

While no one denies that most of the settlers of Iceland came either directly or indirectly from Norway—this has been specifically documented by the *Book of Settlements*—the theory has been put forth by Barði Guðmundsson (1967) that the dominant element among the settlers and in the culture that came to dominate Iceland originated in eastern Scandinavia, most likely in Denmark. He argues that the customs of the early Icelanders and the West Norwegians were so strikingly different on so many counts that they could not have belonged to the same people. He points out that the West Norwegians cremated their dead while the Icelanders never did. Guðmundsson's other examples of the differences include the greater independence and status of women in Iceland, the disappearance of the tradition of Scaldic poetry from Norway after the emigrants left, the absence of primogeniture in Iceland, and the much greater role of the fertility god Frey in Iceland. In addition, he points out numerous lesser differences. Specifically, Guðmundsson considers the Icelanders to be descendants of the Heruli, a particularly migratory group of East Scandinavians who had settled in West Norway but did not assimilate West Norse culture. He challenges the centuries-old assumption that the Icelanders are of West Norwegian origin and culture. But his thesis remains less than fully convincing. Jón Jóhannesson (1974, p. 20), who wrote the most comprehensive history of medieval Iceland, observed that it is "strange" that the "Danish origin [of the Icelanders] should be completely forgotten. Also, it is hard to explain how the Icelanders could have managed to introduce a Danish mode of government into their new society at the same time they founded their laws on the law-code of the Gulathing of western Norway."

What proportion of the early settlers were Scandinavian and what proportion were Celtic is a topic on which there is conflicting evidence (Fridriksson, 1971; Gunnar Hannesson, 1925; Bjarnason et al., 1973). The blood groupings of modern Icelanders more closely resemble those of the Irish than of the Norwegians (in the former, O type is most common; in the latter, A type). The Icelanders also have more redheads and dark-haired people than the Norwegians. On the other hand, the colors of modern Icelanders' eyes and skin are very similar to those of the Norwegians. The culture that took root in Iceland was, however, Scandinavian. Irish influences are apparent in a few proper names, some place names, and a few words in the language (Sveinsson, 1959). Some students of Icelandic literature claim that, while there are few specific Irish influences, Irish culture made a diffuse impact on Icelandic culture and literature (Stefán Einarsson, 1957, pp. 5-6).

THE FOUNDING OF ICELAND

One of the most readily apparent ways whereby new societies differ from old ones is that new societies know their origins and how they came into being and old ones do not. This knowledge assumes major importance in the history and mythology of a new nation. One of the first tasks of new nations is to develop unifying myths, a sense of national distinctiveness and nationhood. Americans celebrate the landing of the first pilgrim settlers and the taming of the West, Afrikaners revere the *trekboers* who conquered and occupied the wilderness of South Africa during the eighteenth century, and Argentines respect the freedom of the pampas typified above all by the gauchos. Icelanders celebrate the founding of Icelandic society and the early history of their island, particularly the century around 930-1030 known in Icelandic chronology as the Saga Age. This is the period during which the sagas of the Icelanders take place. The earliest historical writings also deal with this period. An early version of the *Book of Settlements* (1972, p. 6) even tells us that, among other reasons, it was written to establish for "foreigners" the accurate ancestry of the Icelanders.

> People often say that writing about the Settlement is irrelevant learning, but we think we can better meet the criticism of foreigners when they accuse us of being descended from slaves or scoundrels, if we know for certain the truth about our ancestry. And for those who want to know ancient lore and how to trace genealogies, it's better to start at the beginning than to come in at the middle. Anyway, all civilized nations want to know about the origins of their own society and the beginnings of their own race.

Aside from being great contributions to world literature, the sagas are the folk literature of Iceland—Icelandic equivalents of American Westerns. Their subject is the conflicts of the yeoman farmers who were the original settlers and their children and grandchildren. The sagas are accounts of prototypical frontiersmen in continual strife with their neighbors. They are a kind of historical fiction; many of the characters are known to have lived and many of the events are known to have occurred. Parts of the sagas are close to history, and parts are pure fiction. Even though the origins of Iceland lie farther back in time than those of the other new societies, the mythology of the founding is more coherent and peopled with more concrete figures than is that of any other new nation. Magnus Magnusson (*Iceland Review*, 1968, p. 43), the Icelandic-Scottish translator of many sagas into English, is quite correct in his assertion that "much, much more than the garbled and debased mythology of the Wild West, Iceland is the remembered and continuing land of frontiersmen."

However, there is one major challenge that the Icelanders never had to face: a population indigenous to their new land. Here one of the central themes of new societies is missing, the interplay of settlers and natives. Iceland was in fact the largest uninhabited area settled in historical times. One basic disadvantage the settlers had was that they had no help in adjusting to their new environment. The Icelandic geologist and geographer Sigurður Thorarinsson (1958) is of the opinion that the Icelanders did not adjust very well to their new environment. He noted (p. 21) that they were never able to clothe themselves effectively against the cold and the rain and that "their shoes were inferior to those of any other nation inhabiting a cold country." During famines, they never learned to eat several edible indigenous plants available to them.

Icelanders from the beginning have dwelled on their origins and their genealogy. The enormous number of manuscripts of the sagas that have survived from medieval times and that are known to be only a small fraction of the total confirm that copying and reading the sagas were major endeavors of the people. Scores of eighteenth- and nineteenth-century travelers to Iceland wrote about the pervasive popularity of the sagas in Iceland. Unfortunately, there were no medieval travelers who wrote about such things. Let two examples suffice for many. Two centuries ago, Uno von Troil wrote in his *Letters on Iceland* (1780, p. 27): "Their chief amusement in their leisure hours is to recount to one another the history of former times; so to this day you do not meet with an Icelander who is not well acquainted with the history of his own country; they also play at cards." A century later, in 1872, James Bryce (1923, p. 30) noted that the average Icelander "is certain to be familiar with the masterpieces of his own ancient literature. It is this knowledge of the Sagas that has more than anything else given a measure of elevation as well as culture to his mind."

W. P. Ker, an eminent medievalist and saga scholar, provided a stunning capsule account of the founding of the Icelandic nation in his *Dark Ages* (1904, pp. 314-15), the history that every Icelandic child learns.

> The whole of Icelandic history is miraculous. A number of barbarian gentlemen leave Norway because the government there is becoming civilized and interfering; they settle in Iceland because they want to keep what they can of the unreformed past, the old freedom. It looks like anarchy. But immediately they begin to frame a Social Contract and to make laws in the most intelligent manner: a colonial agent is sent back to the Mother Country to study law and present a report. They might have sunk into mere hard work and ignorance, contending with the difficulties of their new country; they might have become boors without a history, without a ballad. In fact the Iceland settlers took with them the intellect of Norway; they wrote the history of the kings and the adventures of the gods. The settlement of Iceland looks like a furious plunge of angry and intemperate chiefs, away from order into a grim and reckless land of Cockayne. The truth is that those rebels and their commonwealth were more self-possessed, more clearly conscious of their own aims, more critical of their own achievements, than any polity on earth since the fall of Athens. Iceland, though the country is large, has always been like a city state in many of its ways; the small population, though widely scattered, was not broken up, and the four quarters of Iceland took as much interest in one another's gossip as the quarters of Florence.

In the Sagas, where nothing is of much importance except individual men, and where all the chief men are known to one another, a journey from Borg to Eyjafirth is no more than going past a few houses. The distant corners of the island are near one another. There is no sense of those impersonal forces, those nameless multitudes, that make history a different thing from biography in other lands. All history in Iceland shaped itself as biography or as drama, and there was no large crowd at the back of the stage.

The development of Icelandic independence proceeded in a way analogous to that of the American colonies, and it took about the same amount of time, a century and a half from the time of first settlement. The impression from Snorri Sturluson's *History of the Kings of Norway* (1967) is that King Olaf Tryggvason as late as 999-1000, when he was aggressively and cruelly campaigning to Christianize his domain, regarded himself as king of the Icelanders and the Icelanders so regarded him. A quarter of a century later, around 1024-1025, when Olaf Haraldsson (St. Olaf) was king of Norway, the situation had changed. At the 1024 Althing (parliament), a messenger named Thórarin sent by King Olaf spoke (chapter 125) as follows:

> I parted from King Óláf Haraldsson four days ago. He gave me greetings hither to all the people, both men and women, the young as well as the old, the rich as well as the poor—both God's and his greeting—and bade me say that he will be your king if you will be his subjects, and both be friends and help one another in all things of good report.

This message, even if the wording is apocryphal, indicates that the suzerainty of King Olaf was not clear.

The king wanted the Icelanders to pay tribute to him, and he specifically requested that he be given the island of Grímsey, which lies at the mouth of the Eyjafjörd, strategically the most important fjord in the north of Iceland. Some of the chieftains at the Althing favored having the "friendship" of King Olaf; others opposed entering into "bondage" under the king. In the end, the Althing refused both to pay taxes to the king and to grant his request for the island of Grímsey. The chieftains followed the lead of the chieftain Einar Eyólfsson, the leader of the opposition forces. According to Snorri (chapter 125) again, Einar is alleged to have argued that it was

> "best for the people of our country not to subject themselves here to pay tribute to King Óláf, nor to all those taxes such as he has imposed on the Norwegians. And we would impose that bondage not only on ourselves but both on ourselves and our sons and all our people who live in this land; and that bondage this land would never be free or rid of. And though this king be a good one, as I believe he is, yet it is likely to be the case, as always hitherto, that when there is a change in the succession there will be some kings who are good and some who are bad. But if our countrymen would

preserve their freedom, such as they have had ever since they settled here, then it would be best not to let the king get any hold here, whether it be a piece of land or our promises to pay fixed taxes, which might be interpreted as due from subjects. But I would consider it appropriate for those of us who wish to, to send the king gifts of friendship—hawks or horses, tents or sails or other things which are suitable for sending. That would be a good investment if it is repaid by friendship. But concerning the Island of Grímsey I would say this, that even if nothing is taken from it for supplying people with food, yet a host of men could find food there. And if some army from abroad [made it their base and] sailed from there with warships, I think many a cotter would find himself in a predicament."

And when Einar had spoken and made the state of affairs clear, then all the men were agreed that this should not come about, and Thórarin understood what the outcome of his mission would be.

How much this account has been embellished by Snorri is unknown. Still, from his perspective two centuries after the event, this was Iceland's Declaration of Independence. For almost two and a half centuries longer, Iceland was to continue as a republic independent of Norway. Orkney and the Faroes, much smaller in population and less isolated from Norway than was Iceland, did not revolt and they agreed to pay tribute to the king. As England and Spain did later, until the nineteenth century, Norway demanded allegiance to the Crown from emigrants in distant lands.

The sagas of the Icelanders give the impression that the earliest generations of Icelanders had a strong sense of nationality and felt distinct from the Norwegians, but it is necessary to remember that these sagas were written in a world two centuries removed from the Saga Age. Yet there was recognition, even 200 years later, that Norway was the center and they themselves were the periphery; Norway, not Iceland, was the focus of attention. In the sagas and the histories, Iceland is outside while Norway is "home." The Icelanders "sail out" to Iceland but "sail home" to Norway (Ker, 1908). In the sagas, there is avid interest in how Norwegian royalty view the Icelanders. The kings and earls are always impressed by how splendidly handsome, intelligent, well mannered, noble in behavior, and accomplished in sports the Icelanders are. For example, this is the case in *Laxdaela Saga* (introduction, 1969, p. 29) when "the kings of Norway are wheeled on the stage merely to fete and flatter the illustrious Icelanders who visit them." This preoccupation is the same "concern with the 'good opinion' of the elite of the former metropolitan power" that Lipset (1963, p. 72) points out as frequently characteristic of new nations. Continual emphasis is placed on the noble lineage of the Icelandic adventurers, many of whom are alleged to be descended from Norwegian kings. All of this should be take with a grain of salt. No one is so impressed with nobility as republicans!

One peculiar way that the ancient Icelanders continued to see the world from a Norwegian perspective was their terminology for points of the compass. They persisted in calling "inland" northeast. This worked satisfactorily for Norway but was a fiction for most of Iceland. People from Ireland, Britain, and the islands of the North Atlantic are spoken of in the old literature as coming from "the west." Again, this made sense in Norway but not at all in Iceland.

Icelanders continue to remain closest in sentiment to Norway as the mother country and to Norwegians as a people more like them than any other. The feeling is perhaps akin to the feelings English Canadians have toward England. Among the questions I asked my 100 representative Icelanders was one (question 3) inquiring how they would rank order six peoples in order of their similarity to Icelanders. The mean rank orders for the six were the following:

Norwegians 1.59
Faroese 1.91
Danes 3.28
Irish 3.88
English 4.86
Americans 5.08

Later in the interview, I asked them to rank order six countries according to which they would prefer to emigrate to, if they had to leave Iceland (question 28). The mean rank orders for the six countries were the following:

Norway 1.88
Sweden 3.00
Denmark 3.03
Canada 3.66
United States 3.67
Australia 5.76

Note from these results that the Icelanders regard the Norwegians as most like them. This is true in spite of the facts that Iceland was a colony of Denmark from 1380 until 1918, that Danish is the second language in Iceland—the linguistic link to the rest of Scandinavia—and that Denmark for centuires has been the principal country to which Icelanders have gone for specialized education. Also, Denmark is the country to which Icelanders are in fact most likely to emigrate. But note that Norway is clearly first choice for hypothetical emigration. The Irish were put on the list in the belief that the Icelanders feel a greater affinity toward their Celtic neighbors than toward any people other than the other Scandinavians. This seems to be the case even though there has been virtually no contact between the two peoples since Viking times. The Icelanders remain conscious of their dual Norwegian and Irish ancestry, even if the Irish settlers were a numerical minority that had relatively little influence on the Icelandic culture. Mysteriously, as previously noted, the distribution of blood groups among the Icelanders is closer to that of the Irish than to that of the Norwegians.

THE EFFECTS OF OVERSEAS MIGRATION

A factor in the dynamics of fragment new societies is the effects of overseas migration. Arnold J. Toynbee (1962, pp. 84-100) and William H. McNeill (1963, pp. 210-26) have both been impressed with this phenomenon in history and with the stimulation it provides to new societies. In addition to the observation that those who leave the mother country are always special kinds of people and are never representative of the total society is the law that not everything is taken. Only certain property, certain institutions, and certain ideas are transported to the new land. Great migrations are selective in all ways. Also, overseas migrations result in the intermingling and interbreeding of diverse peoples. At the very least, kin groups and communities are broken up. The cake of custom is shattered or at least altered by its ingredients being mixed in new ways. New societies—at least at first— are characterized by the lessened influence of kin and traditional community. The Hobbesian war of all against all so latent in new societies has a tendency to be mitigated by the development of law over kinship as the source of authority. Law tends to assume a central role in new societies, a role greater than in mother countries.

Overseas migration resulting in the breakdown of kinship has been stressed by Toynbee (1962, pp. 99-100) as the explanation for the early development of an English legal polity and for the general political achievements of medieval England. Primitive conceptions of social organization based on kin were disrupted by the overseas migration of the Angles and the Jutes during the fifth century, the Danish invasions beginning in 851, and two centuries later the invasion of those Frenchified descendants of Danish and Norwegian Vikings under William the Conqueror.

It is little wonder that law gained such a commanding role in the new nation of America, settled by overseas migrants from the country where the doctrine of fundamental law, law beyond human control, had been most fully developed. Iceland, in a more primitive way than seventeenth-century New England, also became a polity where law was central. Killing at night for almost any reason, for example, was murder and condemned a person to being an outlaw; killing under appropriate conditions in daylight, however, was not illegal. The respect for legal proceedings was so great in saga times that they came to be regarded as magic charms; any error in following legal formulas could lose a case. (See *Njal's Saga*, 1960, chapters 141-44; see also Homans, 1942, pp. 215-16.) "In no other literature," wrote Bryce (1901, p. 287), "is fiction or history, by whichever name we describe the Sagas, so permeated by legal lore."

Another consequence of the breakdown of traditional kinship and communal ties and the intermingling of people is the homogenization of culture that occurs in new societies. This is particularly observable in language and the breakdown of dialects. American English has always been more uniform than the English of the mother country, just as the Spanish of Latin America shows less variation from Mexico to Argentina than does the Spanish of Castile and Galicia. Iceland is perhaps the most extreme example of this tendency toward the homogenization of language in new societies. Persons from the same area did not have any tendency to settle in the same place in the new country. The Icelandic linguist Hreinn Benediktsson (1961-1962, p. 102) wrote that at the end of the Age of Settlement, in the middle of the tenth century, Icelandic "probably was to the furthest possible degree, uniform and freed of dialect variations." And "it has remained almost as uniform as a language spoken within an area of its size can ever be." This Icelandic was a blend of the dialects of the Norwegian west.

Great migrations, perhaps not necessarily overseas migrations, seem to make people aware of great events and great personages. And it is momentous events and leaders who become the source of epics. The embellished events of the past become more interesting as a source of tales than the mundane present of the descendants of those who participated in the great movement. No greater stimulus exists, it seems, to the development of epics than great overseas migrations. "This explains," in the words of Toynbee (1962, p. 62), following Bertha S. Phillpots (1931), "why the Hellenic epic developed in transmarine Ionia and not, like the Hellenic Drama, in the European Greek peninsula, the Teutonic Epic on the island of Britain and not on the European Continent; and the Scandinavian Saga on the island of Iceland and not, like the Scandinavian Drama, in Denmark or Sweden."

CONSERVATISM OF NEW SOCIETIES

Another general phenomenon of fragment new societies is their tendency toward various kinds of institutional and ideological conservatism. This is the dynamic that Hartz (1964, p. 3) called "immobility" and that Toynbee (1962, p. 96) called "atrophy," and this is the process that Samuel P. Huntington (1968, p. 172) brilliantly described but did not name whereby America adopted "the principal elements of the English sixteenth-century constitution . . . at precisely the time they were being abandoned in the home country." The following sentences from Huntington (p. 172) about the conservatism of the early American polity apply just as aptly to early Iceland.

> The English [Norse] colonists took these late medieval and Tudor [old Germanic] political ideas, practices, and institutions across the Atlantic with them during the great migrations of the first half of the seventeenth century [in the years 870-930]. The patterns of thought and behavior established in the New World [Iceland] developed and grew but did not substantially change during the century and a half of colonihood.

Boorstin (1958, p. 26-27), in a discussion of "Puritan conservatism," observed that their legal proceedings in the early years "give us the impression of a people trying to reproduce what they knew 'back home.' . . . What they produced was . . . a layman's version of English legal institutions." The colonial Icelanders, as I will show, had the same intentions, but they were more careful; they sent a delegate back to Norway to get the laws straight.

Only a part of the old society migrates and not all of the culture is transported. In the new land, the part then becomes the basis for a new whole. The part is simpler, less rich, and less diversified than the whole. It has fewer capacities within itself for change because much of the stimulus for change has been left behind. When there is knowledge of the origins of the society and when there is celebration of its founding, there is a tendency for national institutions to become touched with the sacred. Such seems to be the dynamics of the conservatism of new societies.

As America preserved much of the English medieval in its political institutions, so did the Icelandic Republic keep much of the old Germanic polity at the time when it was disappearing in Norway. England in the seventeenth century modernized its polity by establishing the sovereignty of the monarch and the state, while the ideology of the supremacy of the law disappeared; in America, an antique polity was established, based on the essentially medieval conception of the supremacy of the law, the divisions of sovereignty, and strong local autonomy. "Neither the divine right of kings, nor absolute sovereignty, nor parliamentary supremacy had a place on the western shores of the Atlantic" wrote Huntington (1968, p. 178). To push the point to the extreme, he (p. 185) called the American presidency "the only survival in the contemporary world of the constitutional monarch once prevalent throughout medieval Europe." From the beginning of its existence, America has been a modern society with an antique polity. So, in its time, was the Icelandic Commonwealth.

Knut Gjerset (1925, p. 80), the only non-Icelander to write a scholarly history of Iceland, observed that "in private life as well as in state organization and public institutions the Icelanders adhered with great fidelity to the ways of their ancestors. This conservatism, which had been adopted as a distinct program by the early settlers, was strengthened through the isolated location of the colony." Such an observation might have been made of seventeenth-century New England.

The Icelandic Commonwealth represented the fullest development of the Scandinavian variant of the old Germanic polity. At a time when Norway was beginning its centuries-long development into a Christian and national state—or at least a state under one king—Iceland reasserted the fundamental elements of the diffuse traditional polity and expanded them in ways unknown elsewhere.

First was the institution of the *thing*, the assembly of freemen known to have existed among all the Germanic peoples; it was described as early as the first century A.D. in the *Germania* of Tacitus (1948, chapters 11-13). Immediately after their arrival in Iceland, the settlers established local *things* all over the island for resolving the disputes among the settlers (Jón Jóhannesson, 1974; Njarðvik, 1973; Bryce, 1901). Then, around 927, a man by the name of Úlfljótur was chosen to prepare a code of law for the whole island. He went to Norway for three years and studied the law of the *thing* of Gula in southeastern Norway, which had jurisdiction for Sogn, Hordaland, and Fjordane. On the basis of this Norwegian provincial code, he prepared a law code for all of Iceland. This code was adopted as the law of the land at Thingvellir, a place previously chosen for the national assembly about the year 930. So the Althing was founded, the first and only truly national *thing* of the Germanic peoples. In Norway and everywhere else, the *thing* had been only a local assembly. The Althing was a new growth of a primordial Germanic institution, one that became the preeminent national institution in Iceland for more than three centuries. The Althing was a national legislative and adjudicating assembly, a fair, a marriage mart, a reunion of family and friends, and a national celebration in which a large but unknown proportion of the Icelandic population participated for two weeks each June. During these centuries of the Icelandic republic, the *things* were declining in importance in Norway with the spread of the authority of the Church and the clergy and the beginnings of national kingship.

The same efflorescence of an old Germanic institution is seen in the expansion of the role of the chieftains. Because no one in the new settlement could claim power, the chieftains achieved a dominance under the ancient customs greater than they had ever known before. In Iceland, the chieftains came to be known as *goðar* (singular, *goði*). The *goðar* had overriding, but rather vague, political and religious duties. At the founding of the Althing, the number of *goðar* was established at thirty-six (later increased to thirty-nine). The office could be inherited, sold, divided up, and even loaned. The *goðar*, together with the lawspeaker of the Althing and later the bishops, made up the *Lögrétta* (the English translation of the word "to order the law"), the legislative branch of the Althing. The *goðar* were also responsible for naming the jurors in legal disputes. The *goðar* were indeed the ruling class in the Icelandic Commonwealth. Still, the freemen had a free choice of who their *goði* was to be, and they were not limited to choosing those in their part of the country. Later in the Commonwealth, some families got to own several *goðar* and hence had many supporting farmers. The *goðar* also had the responsibility of maintaining a *hof*, or temple. However, their religious duties were generally secondary to their secular duties. Later, after Christianity was established, the *goðar* kept the churches and chose the priests. The *goði* was a unique institution, but one rooted in the role of the old Germanic chieftain.

There was lots of law but little government in the old Icelandic society. It suffered from the fatal flaw of the old Germanic polity, an inability to develop any ordered and regular hierarchy of authority. The viability of the old English society, by contrast, was its success in overcoming this societal dysfunction (Paul Johnson, 1972, pp. 46-47). The institutions of "the ancient Germans may be said to culminate, and end, in Iceland in the thirteenth century" (Ker, 1957, p. 57).

The first century of the Icelandic settlement also saw a marked return to the "old-time religion" of the Norse gods. Thor above all was favored among Icelanders during the tenth and eleventh centuries. A number of the settlers had been Christians, and some even had Christian names such as Markús, Páll, and Margrét. The *Book of Settlements* (paragraph S399) tells us about the decline of Christianity among the early generations.

> Learned men say that some of the settlers who occupied Iceland were baptized men, mostly those who came from west across the sea. Under this head are named Helgi the Lean, and Orlyg the Old, Helgi Bjola, Jorund the Christian, Aud the Deep-minded, Ketil the Fool, and still more men who

came from west across the sea. Some of them remained faithful to Christianity to the day of their death, but this rarely held good for their families,
for the sons of some of them raised temples and sacrificed, and the land
was altogether heathen for almost a hundred years.

Even after the decision to adopt Christianity was made in 999 or
1000, there was official toleration of some of the old heathen practices.
The Icelanders seem to have adopted Christianity at the Althing for
pragmatic reasons, partly to gain the release of some Icelanders kept
captive by King Olaf Tryggvason in Norway, partly out of the belief that
Icelanders could have only "one law." (See chapter 7.) In any case, the
official adoption of Christianity brought no social or political transformation of any great magnitude in this antique Germanic polity until the
thirteenth century, when Iceland lost its autonomy to the king of Norway and the bishop of Niðarós (Trondheim). With the passing of the
Commonwealth in 1262, Iceland went the way of Christian Europe; the
Church and the king grew in authority, the autonomy of the Althing declined, and the peculiar institution of the *goðar* passed away completely.

RECAPITULATION

So far I have attempted to show that the experience of Iceland can be
considered as that of a "new nation" and a fragment "new society"
in the way these concepts are used by Lipset, Hartz, and others. I also
have suggested that the cultural and structural transmutations resulting
from transmarine migration, as discussed by Toynbee, can contribute
to an understanding of the development of Iceland and other new societies. Also, there are some parallels between the Icelandic and the
American experiences. Both societies preserved and transformed antique political forms, were ideologically conservative, celebrated their
origins, developed homogeneous cultures and languages, and were
characterized from the beginning by a great deal of internal migration.
There is also a striking similarity in the value systems that developed
in the two societies—above all, in the central role played by an egalitarian ethic (chapters 2 and 8). The predominant social types that
were formed in the two rural socieites were essentially variations on
the theme of frontiersman/farmer.

ON ICELANDIC HISTORY

Several factors have worked together to produce the cultural persistence that has been maintained throughout Icelandic history, from

early medieval times to the present. I will show this throughout the book. However, with advanced modernization and the internationalization of the culture, these continuities have been attenuated or transformed. Both geographic and cultural isolation have provided the context for long-term historical continuity. During the early centuries of Icelandic history, up to the mid-fourteenth century, the sagas indicate there was frequent communication and travel between Iceland and Norway and other parts of Scandinavia and the North Atlantic area. However, from the time of the ravages of the Black Death in Norway (1349) through the eighteenth century, Iceland was culturally isolated to a degree unknown in any other Western society. The near absence of Gothic and Renaissance, baroque and rococo influences testifies to Icelandic isolation from Europe (Eldjárn, 1957, pp. 13-14). It is not surprising, then, that Icelanders, as Ólafur Ragnar Grímsson once pointed out, see Icelandic history and "other history" as two distinct categories of knowledge.

The Icelanders possess an extraordinary and unique historical and literary tradition that has bound them to their past and has continually replenished their culture. No European people can see its history with anything like the unity that the Icelanders see, with the partial exception of the Jews but they have had neither the geographical stability nor the cultural isolation of the Icelanders. Americans and the peoples of the other new societies have some of the same sort of national awareness, cultural mythology, and sense of continuity. But the Icelanders' extreme cultural homogeneity, their isolation, and their classical language and literature, combined with the smallness of their society, have intensified the intimacy Icelanders feel toward their national experience. For example, nearly all Icelanders could, if they wished, trace their lineages back to Bishop Jón Arason, the last Catholic bishop in Iceland, who died in 1550; he had nine illegitimate children. Even more Icelanders could trace their ancestry back to the historian and saga writer Snorri Sturluson (1179-1249). Only 10 of the 100 Icelanders I interviewed answered in the negative my question about whether they were related to any of the great Icelanders from the time of Egill Skalla-Grímsson (tenth century) to the present (question 11). (See appendix A.)

A folk culture of free farmers has been preeminent in Icelandic history from its beginning. They have played a role similar to, but greater than, "that 'petit bourgeois' giant . . . the American democrat absorbing both peasant and proletariat" (Hartz, 1955, p. 204). The influences of Christian theology and of Greco-Roman-European culture have not been slight in the development of Icelandic society —even from the very beginning—but their effects have been less than among any other Western people. As Hjalmar Lindroth (1937, p. 98) wrote, "Certain features of the pre-Christian faith have survived in Iceland down to recent times. An authority on the subject has asserted that 'a whole book could be written about it, and not a small one, either,' " As Indriði G. Thorsteinsson (*Iceland Review,* 1968, p. 35) put it, Iceland has existed as "a sort of national park of Nordic culture."

An oversimplified chronology of eleven centuries of Icelandic history based on crucial political, cultural, and economic factors can be found in table 1-1. The Time of Settlement spans the decades 870-930, with 874 traditionally accepted as the symbolic year of the founding of Iceland, when Ingólfur Arnarson, the first settler, "took land" in southwest Iceland. The century 930-1030 is conventionally called the Saga Time (or Saga Age), the period during which the sagas of the

Table 1-1. Icelandic Chronology

	Years	Historical Events
Commonwealth period	870-930	Age of Settlement
	930-1030	Saga Age
	999	Adoption of Christianity
	1030-1120	Time of peace
	1120-1230	Writing time
	1230-1262	Time of Sturlungs, or time of internecine struggle
Dark ages	1262-1380	Rule by king of Norway
	1380-	Rule by Denmark (until 1918)
	1402-1404	Time of Black Death
	1550	Triumph of Reformation
	1602	Establishment of Denmark's trade monopoly
	1662	Absolute power of king of Denmark assumed
	1787	Trade monopoly abolished
	1800	Universal literacy achieved
	1801	Althing (parliament) abolished
Modern period	1801-1845	Cultural renaissance and small improvement in living conditions achieved
	1845-1918	Struggle for home rule
	1918-1944	Period of home rule and development of modern political parties
	1944-	Full independence from Denmark and rapid modernization

Icelanders took place. The sagas are our major source of knowledge of everyday life of the earliest generations; I discuss their historicity at the end of this chapter.

During the years 1030-1120, the Icelandic farmers apparently settled down to their chores and storytelling and there was less feuding. Perhaps Christianity had some effect. In 1117-1118, the laws were first written down in the Latin alphabet. From 1117 to the end of the thirteenth century, Icelandic literature of all sorts reached its highest development, its golden age, the most celebrated period in Icelandic history. The last period of the Commonwealth is conventionally called the Age of the Sturlungs (1230-1262) after the most powerful family in the land. During these decades, power and wealth came into the hands of a small number of families who engaged in internecine struggles with each other and with the Church. The upshot of these bloody years was that the leading chieftains turned to the king of Norway to find peace. So began six and a half centuries of colonial status, from 1262 to 1380 under the king of Norway and from 1380 to 1918 as a colony of Denmark.

The period between the fall of the Commonwealth and the end of the eighteenth century might be called the Icelandic dark ages. These were centuries of worsening climatic conditions aggravated by the country's subservience to Denmark that culminated in the disastrous Danish trade monopoly of 1602-1787. The period from the late seventeenth to the late eighteenth century was the nadir of a millennium of misery for the Icelanders, a century when they lived literally on the fringe of survival. (This is documented in chapter 3.) Still, during those centuries the country was not without cultural creativity, and, amazingly, universal literacy was achieved by the end of the dark ages (see chapter 5).

After the turn of the nineteenth century, the conditions of life began a slow and erratic improvement and there was an increase in cultural activity. A few years into the century, national romanticism came as a flood over the country, a movement that looked back to the Commonwealth and the sagas for much of its inspiration. The first half of the nineteenth century can quite literally be called an Icelandic renaissance. The roots of the modern movement for independence can be found in a number of national poets who came to the fore during the 1830s. In 1845, the old Icelandic parliament (the Althing) was reestablished on a consultative basis—it had been dissolved in 1801 after it became obvious that it served no function—and "became the primary symbol of Iceland's golden age and its lost independence" (Ólafur R. Grímsson, 1970, p. 39). In 1848, the king of Denmark renounced his absolutism. During the next 70 years, Iceland gained increasing autono-

my. With the 1918 Act of Union, Denmark recognized the full independence of Iceland. Iceland's foreign affairs, however, were handled
by Denmark until 1944, when the Icelanders voted overwhelmingly
in a plebescite to discontinue the union with Denmark. The years
1848-1918 saw, in Ólafur Ragnar Grímsson's (1970, p. 510) words,
"the transition from a complete colonial status, when the absolutist
Administration and the Church together with a few literary societies
constituted the only organized activity in the country, to a sovereign
position in all matters, except foreign affairs and defense." This transformation occurred peacefully, without a single incidence of violence.

THE TRAVELERS' ACCOUNTS

Iceland and America are among the few countries in the world to
have rich accounts of themselves written by perceptive foreigners. A
great number of the Icelandic travel books, even some of the lesser
ones, have been translated into Icelandic; this fact indicates that they
are recognized for the national treasure that they indeed are. Throughout this book, I will make continual references to this literature.

"Iceland on the brain" is a condition diagnosed by Richard F.
Burton (of *Arabian Nights* fame), one of the more well known of the
nineteenth-century scholar-travelers. "Iceland on the brain," he wrote
(1875, volume 1, p. x) after his 1872 journey to Iceland, was a special
affliction of many of the Icelandic travelers who preceded him and
were so impressed by "everything and everybody" they saw in this
"most difficult and expensive country in the world." They endlessly
reported "scenes of thrilling horror, of majestic grandeur, and of
heavenly beauty."

Irresistible danger and mystery seemed to lurk everywhere in this
land on the outer edges of the inhabitable world and about which so
little was known in the so-called civilized nations. Some of this feeling of excitement and discovery was suggested by Ebenezer Henderson,
an indefatigable Scotsman who trekked all over Iceland in 1814 and
1815, distributing Bibles for the British and Foreign Bible Society:
"Most of the regions through which [I] passed have never been visited
by any native of Great Britain, and many of them have been wholly
unexplored by foreigners" (1818, p. ix). And, being a particulary pious
man, he got down on his knees and thanked God for his protection
after fording every stream and crossing every ravine. As late as 1860,
an English traveler, no doubt more concerned with impressing his
readers than with reality, wrote: "To get drowned, to break your neck
or your limbs, to be maimed, to be boiled alive, or, at the least to be

prostrated with rheumatism, are quite in the cards" (Metcalfe, 1861, p. 316).

A more appealing variety of "Iceland on the brain" was that of William Morris (1911), who visited Iceland in both 1871 and 1873. The results of these visits, according to one student of Morris, were to make him an egalitarian in his politics, to enhance his passion for the sagas, and to turn him into a bore on the subject of Iceland (according to some of his friends). One of his friends wrote to another: "Morris has come back smelling of raw fish and talks more of Iceland than ever" (cited by Purkis, 1962, p. 28).

Particularly notable in many of the travelers' accounts are the intense descriptions of their first sightings of Iceland. An example, and not one of the most dramatic, is that of Robert Chambers, an Edinburgh publisher and popularizer of evolutionary geology, who arrived in Iceland on the Danish steamer *Thor* in 1855. I choose this example because the *Thor* was the first steamship ever to sail to Iceland. Chambers (1856, p. 33) wrote: "It was almost with a childish wonder and curiosity, that we approached Reykjavík. As the capital of a country so out of the way and peculiar, we hardly know how to paint it to the imagination. With a sort of hush, we clustered together on deck. . . ."

Burton's judgment on the tendency of his predecessors toward overstatement is certainly true. Yet it is equally true, and Burton did not seem to recognize it, that Iceland had been visited by an extraordinarily talented group of observers during the eighteenth and nineteenth centuries. John Barrow, an Englishman who came in 1834, quite realized this fact when he wrote (1835, p. xi) that Iceland "had been visited by some, though not many, of the most intelligent of our countrymen." A number of these travelers achieved great distinction in their later lives. Many who visited Iceland during the early decades of the nineteenth century were young scientists from England and Scotland. But later, travelers came from France, Germany, and Scandinavia. Not until 1852 did the first American visit Iceland and later write a book about it (Miles, 1854).

From the 1870s on, there was a marked increase in the number of author-travelers who came to Iceland and a general decline in the quality of the books they wrote. The age of the scholar-generalist was fast disappearing. The last of this species to visit Iceland was probably the American Samuel Kneeland (1876), who came in 1874. He was the secretary of the Massachusetts Institute of Technology and professor there of both zoology and physiology. He went to Iceland to study volcanic activity, to collect specimens of natural history, and to observe this "curious and remarkable people" (p. vi). And he did all three. However, several of the number of European academics who visited Iceland in subsequent years did write worthwhile accounts of the culture, society, and national character of the Icelandic people. Among these were Konrad von Maurer (1823-1902), professor of legal history at Munich; W. P. Ker (1855-1923), founder of the Department of Scandinavian at the University of London and professor of poetry at Oxford; Andreas Heusler (1865-1940), professor of Germanic languages at Berlin and, later, at Basel; and Hjalmer Lindroth (1878-1945), professor of Nordic languages at the University of Gothenburg (see Sigurður Grímsson, 1946).

The earliest foreign traveler to visit Iceland and write about it may have been the Englishman Andrew Boorde, who went there sometime before 1542. His book, *The Fyrst Boke of the Introduction to Knowledge*, was published about 1547. He wrote that there "is no corne growyng there, nor they have lytle bread or none. In stede of bread they do eat stockefyshe . . . they be beastly creatures. . . . They have no houses, yet doth lye in caues, al together, lyke swyne" (quoted in Seaton, 1935, p. 13). The earliest Briton, however, to write about the Icelanders was probably the Welsh chronicler Giraldus Cambrensis (1146?-1220), who, like some others who have written about Iceland, never visited the country. He wrote that the Icelanders were "sober, truthful, and sparing of speech" (a remark I might make of Icelandic farmers today). (See Phillpotts, 1931, pp. 218-219.)

Most of the few travelers to Iceland who wrote accounts of the country up to the middle of the eighteenth century were merchants; none were scholars or scientists. The first scientist to visit Iceland and write an objective account of the country was the Danish mathematician and astronomer Niels Horrebow. He spent two years in Iceland (1749-1751) for the purpose of making meteorological observations for the Danish government. Fortunately, he also made many observations on the characteristics of the land and the people. Horrebow's purpose in writing *The Natural History of Iceland* was to correct the account of Johann Anderson, mayor of Hamburg, entitled *Nachrichten von Island* (1746). He wrote (p. vii) that Anderson's book is "entirely false, and conveys a wrong idea of the country." In order "to undeceive the public, and make void the severe and false accusations contained in that book against this island, I have made it my business to publish this treatise, which contains a very faithful account of the island, the air, the people, and their various occupations." Anderson had never visited Iceland but rather had based his book on information obtained from ship captains and merchants who traded there.

An English translation of Horrebow's book appeared in London in 1758. This account of Iceland is the work of an objective observer, if not a particularly analytical one; such an impression is strengthened by the congruence of his observations with those of several brilliant observers who visited Iceland in later decades. It is interesting to note that Samuel Johnson had read Horrebow's account of Iceland. Boswell (1893, volume 2, p. 186) reported in his *Life of Johnson* that "Johnson had said that he could repeat a complete chapter of *The Natural History of Iceland* . . . the whole of which was exactly thus: 'Chap. LXXII. Concerning snakes. There are no snakes to be met with throughout the whole island.' " However, either Johnson or Boswell did not quote the chapter quite correctly; the entire chapter reads: "No snakes of any kind are to be met with throughout the whole island."

The tradition of great travelers began in 1772 with the visit of Sir Joseph Banks (at the age of 29), later president of the Royal Society, patron of science, and lifelong friend of Iceland, particularly during its troubles with Denmark (Hermannsson, 1928). He was accompanied by several "learned and ingenious men," one being Uno von Troil (age 26), a Swedish antiquarian who was the archbishop of Sweden when he died. Von Troil's *Letters on Iceland* (1780), originally published in 1777 in Sweden, should probably be reckoned one of the great travel books written before the nineteenth century. Von Troil deals intelligently and objectively with topics as diverse as volcanic activity and child rearing, the diseases of the people and their diet and housing, and the literary bent of the Icelanders. All of these topics, however, had been touched on by Horrebow two decades earlier. Von Troil's book was soon translated into a number of languages and served as an inspiration to many later Iceland travelers. The Scottish botanist William Jackson Hooker (age 24) went to Iceland in 1809 after being directly influenced by von Troil's book and encouraged by Banks, who had loaned him his notes. Hooker went specifically to observe the natural history of Iceland, but fortunately he observed much more. In spite of losing most of his materials and almost his life when his ship burned in Reykjavík harbor, he published a two-volume account (1813) of his travels, largely from memory. So began the career of one of the greatest botanists of the nineteenth century. He became Regius Professor of Botany at Glasgow; a genus of moss, *Hookeria*, was named after him; he died as director of the Royal Kew Gardens in London.

The year after Hooker came George Steuart MacKenzie (age 30), together with Richard Bright (age 20) and Henry Holland (age 21). MacKenzie published *Travels in the Island of Iceland during the Summer of the Year 1810* (1811). MacKenzie became a leading mineralogist; Bright (in addition to having a disease named after him) became, according to the *Dictionary of National Biography*, one of the half-dozen greatest names in English medicine; and Holland became one of the most fashionable physicians of his time and physician extraordinary to Queen Victoria. Shortly before his death in 1873, Holland returned to Iceland with his son, but, unfortunately, he says little about the trip in his autobiography (1872) except to comment on the improvement in the Icelanders' standard of living.

Ebenezer Henderson, previously mentioned, came in 1814 (age 30) and later published (1818) his rambling and eccentric two-volume journal, regarded by many later travelers and many Icelanders as the greatest of all the nineteenth-century accounts. James Bryce and Richard F. Burton were both of this opinion, even though Burton attributed to Henderson a particularly severe case of "Iceland on the brain." Henderson was as energetic as any of those particularly energetic Scottish Presbyterians. By the time he was 22 years old he had mastered seven languages, including Danish and Swedish. Before coming to Iceland, he had been the first British missionary in Sweden and had spent two years preaching in Denmark at the same time he supervised a translation of the Bible into Icelandic. After his venture in Iceland, he went to Russia to distribute more Bibles. He later returned to Britain, where, among other things, he became active in propagating the gospel to Jews.

After 1830, the number and diversity of travelers tended to increase. The first French observers went to Iceland during the summers of 1835 and 1836 as members of a scientific expedition sponsored by Louis Philippe and under the direction of Paul Gaimard, a physician and naturalist. Between 1839 and 1852, the French travelers published eight substantial volumes containing a gigantic amount of largely undigested information on the geology, natural history, and customs of the Icelandic people. In addition, they published four volumes of drawings, most notable of which are the drawings of Icelanders and their houses and everyday lives, done mostly by August Mayer.

The first woman author-traveler to travel to Iceland was Ida Pfeiffer (1852), who came from Vienna in 1845. Unlike most of the nineteenth-century travelers, she was little interested in the sagas or in history or geology; rather she was a collector of plants, butterflies, and insects. Pfeiffer was a strong woman with an intense passion for travel to distant places; she had just returned from a journey to the Holy Land before she set out for Iceland. She was also haughty and critical. She did not like the Icelanders, and apparently they did not like her. She deserves an accolade for writing the most unfriendly book of the century, "a snarling, ill-tempered journal" a later traveler (Miles, 1854, p. 54) called it. (Johann Anderson had published just a century earlier *Nachrichten von Island* [1746], the most scathing anti-Icelandic book of the eighteenth century, but he was not nearly so good a reporter as Pfeiffer.) A sentence, taken not quite at random, suggests her tone:

"I defy the most powerful imagination to conceive anything in the way of filth and disgusting practices, which I have not witnessed in an Icelandic household" (p. 225). She found "selfishness" to be a basic characteristic of the Icelanders (p. 74) and pointed out quite simply that the "men are ugly, the women rather less so" (p. 78). Still, she made many useful observations about the egalitarianism of the Icelanders that agree with the observations of those more favorably disposed to what they saw.

The first American to visit Iceland and write about it was Pliny Miles (1854), who came in 1852. He was as loving of the Icelanders as Pfeiffer was hostile. Only Lord Dufferin, who went to Iceland three years later, approached Miles in admiration for the Icelanders. Miles (p. 29) described them as being a people who are

> more contented, moral, and religious, possess greater attachment to country, are less given to crime and altercation, and show greater hospitality and kindness to strangers than any other people the sun shines upon. . . . They possess a greater spirit of historical research and literary inquiry, have more scholars, poets, and learned men, than can be found among an equal population on the face of the globe.

A few years later, a second American from California, J. Ross Browne, traveled to Iceland. He wrote three long descriptive articles on his Icelandic travels, which appeared in *Harper's Magazine* (1863). From Iceland, in a letter to his wife, he wrote (Lina Browne, 1969, p. 260) that such "a blasted, burnt-up, frozen, scorched, swamped, ice-blistered, rocky, lava-swept, ghost and goblin-ridden country, it was never my fortune to see before." I have found five accounts by Americans written prior to this century, none being among the better ones.

In 1855 came the irrepressible Lord Dufferin (age 29) on his eighty-ton yacht *Foam*. The following year, he published his *Letters from High Latitudes* (1910), the most charming and zesty, if not the most profound, of the nineteenth-century travelers' accounts. He overcame his Victorian rectitude sufficiently to describe getting marvelously drunk at an official Icelandic dinner party, and he suggested what to an imaginative reader was a not completely inactive love life during his visit. Many serious Icelanders apparently were hostile toward his book at the time it was first published, even though, like his American contemporary, he suffered from the positive version of "Iceland on the brain." Indeed, the Icelanders were a people like no other "by all accounts, the most devout, innocent, pure-hearted people in the world. Crime, theft, debauchery, cruelty are unknown amongst them, they have neither prison, gallows, soldiers nor police" (p. 28). Through one of the small good fortunes of history, Dufferin was governor-general of Canada during the 1870s, the time of the early Icelandic emigration to Canada, and he extended his help in relocating the people from the country he so admired.

Frederick Metcalfe suffered from a rather quaint case of "Iceland on the brain." He visited Iceland in 1860 and the following year published *An Oxonian in Iceland*. He was a student of Scandinavian studies utterly carried away by the Teutonic romanticism of his time. Indeed, he felt that it was to the Scandinavians, most magnificently represented by the Icelanders, that the English owed "their dash, their love of enterprise, their frankness, their liberty" (p. 393). Elsewhere, he also noted "their pluck" (p. 79). Yet we have it on good authority from Bryce (1923, pp. 25-26) a dozen years later that the Icelanders were "wanting in dash" and were characterized by a certain "sluggishness."

Two years after Metcalfe, Sabine Baring-Gould, composer of "Onward Christian Soldiers" and prolific writer on werewolves and saints, traveled to Iceland. He wrote a credible and balanced book (1863) on the Icelanders and did not suffer from any version of "Iceland on the brain." Baring-Gould was one of the few nineteenth-century travelers, another was Burton, who used the vital statistics readily available.

In 1871 and 1872, Iceland was visited by Morris, Bryce, and Burton, an impressive trio of observers for any country. Morris's *Journals* (1911) of his 1871 and 1873 visits to Iceland apparently were admired by some students of Morris (Purkis, 1962, p. 5) and by W. H. Auden (1937). I did not find Morris's journals very useful because they lacked social observations. For the most part, they are day-by-day accounts of his overland treks and visits to saga sites. Bryce, probably exceeded only by Alexis de Toqueville as the most cited observer of nineteenth-century democracies, wrote a 43-page essay (1923) on Iceland as of 1872; the essay is sociologically perceptive and has the advantage of serving as a check on less critical observers. He also became a student of ancient Iceland and once wrote that he wished he could have written a history of Iceland, a "fascinating" topic (1901, p. 296). Burton's account, too, serves as a corrective for the overstatements of his predecessors because of his hard-nosed determination not to be impressed by the Icelanders. Burton's (1875) two-volume *Ultima Thule, or A Summer in Iceland* is, excepting Gaimard, the most scholarly and the longest of all the nineteenth-century accounts, but it is marred by a racism that was becoming increasingly common in the 1870s, a great deal of careless writing, and an upper-class English snobbism (even a nastiness) of which both Morris and Bryce are totally free.

The 1870s saw the end of the tradition of great travel writers. I have already noted that the American Kneeland was the last of the scholarly generalists to go to Iceland. His book, *An American in Iceland*, is intelligently descriptive, but he was not as keen an observer as Bryce nor as good a scholar as Burton. The work is noteworthy, however, for its discussion of the similarities between Icelanders and Americans and of the comparable foundations of the two societies. Bayard Taylor, a well-known American traveler and man of letters, went to Iceland in 1874 as a correspondent for the *New York Herald*. His purpose was to report on the thousandth-anniversary celebration of the founding of Iceland, an event that gave Iceland more worldwide publicity than the country had ever received before. He also wrote a much celebrated poem, "America to Iceland," translated into Icelandic by Matthías Jochumsson, national poet and author of the Icelandic national anthem. Later that year, Taylor published a book with the unlikely title *Iceland and Egypt in the Year 1874*.

Anthony Trollope in company with a dozen of his countrymen took a trip to Iceland in June of 1878 on the maiden voyage of a yacht called the *Mastiff*, but they stayed only a week. Still, as late as 1878, a trip to Iceland justified a book and certainly one by a writer of Trollope's stature. *How the "Mastiffs" Went to Iceland* (1878) has even been translated into Icelandic. It is an indication of the general interest of Icelanders in how foreigners see them when such a thin and inconsequential book as this one is translated.

From here on out it is rather downhill for the quality of travelers' accounts. The following decades saw the publication of a shelfful of books with titles like *A Summer in Iceland*, and there is one by C. A. de Fonblanque (1880) quite specifically entitled *Five Weeks in Iceland*. The first chapter is *"Northward Ho!"* and the last *"Good-by to Iceland."* A number of accounts of pony treks across Iceland also begin to appear at this time, one is Ethel B. Harley's *A Girl's Ride in Iceland* (1889). An enormously informative book on Icelandic culture, one of the best, appeared in Sweden in 1930, after a number of lean decades. This is Hjalmar Lindroth's *Iceland: A Land of Contrasts*; an English translation appeared in 1937. The author, a professor of Scandinavian languages, had a long-time and intimate knowledge of the language and culture of Iceland. In 1937, W. H. Auden and Louis MacNeice published their whimsical *Letters from Iceland* (1967). Auden had a lifetime involvement with ancient Icelandic literature and once claimed that the "memory" of Iceland "is a constant background to what I am doing" (quoted by Sigurður A. Magnússon, 1977, p. ix). Typical of the kinds of observations in *Letters* is the following on national character: "I found the Icelander, certainly as compared with the Englishman, very direct, normal, and free from complexes, but whether this is a good or bad thing, I cannot decide" (p. 213).

One of the low points in the travelers' accounts was reached in 1945 by an American who was brought to Iceland by the military during the Second World War. Let him be nameless. In the preface to his book, he wrote that until coming to Iceland "America was enough for me." And he summed up the cultural history of Iceland in 25 remarkable words: "The Icelandic people actually have no philosophy or logical thinking. Everything comes from and is based on the Sagas. However, Icelandic literature is very rich." In 1969, John C. Griffith's *Modern Iceland* appeared; an intelligent, readable, journalistic account of its subject, it was the first one of its kind to appear in a long time. Katherine Scherman's (1975) *Fire and Ice* is a rambling account by a woman who knows a little about the sagas, wildlife, and islands but not much about Icelandic society and culture.

There are scores of other travelers' accounts of Iceland, some of which were useful to me and are listed in the bibliography; the greatest number are in English, followed by those in the Scandinavian languages, German, and French. Accounts exist too—and these I have not included—in Dutch, Italian, Czech, Serbo-Croatian, and a few other languages.

A NOTE ON THE HISTORICITY OF THE SAGAS

The sagas are a unique medieval literature to which I will continually refer and sometimes quote throughout this book. The word *saga* can be translated into English as "history;" hence, the Icelandic series *Íslendinga Saga* would be translated as *History of the Icelanders*. In English, however, sagas are the histories written down in Iceland from the twelfth through the fourteenth, but particularly the thirteenth, centuries.

There are various kinds of sagas from this time: those that deal with ancient, former, and contemporary times, and those that are more self-consciously historical. The sagas of ancient times are heroic accounts of the Germanic peoples during the migration period (the fifth and sixth centuries), while the sagas of former times deal with the first settlers and the early generations of Icelanders. This latter category is conventionally called the sagas of the Icelanders or the family sagas or just the sagas; there are about forty of them extant, ranging in length from a few pages to 300 or 400 pages in conventional book form. They describe in a highly realistic and exterior way, in a style similar to Hemingway's, the tumultuous lives of leading Icelandic farming families during the tenth and eleventh centuries, their feuds and their alliances. However, these accounts were not put down on parchment until the late twelfth and thirteenth centuries, two centuries after the purported events they describe. How much they are historical accounts and how much fiction has been a point of intense controversy for the better part of a century. Peter Hallberg (1962, p. 2) neatly summarized the polar positions.

> On the one hand, the sagas are believed to be essentially historical; according to this theory they developed in close connection with the described events, were transmitted from generation to generation by storytellers, and were finally committed to parchment, generally sometime during the thirteenth century. Such an attitude toward the sagas scarcely permits one to talk about their authors; their writings would merely be a matter of recording a fixed oral tradition. On the other hand, they have been regarded by some scholars primarily as works of fiction. From this it naturally follows that one must accord to their writers a decisive role as true authors.

The overwhelmingly dominant opinion among current literary and historical scholars of the Icelandic middle ages is that the sagas are fiction—works of art, not historical accounts (see, for example, Sigurður Nordal, 1958; Hallberg, 1962; Andersson, 1964; Claiborne Thompson, 1973; and Byock, 1978). A persuasive demonstration of the lack of literal historicity of the sagas is Sigurður Nordal's (1958) celebrated study of *Hrafnkel's Saga*, a short, particularly realistic, unexaggerated, believable account of the conflicts among farmers in the eastern fjords. Through close internal and external analysis, Nordal effectively demolished the historicity of this saga, previously thought to be among the most historically reliable, and showed it to be an elegantly crafted short story.

However, even Nordal, who was extreme among saga scholars in his argument that the sagas must be regarded primarily as works of fiction, would never have denied the historicity of most of the leading saga personalities nor that the sagas are, to various degrees, based on actual historical events. Most significantly, he regarded the artistic success of the thirteenth-century saga authors to be the result of their ability to create the appearance of historical reality. Thus, he (1957, p. 29) said:

> Not only through their access to older written sources, but in certain other ways too, the writers of the Family Sagas were better off than might be expected when describing times so long past. The changes in the social and material conditions, in housing, clothes, weapons, seamanship, and so on, were not very remarkable from the tenth to the thirteenth century, and obvious anachronisms in such descriptions are rare. The writers were quite conscious of the distance in time, and they had a considerable historical sense.

One saga scholar, Jesse Byock (1978, p. 19) noted that Nordal and "so many" of his contemporaries were "virtually blind to the fact that the sagas would be an important resource for today's interest in societal functioning and traditional patterning." But the saga scholars are not alone in this. The anthropologist Rosalie H. Wax (1969, p. 7) noted that "most of those Old Icelandic and Old Scandinavian materials [fall] squarely into an area of investigation to which anthropologists and sociologists have been selectively inattentive." She later noted (p. 17) that she does "not believe that there is any other record of comparable richness, volume, and interest in the world." Her sentiments are echoed by another anthropologist, Victor W. Turner (1971, p. 351), who observed that the sagas "are many and rich and full of the very materials that anthropologists rejoice in when vouchsafed to them by informants in the field." In one place (p. 361), he calls *Njal's Saga* an "anthropological paradise.'" Turner's view (p. 358), the same as that reflected in this book, is that the "major continuities" between the Saga Age and the thirteenth century are "so many" . . .

> at the basic levels of kinship and territorial organization, mode of subsistence, forms of adjudication and arbitration, and norms governing relations between individuals and groups, that sagas treating of both the earlier and later periods can be regarded equally as models of and for Icelandic social life as it lasted over several centuries.

The sagas are used in this work as a source of information—the only source of information—on pre-Christian Iceland, its legal system, relationships between the sexes, kinship, names and naming patterns, and social structure in general.[1]

CHAPTER 2

Modern Iceland and Its Making

An Icelandic scholar fixed the year 1906 — the year in which a submarine telegraph cable finally brought Iceland into direct communication with the outside world — as the end of the Middle Ages in Iceland.

Jóhann S. Hannesson (1964)

The history of the Icelanders in the present century provides an unequivocal example of the speed with which a technical culture can take root where a culture of the mind has prepared the soil.

Gylfi Th. Gíslason (1966)

With a population of fewer than a quarter of a million people, Iceland is the smallest nation in the world with a full panoply of the institutions of modern nationhood: a national language, a distinctive history and literature, a strong national consciousness, governmental institutions, a full-fledged university, and diplomatic relations around the world. Only the military is missing. Iceland is a minination, much smaller even than the "small countries." Nonetheless, Iceland has institutions as legible and distinct as those of larger societies.

THE ECONOMY

This island nation bordering the Arctic Circle has one of the highest standards of living in the world, with a 1978 per capita income of $9,100 and more private automobiles (314.8 per 1,000 in 1977) than any Nordic country except Sweden (Nordic Council, 1979, p. 205). The life expectancies of Icelanders are at the highest levels in the world, 73.0 years for males and 79.2 years for females in 1975-76 (p. 60). Newspaper circulation, at 555 copies per 1,000 population

32

per day in 1977 (p. 296), is also at the highest level in the world. The modal size and quality of housing are probably unsurpassed in the world; the average-size dwelling unit has about 1,300 square feet (Nordal and Kristinsson, 1975, p. 300). Sixty-six percent of the dwellings completed in 1976 had five or more rooms (Nordic Council, 1979, p. 146). Few people are either very rich or very poor in this isolated but modern nation.

Yet modernization and affluence are recent phenomena. Before the Second World War, Iceland was a poor fishing and sheep-ranching society. The country prospered in a number of ways from the British and American occupations during the Second World War, and in the postwar period there was a rapid modernization and expansion of the fishing and fish-processing industries, particularly the processing of frozen fish. While Icelanders have always depended on the sea to supplement their meager livelihood from the land, today their very survival as a modern society depends on the export of fish. Only 1 percent of the land is cultivated; 23 percent is usable for grazing; and 76 percent is made up of wasteland—mountains, glaciers, deserts, and lava fields. Half of the population is concentrated in the Reykjavík metropolitan area; most of the other half, in towns and villages around the perimeter of the island. Iceland, according to the calculations of Taylor and Hudson (1972, p. 222), has the fourth highest concentration of population in the world after Hong Kong, Singapore, and Uruguay. Less than 10 percent of the population is engaged in agriculture. Yet, the economic base of modern Iceland is precarious.

An awareness of the rigorous environment, the lack of nearly all natural resources, the short growing season, and the near absence of agriculture except for the growing of hay is fundamental to an understanding of the obsessive and aggressive concern the Icelanders have with the state of the fish stocks in their waters. And the waters around Iceland are among the richest fishing beds in the world, the result of of a large and shallow continental shelf where warm and cold ocean currents meet and where there is an abundance of oceanic plant life. These are ideal conditions for spawning areas and nursery grounds.

But these fishing grounds are in danger of becoming depleted. This explains the militancy of the Icelanders in unilaterally and repeatedly extending their fisheries limits. These limits were extended from 3 to 4 miles in 1948, to 12 miles in 1958, to 50 miles in 1972, and to 200 miles in 1975. In 1958, 1972, and 1975-76, much publicized "cod wars" broke out between Iceland and Britain over the extensions. In all of these unilateral decisions, Iceland was the first North Atlantic nation to act and to establish a precedent for a number of other countries.[1]

On 14 October 1975, the day before the extension of the fisheries limits to 200 miles took effect, Prime Minister Geir Hallgrímsson spoke to the nation in a radio address (Ministry for Foreign Affairs, 1975) and asserted that "the fish stocks in the waters adjacent to Iceland are in such danger of extinction that it would, indeed, be a matter of heavy responsibility to wait any longer. . . . Our livelihood is at stake and our cause is so strong and just that victory will be won." This extension of the fisheries limits was unanimously supported by the Althing, as were all the previous extensions. Public opinion too was unanimously in support of all the extensions. The singlemindedness and vehemence of the Icelanders on this issue are reflected in the Prime Minister's statement: "We shall not enter into any agreements which do not fully conform with our interests, and we shall either negotiate for full victory, or, if such is our fate, fight until victory is won."

The overwhelming importance to Iceland of the export of fish and fish products for earning foreign exchange is indicated by the export figures in table 2-1. Marine products accounted for 78 percent of the value of exports in 1978, a figure that has been relatively constant for a number of years.

The founding in 1966 of the Icelandic Aluminum Company (ISAL), a subsidiary of the Swiss Aluminum Company (Allsuisse), was the first large-scale attempt to diversify the economy. It was also the first industrial utilization of Iceland's abundant hydroelectric power. ISAL has proved that it is profitable to import bauxite to Iceland and reduce it to aluminum (a process that takes vast amounts of electrical energy) and then export it to Britain, Switzerland, and China. Yet, aluminum earns only 25 percent as much as the foreign exchange of fish. So it would not be far off to assert that about 85 percent of Iceland's foreign exchange is earned by the fishing industry. No other country in the world remotely approaches Iceland in fish and fish products as a percentage of its total exports; Norway is probably second, with less than 10 percent (Nordic Council, 1979, pp. 158-63). Nor does any other modern society rely so heavily on one industry.

Iceland is enormously sensitive to the ups and downs of the world economy and to the volatility of foreign markets. For example, the market for dried unsalted fish declined by more than 50 percent as a result of the Civil War (1967-1970) in Nigeria, Iceland's major market for this product. Between 45 and 50 percent of Iceland's gross national product (GNP) is accounted for by foreign trade, a very high figure even by European standards. Nearly all foodstuffs except fish, lamb and mutton, and dairy products must be imported. Iceland paid a little over $19 million in the world market for fuel in 1973 and $75 million in 1977. Thus, the fuel crisis has put further pressure on the economy,

Table 2-1. Icelandic Exports in 1978

Type of Product	Percentage
Marine	
Frozen fish	37.0
Salted fish	10.5
Processed stockfish	4.3
Salted herring	2.4
Fish meal and oil	16.7
Canned fish	1.1
Other processed fish	1.6
Fish landed abroad directly	3.2
Processed whale	0.7
Total marine	77.5
Agricultural	
Meat	1.5
Dairy	0.5
Wool	0.1
Other	0.2
Total agricultural	2.3
Manufacturing	
Fur, hide, other tanned goods	1.2
Wool	2.6
Aluminum	13.4
Diatomite	0.7
Other	0.7
Total manufacturing	18.6
Other	
Total other	1.6

Source: Statistical Bureau of Iceland, *Hagtíðindi*, 1979, p. 109.

already for many years the most inflationary in Europe. Consumer prices increased by 49 percent in 1975, 30 percent in 1976, and 37 percent in 1977, far and away the highest rate of inflation among member nations of the Organization for Economic Cooperation and Development (OECD). Between January 1968 and August 1979 the cost-of-living index for Reykjavík leaped from 100 to 1,649, almost a seventeenfold increase. In December 1946, the official exchange rate was 6.5 Icelandic krónur to each United States dollar; by 30 June 1979, it was 344 krónur to each dollar. The most important single factor in explaining this inflation is the great year-to-year fluctuation in Iceland's earnings from exports. Indeed, Iceland can provide the world with a lesson in how to maintain a high level of social stability under conditions of permanent high-level inflation.

Fish is an unstable commodity on which to base an economy. During the late 1960s, the profitable herring disappeared from Icelandic waters because of overfishing and the mysterious way herring have of changing their habitat. The loss of the herring, combined with a decline in the export prices of fish and a decline in the market for dried unsalted fish, brought a drop in real per capita income in excess of 16 percent between 1966 and 1968 — a severe decline in the standard of living. Then the fish catch increased, and value of exports increased sharply and by 1970 exceeded that of 1966 in constant krónur. Good years continued until 1973, when a period of great fluctuation in foreign trade prices began. A particularly bad year, 1974, saw a decline of 15 percent in real earnings of all workers (OECD, 1978, p. 13) as a result of low prices and a poor catch. The downturn continued until mid-1976, when there was an upturn that accelerated in 1977 but slowed down again in 1978. And so it goes.

Should more species like the herring disappear or become depleted — particularly the cod and other demersal, or bottom-feeding fish (for example, haddock, saith, redfish) — Icelanders would face the prospect of mass starvation or mass emigration. While the catch of demersal species has remained fairly stable in recent years, catching them now requires more sophisticated equipment and greater effort. But the Icelanders have begun to monitor the activities of the domestic fleet as never before, and specific areas of Icelandic waters are now being closed to fishing at certain times. The fish stock in the Icelandic waters, above all that of cod, is regarded to be at a dangerously low level, and great efforts are being made to rectify this situation. The extension of the fisheries limits to 200 miles in 1975 for the purpose of getting rid of foreign fishing efforts was only the beginning. The Ministry of Fisheries increasingly is controlling the magnitude of the catch, prohibiting fishing in certain areas and at certain times, and utilizing other measures to prevent overfishing, such as heavily fining those who violate the law.

Yet, the overall economy has been quite stable. The goal of full employment was realized during the early 1940s and has been maintained ever since. The rate of unemployment has rarely exceeded 1 percent, and, when it has, it has been mostly of a seasonal sort. In the first half of 1977, unemployment was 0.4 percent. This is indeed an unusual economic phenomenon, considering the enormous fluctuations in total demand and the fact that the labor force has been growing at about 2 percent a year as a result of natural demographic trends and an increase in female participation in the labor force. A recent OECD economic survey (1978, p. 14) suggested the various reasons the structure of the Icelandic economy facilitates full employment.

There is a small relatively homogeneous population and very few enterprises employing large numbers of people. The social pressures in favour
of retaining labour are undoubtedly significant. The mobility of labour is
traditionally high: the agricultural sector is fairly large (10 percent of the
working population) and for climatic reasons notably seasonal. There are
also strong seasonal variations in fishing and construction. It is consequently
fairly usual for young workers in particular to switch jobs frequently. Last,
but probably not least, real wage flexibility has been enforced by official
policies.

No other western economy is more regulated to insure full employment, and none heretofore has been so successful.

The economic modernization of Iceland is a phenomenon of this
century, and it is a simple story. It can be seen as having occurred in
three stages (Dóra Bjarnason, 1977). First was the period around the
turn of the century when the number of decked fishing vessels had
greatly increased, making fishing in distant waters possible. Prior to
this time, fishing was mostly a part-time activity. In 1876, the entire
Icelandic fishing fleet consisted of 38 decked vessels and 3,208 open
rowboats; by 1904, there were 160 decked vessels and fewer rowboats
(Ólafur Björnsson, 1964, pp. 149, 151). In 1906, Iceland acquired its
first fishing trawler; by 1915 the country had 20. Underlying this expansion of the fishing industry were the improved trading conditions
of the nineteenth century, the founding of the National Bank of Iceland (the first bank in the country) in 1885, and the development of
the Cooperative Movement, "the most highly advanced and the best
consolidated in the world" (Odhe, 1960, p. 9).

The second phase was the brief period between 1914 and 1917
when world fish prices boomed as a result of the First World War,
wages were low, and the country had a fishing fleet large enough to take
advantage of the situation. Iceland profited still more by the Second
World War; during the early years of the war, there was a combination
of high fish prices, good catches, and continuing low wages. During
the same period, Iceland was occupied by the British and then the
Americans, who poured large amounts of money into the economy;
they improved roads, built airports, and employed large numbers of
Icelanders at high wages. Opportunities for work were unlimited, and
entrepreneurs of all sorts flourished. "The Icelanders had become
wealthy overnight" (Dóra Bjarnason, 1977, pp. 7-8). By the time Iceland became a republic in 1944, the structural transformation of the
economy, led by the fishing sector, was well underway.

The economic development of Iceland was carried out by individual entrepreneurs, not by the state, in a way similar to development
in the United States. Many small entrepreneurs mobilized the savings

of the people, borrowed, and invested. The people in general, too, were a factor in the rapid modernization of Iceland: "(1) they were literate, flexible, and modern in outlook, (2) no great specialized or sophisticated skills were needed, (3) they were familiar with a cash economy, and (4) they were hard-working" (Dóra Bjarnason, 1977, p. 8).

POLITICS AND POLITICAL PARTIES

Of all the institutions of a modern society, none is more a simplified microcosm of the whole of a society—of its values, social structure, and cleavages—than its politics and its political party system. This is particularly true of a complex multiparty system like Iceland's, in which interests and values can be more finely articulated than in less complex systems.

Three factors stand out as having shaped Iceland's politics and political party system: the country's size, the homogeneity of its population, and its isolation. As a result of the country's small size, Icelandic politics have always been strongly personalistic and ideology has generally counted for less than the personalities of a small number of well-known leaders. There have never been any religious or ethnic differences among Icelanders to complicate their politics. Of the more than 20 groups that might be called political parties in nineteenth- and twentieth-century Iceland, none has ever developed along religious or ethnic lines. There are, however, four basic cleavages in this homogeneous society: (1) the dominant capital versus the rest of the country, the center-periphery conflict; (2) the class cleavage, largely that between employers and employees; (3) the commodity market conflict, that between the primary producers (fishing, agriculture) and consumer interests—to some extent, this is an urban/rural-small village cleavage; and (4) national versus international values conflict, a cleavage of particular salience in the island nation. Iceland is isolated in the North Atlantic, the most geographically isolated modern society in the world. A consequence of this isolation has been the focusing of Icelandic politics on domestic issues. The major exceptions to this concentration since the Second World War have been NATO membership and the United States' military presence together with the issue of extending the country's fisheries limits. Both issues have become less central in Icelandic politics during the late 1970s.

Modern Icelandic political history can be conveniently divided into three periods: (1) before 1845, when Iceland was a colony under Danish absolutism; (2) 1845-1918, when the central issue in Icelandic politics was home rule; and (3) the period since 1918, after Iceland achieved home rule and developed a modern political party system.

While the independence movement was central to Icelandic politics before 1918, it was never carried out with much popular passion. Until the election of 1902, only a small minority of the eligible electorate even bothered to vote. In the election of 1874, a mere 19.6 percent of the eligible electorate voted in the Althing elections (Statistical Bureau of Iceland, 1976, p. 230)—and this was a population in which literacy was universal. The eligible electorate was expanded in 1903, and in 1915 suffrage was made universal for all men and women over the age of 25, excluding only those who received community assistance. The secret ballot was introduced in 1903 and was first put into practice in the 1904 by-elections.

The development of political parties, and of other associations of interest aggregation, was primitive until home rule was achieved in 1918. Those parties that existed, and there had been eight or ten of them, were mostly parliamentary groupings. The Social Democratic Party, founded in 1916, was the first political party in Iceland (and in the other Scandinavian countries) to be organized outside of parliament for the express purpose of electing members to it.

The main values and structural characteristics that shape the political culture of the Icelanders can be summarized as follows:

1. There is a pervasive social and political egalitarianism. In comparison to other modern societies, Iceland must be termed radically egalitarian in ideology. Yet, there has been a tendency for leading political figures to come from a few high-status families or for a few individuals to be politically dominant for long periods; also, there have been almost no women in leading political positions.

2. There is a strong and pervasive belief in freedom and individualism combined with norms of tolerance and a general absence of fanaticism of any kind, except in politics.

3. The population has a high level of literacy and political awareness. In all the national elections since 1956, over 90 percent of the electorate has voted, a level achieved only by Sweden in northern Europe.

4. In spite of highly acrimonious, partisan, and personalistic politics, there is a high level of consensus on the legitimacy of the nation's political institutions (see appendix A, question 20). There has been an absence of serious violence in Iceland since the Protestant Reformation.

5. Because of, or perhaps in spite of, an extreme cultural homogeneity, the Icelanders have strong "primordial sentiments" (to use

Clifford Geertz's term) growing out of their isolated and misery-filled history, their unique literary tradition with its historical continuity of language, and their common descent.

6. There is a strong "help thy neighbor" attitude, most notable when disaster strikes, which can be traced back to the beginnings of Icelandic society.

7. Icelanders are provincial in a way similar to the way people of large nations are provincial. They read their own literature more than any other, are intensely patriotic (perhaps ethnocentric is a better term), and often have little awareness of the insignificance of Iceland in the world. Politics center on domestic issues and domestic issues often shape foreign policy positions.

Seven parties have dominated Icelandic politics since the close of the Second World War. What they stand for, who supports them, and how they have changed are discussed below. Table 2-2 is a list of the parties in power since home rule was achieved in 1918; table 2-3 lists the party composition of the Althing since 1946.

Independence Party (Sjálfstæðisflokkur). The Independence Party came into being in 1929 as a result of the merger of the Conserva-

Table 2-2. Parties in Power in Iceland Since 1918

Years in Power	Party or Coalition
1918-1920	Home Rule, Progressive, Independence parties
1920-1922	Home Rule Party
1922-1924	Home Rule, Independence parties
1924-1927	Conservative Party
1927-1932	Progressive Party
1932-1934	Progressive, Independence parties
1934-1938	Progressive, Social Democratic parties
1938-1939	Progressive Party
1939-1942	Progressive, Independence, Social Democratic parties
1942	Independence Party
1942-1944	Nonpartisan cabinet (no ministers in Althing)
1944-1947	Independence, Social Democratic, Socialist parties
1947-1949	Social Democratic, Independence, Progressive parties
1949-1950	Independence Party
1950-1953	Progressive, Independence parties
1953-1956	Independence, Progressive parties
1956-1958	Progressive, Social Democratic parties, People's Alliance
1958-1959	Social Democratic Party
1959-1971	Independence, Social Democratic parties
1971-1974	Progressive Party, People's Alliance, Union of Liberals and Leftists
1974-1978	Independence, Progressive parties
1978	Progressive, Social Democratic parties, People's Alliance

Note: The first party named in a coalition is the party of the prime minister.

Table 2-3. Composition of the Althing, 1946-1978

Years	Total Elected Members	Independence Party	Progressive Party	Social Democratic Party	Socialist Party	People's Alliance	National Preservation Party	Union of Liberals and Leftists
1946	52	20	13	9	10	—	—	—
1949	52	19	17	7	9	—	—	—
1953	52	21	16	6	7	—	2	—
1956	52	19	17	8	—	8	—	—
1959(1)	52	20	19	6	—	7	2	—
1959(2)	60	24	17	9	—	10	0	—
1963	60	24	19	8	—	9	0	—
1967	60	23	18	9	—	10	0	—
1971	60	22	17	6	—	10	—	5
1974	60	25	17	5	—	11	—	2
1978	60	20	12	14	—	14	—	—

tive Party and the Liberal Party. Since the election of 1931, it has been, without exception, the largest party in the country, with generally around 40 percent of the popular vote and of the mandates. It is the dominant party in Icelandic politics. The party has participated in the government for more than two-thirds of the years 1932-1978. In 22 of the 33 years 1945-1978, Iceland has had a prime minister from the Independence Party. The party was originally committed to an ideology of laissez faire individualism, low taxes, and minimal governmental interference in the economy. However, since the 1930s, it has come increasingly to discard its laissez faire ideology and to accept economic planning and regulation and the principles of the modern welfare state. As a result of these changes, right-wing dissidents have left the party on two occasions: in 1941 to form the Commonwealth Party and in 1953 to form the Republican Party. Both were unsuccessful in electing members to the Althing and were short-lived. The Independence Party has been the most positive, and at times the least hostile, of the Icelandic parties in its attitude toward the United States military presence and toward international cultural influences. The party is particularly strong in Reykjavík and the larger towns, and weaker in the rural and outlying areas of the country. It is supported by *Morgunblaðið* (*Morning News*), by far the most important of the six national daily papers in Iceland, all of which are published in the capital city. *Vísir,* the sole afternoon daily in the country, also supports the Independence Party, giving it the support of two-thirds of the daily newspaper circulation (which on a per capita basis is among the highest in the world). The party has occupied a more important position in the political life of Iceland than have the conservatives, or perhaps even the conservatives plus the liberals, in the other Scandinavian countries. It is also probably a little less conservative on economic and social issues than its Scandinavian counterparts. More than any other Icelandic party, the Independence Party's leadership tends to come from the ranks of distinguished families. The party is highly pragmatic, as are all of the Icelandic parties, and has entered into coalitions with the Progressives, the Social Democrats, and even the Socialists (communists plus left Social Democrats).

Progressive Party (Framsóknarflokkur). The Progressive Party came into being in 1916 as a farmers' party, reuniting the old Farmers' Party and the Independent Farmers that had split from the former. Effective political party organization among farmers has been a general characteristic of Nordic political party systems, and Iceland's is typical in this regard. Through the years as the proportion of farmers in Iceland has declined, the party has expanded its appeal to include more and more nonfarmers; nonfarmers now make up the majority of its supporters. The closest counterpart to the Icelandic Progressive Party is the Swedish Center Party, which has also greatly expanded its support beyond farmers with an antibureaucratic appeal. The Progressive Party has always been relatively weak in Reykjavík and its environs and has obtained most of its support in the rest of the country, where it is generally the strongest party. The Progressives have a close relationship with the Cooperative Movement, which has been particularly strong and well organized in Iceland. As a result of the party's attempt to broaden its appeal, a dissident faction formed the new Farmers' Party in 1933 in an attempt to appeal to all the farmers in the country. This dissident party collapsed in 1942, but it did succeed in electing three members to the Althing in 1934 and two in 1937. The Progressive Party is supported by the fourth largest paper in the country, *Tíminn (The Times),* which has most of its circulation outside of the Reykjavík area. The party has been enormously successful in forming coalitions with other parties; this has enabled it to be in the government most of the time since 1927, except for the 1959-1971 period.

Social Democratic Party (Alþýðuflokkur). The Social Democratic Party of Iceland is far and away weaker than its sister parties elsewhere in the North (not excluding the Faroe Islands) and in western Europe in general. Its place declined drastically after 1956 and 1967 peaks, when it got 18 and 16 percent of the popular vote, and it dropped to 9 percent in 1974. Then, in the 1978 elections, the party's share of the popular vote increased to 22 percent, the highest ever. The party generally did better during the 1930s, when it averaged 20 percent of the vote. The Social Democrats, along with the Icelandic Federation of Labor of which it was to be the political arm, came into being in 1916. As it was previously noted, the Social Democrats were the first Icelandic political party founded outside the Althing to elect members to it. The party adopted the principles of socialism, as had all of the European social democratic and labor parties at an earlier time. Differences between the moderates and the radicals became immediately apparent. However, the communists did not break away to form their own party until 1930, a decade later than in most other countries. A high level of internal conflict has characterized the Social Democratic Party from its beginning. In 1938, a radical faction of the party broke away and joined the communists to form the People's Alliance. After this last major eruption to the nationalistic left, the Social Democrats became more moderate, giving up ideas of nationalizing industry, and have gone the way of other Scandinavian social democratic parties. The party has been less anti-NATO than the Progressives or the left parties. On foreign policy issues in general they have been closest to the Independence Party. Most of the support for the Social Democrats is in the towns, with little from rural areas and least of all from the eastern part of the country, where it is less than 5 percent.

Socialist Party (Sósíalistaflokkur). The Socialist Party was founded under the name People's Unification Party-Socialist Party by a group of left Social Democrats and communists in 1938. This coalition was accomplished at the initiation of the communists. The new party continued to support the policies of the Soviet Union. It and its successor, the People's Alliance, have always received more support than the Social Democrats. Iceland, along with Finland, France, and Italy, are the only Western countries with large communist parties. However, Iceland, along with Finland, is the only one in which the communists have been included in coalition governments (1944-1947, 1956-1958, 1971-1974, and 1978-   ). Between the elections of 1942 and 1953, the party's support, most of which is in the towns, fell to between 16 and 20 percent, more than twice what the old Communist Party received in the elections between 1931 and 1937.

People's Alliance (Alþýðubandalag). An electoral alliance was formed before the 1956 national elections by the Socialist Party, some Social Democrats, and some members of the National Preservation Party. It did not become a full-fledged party until 1970, when the Socialist Party disbanded. Like other communist parties in western Europe, it has moved to a position of independence from the Soviet Union and adheres to a democratic philosophy at the same time it proclaims a socialist program. Its opposition toward the United States' military presence is less salient than it previously was. It continues to be the third largest party, as was its predecessor, the Socialist Party.

National Preservation Party (þjóðvarnarflokkur). The National Preservation Party was founded in 1953 by wings of the Progressive, Social Democratic, and Socialist parties. The party's central aim was to have Iceland follow a policy of strict neutrality in foreign affairs, a policy followed between 1918 and 1940, when such was considered to be an everlasting policy (like that of Switzerland). The party advocated pacifism and national cultural values rather than international ones, and it vigorously opposed Iceland's membership in NATO and the United States' military presence in the country. In domestic affairs, the party held to a liberal social democratic policy. The party maintained an electoral alliance with the People's Alliance but in 1970 reconstituted itself as the Union of Liberals and Leftists.

Union of Liberals and Leftists (Samtök frjálslyndra og vinstri manna). In 1970, when the People's Alliance became a full-fledged party, the National Preservation Party formed a new party, the Union of Liberals and Leftists. The party continues to advocate the same policies as its predecessor, except in a more moderate form. Most of its support comes from townspeople.

THE 1978 ELECTIONS

The 1978 general elections in Iceland showed by far the largest shifts in party voting in Icelandic history. The two parties in power fell dramatically to the lowest points in their histories. The Independence Party lost five representatives in the Althing, going from 25 to 20, declining from 42.7 percent of the popular vote in 1974 to 32.7 percent in 1978. The Progressive Party also lost five seats, going from 17 to 12 with a decline in the popular vote of from 24.9 to 16.9 percent. The two major opposition parties, by contrast, reached the high points of their histories.

Table 2-4. Results of the 1974 and 1978 Icelandic Elections

	Percentage of Vote	Candidates Elected
	1974 Elections	
Parties in office		
Independence Party	42.7	25
Progressive Party	24.9	17
Opposition parties		
Social Democratic Party	9.1	5
People's Alliance	18.3	11
Union of Liberals and Leftists	4.6	2
Other	0.4	0
	1978 Elections	
Parties in office		
Independence Party	32.7	20
Progressive Party	16.9	12
Opposition parties		
Social Democratic Party	22.0	14
People's Alliance	22.9	14
Union of Liberals and Leftists	3.3	0
Other	2.2	0

Source: Statistical Bureau of Iceland, 1978, p. 9.

The lagging Social Democratic Party almost tripled its number of seats, from five to 14, taking more than double the popular vote it had in 1974, going from 9.1 to 22.0 percent. The People's Alliance (communist) increased its number of representatives from 11 to 14 with their share of the popular vote increasing from 18.3 to 22.9 percent.

The Icelanders demonstrated in the 1978 elections that they have become as volatile and changeable in their voting behavior as the voters of any modern society; traditional party affiliations have become less salient, and specific issues and the state of the economy have become more important. The preeminent issue in the period between 1974 and 1978 was the precarious state of the economy, with inflation most of the time galloping at an annual rate of between 40 and 50 percent, an intolerable level even for the most persistently inflationary economy of all OECD nations. The new leftist government is now taking strong steps to control inflation—freezing wages after some adjustments, increasing income taxes, and abolishing the sales tax on food. In late 1978, the government further devalued the króna by 15 percent.

Of importance in getting the three government coalition parties together were the perennial issues of continued Icelandic membership in NATO and the presence of United States military forces at the NATO base in Keflavík, 40 kilometers east of the capital. The People's Alliance opposes both. The government finally agreed on the following statement (quoted in Ivar Guðmundsson, 1978, p. 77):

> The foreign affairs policy will be unchanged in all fundamental matters [from that of the previous government] and will not be altered except with the consent of all cabinet members. However, it is pointed out that the People's Alliance is against Iceland's membership in NATO and the stationing of military forces in the country. New major constructions at the military base will not be allowed.

What this means, in effect, is that there will be no change in Iceland's relationship with NATO and that the United States' military presence will continue to be tolerated, even by the People's Alliance. It is crucially important to understand the underlying economic realities here: it would be quite impossible for Iceland to leave NATO and force out the American military without doing enormous damage to its fragile economy. It is doubtful that Icelandic Airlines (Loftleiðir), the country's largest wholly owned industry and its chief means of communication with the outside world, could profitably survive without the American personnel and American support at the Keflavík airfield. The base also employs a large number of Icelanders and is a diverse source of revenue for the country.

THE TRADITIONAL SOCIETY AND ITS HERITAGE

Until the last two decades of the nineteenth century, the overwhelming majority of Icelanders lived on farms. Indeed, up until about 1880, nearly the entire population was involved in farming, as it had been for a thousand years. Table 2-5 shows that in 1880 only some 7.4 percent of the population lived in towns and villages of over 300 people. Not even commercial fishing achieved much importance until the end of the nineteenth century.

The traditional Icelandic farm has always been large and isolated. The farmers raised sheep, cattle, and horses, and many fished for a portion of each year. The farms were in effect tiny, self-sufficient communities of an extended family, frequently with a servant, or two or three. Probably from five to ten people lived on most farms. From the twelfth century until the mid-1950s, the number of farms varied only between 5,350 and 6,150; the number had declined to 4,660 by 1970 (Jóhannes Nordal and Kristinsson, 1976, pp. 179-91). Most farms range between 450 and 3,000 acres, exclusive of mountains, with an average size of around 750 acres. The most important crop has always been hay for fodder.

In the centuries since the fall of the Commonwealth, there have been marked changes in the patterns of land ownership, but the significance of these changes has not been great (Jóhannes Nordal, 1953).

Table 2-5. Percentages of Icelanders Living in Towns and Villages of 300 and More Inhabitants and in Smaller Places and Rural Districts, 1703-1978

Year	Towns and Villages of 300 and Over	Smaller Places and Rural Districts	Total Population
1703	0	100.0	50,358
1801	0.6	99.4	47,240
1880	7.4*	92.6*	74,445
1890	11.1	88.9	70,927
1901	19.8	80.2	78,470
1910	32.2	67.8	85,183
1920	42.7	57.3	94,690
1930	54.6	45.4	108,861
1940	61.3	38.7	121,474
1950	72.8	27.2	143,973
1960	79.7	20.3	177,292
1970	84.1	15.9	204,578
1975	86.1	13.9	219,033
1978	86.8	13.2	224,384

Source: Percentages calculated from official data of the Statistical Bureau of Iceland.
*Estimates

During the period 1695-1760, some 90 percent of the farmers were tenants; a third of the farmland was owned by the Church and a third by the Danish Crown. From this low point, the proportion of farms individually owned increased to almost three-quarters by the mid-1960s. Still, the distinction between landowner and tenant has had little status or cultural significance throughout Icelandic history. Tenants have generally been isolated from, and largely independent of, whomever owned their land.

The social structure of Iceland until well into the nineteenth century was both strikingly simple and in various ways relatively egalitarian. Two classes found in almost every other Western society hardly existed: a trading class and a ruling class. Trade was wholly in the hands of the Danes after the establishment of their trade monopoly in 1602; earlier the Danes had shared trade with the English and the Germans. The wealth and influence of the native ruling class declined after the Reformation as a direct result of Danish policy. As late as the middle of the nineteenth century, there were only 25 full-time officials in the internal administration of the whole country (Ólafur R. Grímsson, 1970, p. 110).

At the top of the Icelandic class structure were the landowners with larger holdings, the clergy, and the sheriffs (who typically were respected farmers). Then came the great majority of the population, who were free farmers or members of their families. Under them were three categories: subtenants, servants and farm workers, and paupers. While there was little distinction between landowners and tenants, being a subtenant conveyed inferior status. Most servants and farm workers were young people who later married when a farm became available to them; few ever married before acquiring a farm. This is a kind of age mobility that has always been common in Iceland. The pattern was to contract with a farmer in the spring for a year of service at a time. There have always been few casual laborers in Iceland. At the bottom of this simple class system were the paupers, whose care has been the responsibility of the *hreppar* (parishes) from the beginning. In the 1703 census, carried out in a time of great depression, the number of paupers was put at 15.5 percent of the population (Statistical Bureau of Iceland, 1960). The proportion of paupers declined throughout the eighteenth century, and, during the nineteenth century, the proportion never rose above 3.4 percent in any census except that of 1870, when it reached 5.6 percent. In brief, Iceland had, until close to the end of the nineteenth century, a strikingly homogeneous occupational structure in which the overwhelming majority of the population consisted of independent farmers and their families. As late as 1867, an Icelandic physician and scholar could report to an English audience that the Icelanders "at present are not much further advanced in industry or the arts of life than our earliest ancestors" (Hjaltalín, 1867).

Jón Sigurðsson, a scholar and the leading figure in Iceland's struggle for independence from Denmark, wrote in 1842 that there were "mainly two classes or groups" in Iceland, "the common people and the learned men, but we mostly lack a middle class" (quoted by Jóhannes Nordal, 1953, p. 33). The process of increasing equality of condition had so reduced the distinctions between farmers that the sharpest distinction in society had become between the "learned" and the "unlearned." Differences in formal education, not wealth, increasingly emerged in the rural society of the nineteenth century as the most important determinants of status.

The major pastimes that have occupied the Icelanders for centuries grew out of the one commodity the Icelandic rural economy provided in abundance: *time*. Time, at least for Icelandic men, was plentiful for a large portion of the year, when darkness filled most of the day and the weather was raw. With an economy devoted so singularly to raising hay for livestock, the farmers had no fields to clear and no land to till. Some fished for part of the year, and many were part-time smithies of various sorts. The sexual division of labor on an Icelandic farm was such that the men were in charge of the work outside the house and the women were in charge of work inside the house. But the women were far more likely to do haying and milking and to help in the sheep roundups in the fall and with the shearing in the spring than the men were to be involved with domestic chores. So we may assume that leisure was a commodity that was unequally allotted to men in this otherwise egalitarian society. The paucity of women among Icelandic writers and versemakers from the beginning until into this century attests to this unequal distribution.

The Icelanders developed a unique literary tradition (chapter 5) in which reading, reading aloud, storytelling, and versemaking were all popularly developed as perhaps nowhere else on earth. As John Barrow (1835, p. 237), who visited Iceland in 1834, put it: "There is not probably, in any part of the world, an agricultural or pastoral peasantry so well informed and enlightened as those of Iceland." And Barrow was one of dozens of eighteenth- and nineteenth-century travelers who made such an observation. The development of such a popular tradition required first of all time.

Similarly, a lot of time was devoted to the game of chess, a very popular pastime in Iceland. In 1905, Willard Fiske published a volume of 400 pages entitled *Chess in Iceland and in Icelandic Literature* and it was his intention that there be a second volume, although a second volume was never published and probably was never written. Even to-day, there are two magazines devoted to chess published in Iceland. Few popular games require as much time to play well as chess, and it seems to be most popularly developed in the northern "indoor" countries from Iceland to Russia. It is perhaps notable that the most northerly and the most isolated place in Iceland, the island of Grímsey (with a population of 91 in 1977) through which the Arctic Circle passes, has long been regarded as the most chess-obsessed place in Iceland (Fiske, 1905; Jack, 1957). When 21 Icelandic youths aged 9-15 years came to America after Christmas 1978 to play New York City's most promising young chess champions, the Icelanders trounced the New Yorkers just as the Icelanders had the previous year in Reykjavík (*New York Times*, January 1, 1979, p. 19).

Another pastime that was cultivated and popularly practiced in rural Iceland for centuries and that takes a long time to perfect is *glíma*, a sophisticated form of wrestling that dates from at least the twelfth century and was never practiced in any other Scandinavian society. Indeed—as Jóhannes Jósefsson (1908), an Icelandic *glíma* champion, pointed out in a manual on the sport—until a century ago it was kept secret from foreigners just the way ju jitsu was kept a national secret by the Japanese. *Glíma* probably grew out of the techniques of self-defense used in late Viking times, most likely as a way of disarming a man of his sword. It is played by the two opponents who face each other with a grip on the left hip and right thigh of the other; this is accomplished by using a special *glíma* belt. The object of the game is to make one's opponent lose his balance. Jósefsson (1908, p. 8) wrote that the game "has absorbed a tremendous amount of time. The balancing principle is not acquired in a day, nor a month, nor a year, in fact, some men spend all their lives at it and never manage it. No other sport requires so much practice. Clever acrobats have spent a lifetime at it, and not reached anything like perfection." Incidentally, *glíma* itself is a stunning manifestation of cultural continuity. The game has changed hardly at all in eight centuries. All of the maneuvers of the game even bear the original names. However, like reading aloud, versemaking, and even chess, *glíma* is less popular among Icelanders today than it was in the past.[2]

Besides time, there is one other crucial commodity that the traditional Icelandic economy produced in abundance: calfskins and sheepskins, the only practical writing materials that Iceland produced. Even the copying of one of the shorter sagas required the skins of a number of animals. As late as the eighteenth century, many Icelanders relied on parchment manuscripts for their saga reading. Had it not been for the ubiquitousness of skins, together with an abundance of time for part of the year, it is not conceivable that the 70,000 or 80,000 Icelanders could have produced an intellectual golden age in the thirteenth century or that they would have developed their eight-century-long tradition of popular literacy.

ICELANDIC EGALITARIANISM

Among the values that took shape during the early period of the Icelandic settlement and that have been passed down through the centuries in the folk culture are egalitarianism, individualism, freedom, skepticism toward authority, empiricism, and pragmatism — a configuration of values close to those developed in America.[3] Indeed, the frontiersman/farmer social type that came to predominate in America some centuries later shows a marked similarity to that earlier "new man" — the Icelander. But this is explicable because, as I am trying to demonstrate here and as Ellsworth Huntington (1924, p. 301) noted years ago, "much of the story of Iceland is repeated in that of the early white settlers in America."

If we look at the accounts of the social character of Icelanders during Saga Times (as written about in the thirteenth century) through the numerous travelers' accounts written during the nineteenth century before the advent of modernization, a consistent type emerges. The male form is the yeoman farmer; the female form is the independent household manager. These types certainly bear a resemblance to the independent farmers of Scandinavia and Britain. But there is one overriding difference: the Icelanders existed in a much less differentiated social structure. Even the simple distinction between the farmer and the cotter class in Norway, as described by Eilert Sundt during the 1850s, had little significance in Iceland (Drake, 1969, pp. 138-49).

From the beginning, the Icelanders have been egalitarian and class distinctions have been minor, both characteristic more of new societies than of old ones. This must not be taken to mean that Icelanders have not and are not given to making all sorts of invidious distinctions among themselves. They certainly are. It is only that such distinctions are not commonly made on the basis of class criteria. Obviously, Alan E. Boucher (1949, p. 35), an English translator of Icelandic literature living in Reykjavík, overstated the case when he wrote some years ago that "class distinctions simply do not exist in Iceland." So did Prime Minister Jóhann Hafstein, who asserted in a speech he gave on New Year's Eve 1971 that "Iceland is a classless society" (quoted in Dóra Bjarnason, 1974, p. 34). Still—and it has been noted by many travelers to Iceland—a low degree of class consciousness combined with a radically egalitarian ethic have been fundamental to Iceland's folk society. This situation grew out of the conditions under which Iceland was settled, the harshness of pioneer life because of which everyone had to work, and, above all, the undifferentiated agricultural social structure that existed. Just like the language, the rural social structure has not changed much since medieval times. This folk society, in the words of Jóhannes Nordal (1953, p. 33), "is the fountainhead from which the new urban social classes spring, and its values have been carried to the towns, usually in an idealized form. From this class spring the egalitarian values which are so very strong in Iceland today."

The sagas show, I believe, an egalitarianism found in no other literary or historical body of writing produced before the seventeenth century.[4] They portray a society with an egalitarian ethic and are written from an egalitarian viewpoint by their generally anonymous authors. They are crammed with diverse personalities. *Njal's Saga*, for example, the most renowned and the longest of the sagas of the Icelanders, contains at least 36 rich character portrayals (Sveinsson, 1971, p. 85). In it wives and thralls are dealt with as personalities worthy of description, inherently just as interesting as their husbands and masters. Dorothy M. Hoare (1937, p. 10) in comparing the very different Icelandic and Irish sagas wrote: "In Iceland the chieftain represents the common characteristics of the race more eminently; in Ireland the chief seems to be distinct from the masses, as in Beowulf." The major protagonists in *Njal's Saga* are in fact not even chieftains, they are just esteemed farmers.

Even the central characters in the sagas do mundane, everyday tasks. In *Njal's Saga*, Hallgerd and Bergthora, the wives of the two most illustrious men—Gunnar and Njal—serve meals and are involved in performing household tasks. Gunnar, perhaps the most admired of all saga characters, sowed his own grain. In *Njal's Saga* (chapter 53), we read this matter-of-fact description: "That same day Gunnar had left home by himself, carrying a seed-basket and armed only with a hand-axe. He walked to his cornfield, and started sowing grain. . . . He was busy sowing when Otkel came galloping out of control across the field."

In the sagas, only kings and queens, parents and grandparents are addressed with titles. With everyone else, regardless of their age or station, given names are used. There is little deference to status to be found in the dialogue, and a mode of equality permeates interpersonal relations that appears strikingly modern and not at all medieval. Not even in the frequent and mostly fictional encounters with Norwegian kings and kinglets are the Icelanders deferential.

Most of the eighteenth- and nineteenth-century travelers to Iceland were impressed with the equality of material conditions and social relations that prevailed there. Some commented on the Icelanders' dislike for authority, their failure to show deference to rank, the absence of any stigma attached to physical work, and their concern with the opinions of others. These observations are similar to those of nineteenth-century travelers to America (Toqueville and Bryce, for example), but the egalitarianism observed in Iceland was simpler and more radical than that noticed in America, and class distinctions were smaller. Another difference was that the Icelanders were often regarded as poor, yet without any abject poverty. As von Troil (1780, p. 20) put it two centuries ago, the Icelanders "are not very rich, neither have they any beggars." Such observations were repeated dozens of times in other travelers' accounts.

The radical egalitarianism of the Icelanders was often commented upon, and not always favorably, by the educated travelers who visited the country. Henderson (1818, p. 28) noted that "both at meeting and parting, an appropriate kiss on the mouth, without distinction of rank, age, or sex, is the only mode of salutation." Thirty years later the snobbish Ida Pfeiffer wrote negatively about her experiences (1852) among these isolated people. She disliked their "loud" kissing, their republican sentiments, their lack of courtesy among the "better classes," and much else. At some assembly in Reykjavík, she observed (p. 95) that "all ranks meet there, and everything is said to be on a very republican footing. The shoemaker invites the wife of the *Stiftsamtmann* (governor) to dance, and that great personage himself leads out the wife or daughter of the shoemaker and baker."

In 1872, the sensitive Bryce, who even learned to read the language, noted that "there is really no distinction of ranks" (1923, p. 33) and was much impressed with their "social equality which involves no obstrusive self-assertion by the poorer, since it is the natural result of the conditions under which life goes on" (p. 38). Burton (1875), whose account was almost as snobbish and prejudiced as that of Pfieffer but who was more intelligent and informed, was negatively impressed by the "rude equality" of what he mistakenly called "the servant class" (volume 2, p. 363). Morris, like Bryce and Burton, was impressed by the social equality he found, so much so that it was a factor in the transformation of his political and social views and "he talked about it for years to the alarm of many of his friends" (Purkis, 1962, p. 28).

A skepticism toward authority and a failure to be impressed by rank characterize the Icelandic as much as the American variety of egalitarianism. James Nicoll (1841, p. 211) noted that the distance between the clergy and the people in Iceland was smaller than in other countries and that "the Icelander pays little deference to his pastor on account of his office, and unless his personal character secures respect, he is soon treated as a common peasant, in whose labours he is often compelled to join." Valtýr Guðmundsson, who wrote a book explaining his fellow Icelanders to the Danes, observed (1902, p. 19) that the Icelander "has no respect for authorities, but wants always to be his own master or lord, in thought as well as in action." Lindroth (1937, p. 16) commented that the Icelander "does not like to subordinate himself in any way." The treatment of the king of Denmark was described by Kneeland (1876, p. 125), who noted that the king mingled with the people in a "friendly, yet dignified way; but must have been disappointed by, and perhaps wounded by, the sturdy, democratic, independent spirit degenerating sometimes into stolid disrespect, with which he was met in public."

The clergy in most of Lutheran Europe held high status, were deferentially treated, and generally had the accoutrements of the well-off. This was much less the case in Lutheran Iceland. In the middle of the eighteenth century, Horrebow (1758, p. 132) observed that the Icelandic clergy "are obliged to have recourse to manual labor for maintaining their families, or to go fishing like the common people." John Barrow noted in 1835 (pp. 239-40) that "there is little doubt that the pastor and his flock are nearly on an equality as to worldly concerns." Burton observed (1875, volume 1, p. 141) that as "in the United States, there is no gentlemen class except the liberal professions, and even the clergy until the present generation were farmers and fishermen, labourers, mechanics, and so forth, often poorer and shabbier than the laity." But in Iceland there never was much, if any, status inhibition associated with doing physical work. The Scottish geologist George Steuart MacKenzie (1811, pp. 149-50), for example, in observing the "habits and modes of life among the Icelanders of the highest class," noted "that almost every man in the country knows how to shoe a horse; even the son and heir of the Chief Justice of Iceland having been seen thus occupied." Bryce noted (1923, p. 33) in 1872 that "everybody has to work for himself, and works (except, to be sure, a few storekeepers in Reykjavík, and at one or two spots on the coast), with his own hands."

In the predominantly agricultural society that was Iceland until the 1920s, the majority of Icelanders were engaged in agriculture; even most of the clergy had to farm to supplement their meager salaries. Students were farm workers or fishermen during the summer, and most of the few professionals had been workers or fishermen at some time in their lives. The enormously fluid occupational structure of premodern Iceland—which is still somewhat characteristic of modern Iceland—was described by Andreas Heusler (1946, pp. 321-22), a Swiss saga scholar who toured Iceland in 1895, when only 15 percent of the population lived in communities of more than 300 people. He wrote:

Occupational differences which result in horizontal societal clefts among us are here peacefully parallel.

Let me cite some examples. The man who so carefully led our pack horses over mountain and fen and did all the hard work for us, Thorgrímur Guðmundsen, is the brother of a sheriff (*sýslumann*), a prefect with a legal education. This Throrgrímur, who is a guide for foreigners, is also a teacher in a girls' school in the winter. For years he had pursued fishing at sea. At the same time a young doctor, who had recently arrived from Copenhagen and was on his way to his place of practice, had requested to act as our guide. Also, at this time, a son of one of the richest farmers in the North repeatedly led foreigners about the country. On our travels through the desert we were accompanied by two fifteen year old boys, one a carpenter's apprentice, the other a student in the Latin School who intended to study medicine. In the summer he supported himself by working in a store. The brother of the carpenter's apprentice is a priest, an organist in the Cathedral in Reykjavík who previously had been an iron-worker. On one occasion a man visited our hotel selling eiderdown who, we were informed, was a well-known poet. Also, all priests in the country are farmers—they don't get drawn away from everyday life because of their meager stipends —and some of them are among the leading breeders of sheep. Icelandic scholars, including teachers at the University of Copenhagen, are, just like those in leading political and judicial positions, the sons of farmers who grew up in the country knowing about farming from their own experience.

These are only a sample of quotations that illustrate the egalitarianism and the low degree of class consciousness that appear so pervasively in the travelers' accounts. I have come by only one set of empirical data that demonstrates the relative absence of class distinction that existed in the older Icelandic society. Jóhannes Nordal in his 1953 dissertation at the University of London studied the social mobility patterns of 405 leading Icelanders born in the years 1651-1850 and who had completed an academic education. Of the marriage pattern of these "learned" Icelanders he wrote (p. 67): "It is striking to see that the social origin of the subjects seems to have no influence on their marriage pattern: those having both a father and a grandfather in Class I are no more likely to marry into that class than those whose fathers and grandfathers belonged to Class III." (Class III, it should be noted, consisted of all the rural population except the "learned class" [Class I] and "landowners and farmers holding important posts," together with a few minor categories [Class II]).

This traditional equality and the pervasive belief of Icelanders in its existence is being eroded or is being changed through the Icelanders' increasing awareness of how much material, educational, and sexual inequality there in fact is in their modern society. This topic is dealt with in chapter 8, a discussion of contemporary values.

CHAPTER 3

The Demography of
an Isolated People

*To no other country in Europe have the vicissitudes of fate
. . . brought such boundless grief and sorrow.*

Alfred Nawrath (1959)

*The past of the Icelandic people can never be unraveled by
historians alone. The story must to a higher degree than the
story of most other civilized nations be read in the light of
their struggles with the elements, of the changes in the geographical environment due to fluctuations in climate and
drift ice, glacier oscillations, soil erosion, and catastrophic
events such as volcanic eruptions, "glacier bursts," and earthquakes. Since the first days of its settlement Iceland has been
rather near the verge as a possible habitation for people trying to maintain a Scandinavian cultural standard.*

Sigurður Thorarinsson (1961)

It may be that more information is available about the history of the
Icelandic population than about any other national population. The
Icelanders are the only European people whose origins have been recorded in history. We know that the island was settled between the
years 870 and 930, and we know the names of some 400 of the original settlers excluding wives, children, and followers from the *Book of
Settlements* (1972), which contains approximately 3,500 personal
names and more than 1,500 place names (Jakob Benediktsson, 1969).
From the *Book of Settlements* and from other sources, we know where
many of the settlers came from, where they settled, who accompanied
them, what their culture was, and much else. The avid concern of the
Icelanders with genealogy from the beginning, together with the unique
development of popular literacy during the late twelfth and thirteenth
centuries, resulted in unparalleled written records, many of which have

56

survived. Indeed, we know more about many twelfth- and thirteenth-century Icelanders than we do about the kings and queens of the same period elsewhere in Europe.

In this chapter, I give a demographic account of the Icelandic population over eleven centuries. During the country's existence I estimate that fewer than two million Icelanders have been born and that, until the middle of the nineteenth century, fewer than half of those born survived to age 15. The earliest infant mortality rates from the 1830s and 1840s (table 3-6) indicate around 35 percent of all infants born alive died before their first birthdays; this was perhaps the highest rate of infant mortality in Europe during the nineteenth century (United Nations, 1953, pp. 64-67), a rate almost *twice* as high as that reported for Sweden in the middle of the eighteenth century (Sweden, 1969, p. 91). Of particular note in comparative historical demography is the observation that no other European people has been been so persistently ravaged by natural calamaties—famines, epidemics, volcanic eruptions, floods, shipwrecks, and drownings—singly and in combination as have the Icelanders.[1] Indeed, there were fewer Icelanders in the middle of the nineteenth century, before the great emigration to Canada and the United States, than there had been in 1100; and there were only half as many during much of the eighteenth century as there had been in the twelfth century.

A DEMOGRAPHIC HISTORY

Iceland represents the most extremely inhospitable environment in which a European people has been been able to survive and maintain its culture. In the half-millennium from the end of the thirteenth to the end of the eighteenth century, it is not much of an exaggeration to say that the Icelanders just managed to survive. In fact, the eighteenth century was the worst century in Icelandic history in terms of natural catastrophes and climatic conditions. After the famine and the disease that followed the Laki eruptions of 1783-1784, there was public discussion of whether the Icelanders could survive on their isolated island and proposals to evacuate the old and weak to Denmark were made (Bjarnar, 1965).

The most difficult environment for the maintenance of Western culture, the utter outpost of the Western world was, however, Greenland. The Icelanders under Erik the Red settled that desolate country with the attractive name late in the tenth century (Gwyn Jones, 1964, pp. 44-76, 143-62; 1968, pp. 269-311). The colony began with probably fewer than 500 Icelanders and grew to a high point of perhaps 3,000

Table 3-1. Populations of Iceland and Norway, 965-1860

Year	Iceland	Norway	Comparative Ratio*
965	60,000	. . .	
1100	50,000 to 104,000	250,000	3
1311	72,000 to 95,000	. . .	
1349	. . .	400,000†	
1351	. . .	270,000‡	
1371	. . .	250,000§	
1402	120,000†	. . .	2
1404	40,000‡	. . .	
1515	. . .	180,000	
1600	. . .	400,000	
1665	. . .	444,000	
1695	54,000**	. . .	
1703	50,358	504,000††	10
1734	43,845	616,109 §§	14.1
1762	44,845	715,154	15.9
1769	46,201	739,180	16.0
1785	40,623	790,325	19.5
1801	47,240	882,751	18.7
1840	57,094	1,241,140	21.7
1850	59,157	1,391,941	23.5
1860	66,987	1,596,089	23.8

Sources: Estimates of the population of Iceland through 1695 are from Ólafur Lárusson, 1936, pp. 121-37; Steffensen, 1968, columns 390-92; figures for 1703 through 1860 are from Statistical Bureau of Iceland; 1967, p. 19. Estimates of the population of Norway from 1100 through 1600 from Johnsen, 1936, pp. 58-105; Torgersen, 1968, columns 388-90; and Holmsen and Jensen, 1949, p. 517; estimates for 1665 through 1785 are from Drake, 1969, p. 41, 164-65; figures for 1801 through 1860 are from Norway, 1969, p. 33.

Note: Icelandic figures from 965 through 1695 are the estimates of historians; those from 1703 are official population figures. Norwegian figures from 1100 through 1600 are the estimates of historians, those for 1665 through 1762 are also estimates but are based on partial enumerations; and those from 1769 are official population figures.

*Ratios computed by dividing the population of Norway by the population of Iceland.
†Before the Black Death.
‡After the Black Death.
§ Approximate figure; actual figure would be lower.
**Approximate figure; actual figure would be higher.
††Figure is for 1701.
§§ Figure is for 1735.

in two settlements. They developed a popular assembly, a code of law, even a literature. Sometime around 1500 the European Greenlanders disappeared completely. What happened is unknown, but what is remarkable is that they were able to survive so long. Gwyn Jones (1968, p. 311) after discussing virtually every theory about their disappearance concludes

> that the Greenland colony died out for no one reason but through a complex of deadly pressures. Of these its isolation from Europe, the neglect it suffered from its northern kinsmen, the lack of trade and new blood, the worsening conditions of cold, and above all the encroaching Eskimo, were the most important. Even in theory they sound more than enough to bring down the curtain on this farthest medieval outpost of what had been the Viking and was now the European world, and extinguish it with all the trappings of an inexorable and heart-chilling doom.

Iceland lies just south of the Arctic Circle; it is almost half as large as Britain and a fifth larger than Ireland. The shortest distance to Norway is just over 600 miles and to Scotland just under 500 miles. The climate is mild maritime and is made temperate by the warm waters of the Gulf Stream, but the growing season is short, only four to five months, and, more important, the average temperature for July (the warmest month) averages only in the low 50s. As can be seen in table 3-2, the average July temperature in Reykjavík for the years 1931-1960 was 52.2° F (11.2° C). How low this is can be seen by comparison with Tromsö, a Norwegian coastal town north of the Arctic Circle, which recorded an average July temperature over this period of 54.3° F (12.4° C); for Oslo the average was 63.1° F (17.3° C). It also should be noted that the average temperature in Reykjavík is

Table 3-2. Average Temperatures in the Nordic Countries, 1931-1960
(In °Fahrenheit)

	Annual Average	Average Warmest Month	Average Coldest Month	Average Difference between Warmest and Coldest Months
Reykjavík, Iceland	41.0	52.2	31.3	20.9
Copenhagen, Denmark	47.3	64.0	31.8	32.2
Helsinki, Finland	41.7	64.0	21.2	42.8
Joensuu, Finland	36.5	62.1	13.1	49.0
Oslo, Norway	42.6	63.1	23.5	39.6
Tromsö, Norway	37.2	54.3	24.8	29.5
Stockholm, Sweden	41.9	64.0	26.4	37.6
Umeå Sweden	37.6	61.0	16.5	44.5

Source: Temperatures converted from data in Celsius degrees in Nordic Council, 1979, p. 29.

Note: The warmest month is always July; the coldest, January or February.

warmer than that in eight of the eleven official weather stations in Iceland (Statistical Bureau of Iceland, 1967, p. 16).

Overwhelmingly, the most important crop in Iceland from the beginning has been fodder for livestock. This is an understatement. The size of the Icelandic population until the end of the last century was determined by how well the grass grew (Fridriksson, 1972). And how well the grass grew was directly dependent upon the temperature and the length of the growing season, which in turn were related to the magnitude of the ice floes off the coasts of the island. When the grass could not grow, the results were catastrophic. One of the most popular poets in Icelandic history, Matthías Jochumsson (1835-1920), wrote with more than poetic truth:

> When the grass dies,
> The beasts die too;
> First the horse,
> Then the sheep,
> Then the cow,
> After that the beggar,
> Then the farmer,
> Then his wife,
> And finally his child.[2]

The raising of grain in Iceland was most unpredictable, and it was abandoned completely in the sixteenth century, partly as a result of the long-term decline in the temperature that began around the beginning of the thirteenth century. Average temperatures probably did not again reach the levels of the Age of Settlement until the twentieth century (Gwyn Jones, 1964, pp. 54-61; Utterström, 1955).

Less than a fifth of the land surface of Iceland is now arable. About 12 percent of Iceland is glacier and two-thirds is desert, mountain, lava field, and wasteland. In the eleven centuries that Iceland has been inhabited, much of the grassland has been eroded as a result of the introduction of domestic herbivorous animals, which have produced the major sustenance for the human population. Domestic animals drastically altered the natural balance between the native vegetation and the fauna that had existed in Iceland without humans and domestic animals. Sturla Fridriksson (1972, pp. 786-87) has estimated that at the Time of Settlement twice as much of Iceland was covered with vegetation as at present. He also has reckoned that approximately nine sheep were necessary to support one human (with six sheep being the equivalent of one cow). The population of Iceland, until the twentieth century, he maintains, has been directly limited by the amount of available fodder. Fishing, it is important to note, is disregarded in his

Table 3-3. Crude Deathrates for Iceland, Norway, and Sweden, 1735-1977

Years	Iceland	Norway	Difference between Iceland and Norway	Sweden
1735-1740	27.4	22.5	4.9	31.5*
1741-1750	25.3	29.0	-3.7	29.8
1751-1760	39.1	24.2	14.9	27.2
1761-1770	28.0	25.4	2.6	27.6
1771-1780	26.4	25.9	0.5	28.9
1781-1790	48.6	25.1	23.5	27.9
1791-1800	24.4	22.6	1.8	25.4
1801-1810	29.0	25.4	3.6	28.2
1811-1820	25.3	21.4	3.9	25.8
1821-1830	28.3	18.9	9.4	23.6
1831-1840	30.7	20.4	10.3	22.8
1841-1850	29.9	18.2	11.7	20.6
1851-1860	28.3	17.1	11.2	21.7
1861-1870	31.6	18.0	13.6	20.2
1871-1880	24.0	17.1	6.9	18.3
1881-1890	24.4	17.1	7.3	16.9
1891-1900	17.9	16.3	1.6	16.4
1901-1910*	16.2	14.2	2.0	14.9
1911-1920	14.2	13.8	0.4	14.3
1921-1930	12.7	11.3	1.4	12.1
1931-1940	10.7	10.3	0.4	12.1
1941-1945	10.1	10.5	-0.4	10.6
1946-1950	8.2	9.2	-1.0	10.2
1951-1955	7.3	8.5	-1.2	9.6
1956-1960	7.0	8.9	-1.9	9.7
1961-1965	6.9	9.5	-2.6	10.0
1966-1970	7.1	9.8	-2.7	10.2
1971-1975	6.9	10.0	-3.1	10.5
1976	6.1	10.0	-3.9	11.0
1977	6.5	9.8	-3.3	10.7

Sources: Rates for Iceland through 1800 are from Gille, 1949-1950, appendix III; rates for 1801 through 1826 are calculated from data in Indriði Einarsson, no date. The numbers of births used as a basis of the birthrates in table 3-4 were reduced by 3 percent because stillbirths were not separated from live births before 1827. The numbers of deaths were reduced by same estimated number of stillbirths before the death rates were calculated. Rates for 1827-1960 were calculated from data in Statistical Bureau of Iceland, 1967, pp. 36-39. Rates for Norway through 1865 were calculated from Drake, 1969, pp. 192-98. Drake's estimates are a hairbreadth below the official rates calculated by Anders Kiær through 1795, after which time Drake's estimates run slightly higher. Rates from 1866 through 1965 were calculated from Norway, 1969, table 20, pp. 44-47; rates from 1966, from official statistics. Rates for Sweden through 1967 are from Sweden, pp. 86-99, 1969; rates from 1968 are from official statistics.

Note: Figures are annual averages of deaths per 1,000 population.

*Data for years 1736-1740 only.

calculations because it was not an important source of food until the second half of the nineteenth century. During the eighteenth and nineteenth centuries, when frequent enumerations of the human and animal populations were taken, the population of Iceland averaged about 50,000, with around 300,000 sheep and just over 25,000 cattle. In the seven centuries between 1100 and 1800, the population of Iceland declined by about half; so, too, Fridriksson has calculated, had the available fodder for animals. The only other existing European population that has faced an isolated and rigorous environment comparable to the Icelanders' is the 40,000 Faroese, but almost nothing is known of them prior to the Reformation and they have had a milder climate and have lacked a heritage of natural disasters comparable to the Icelanders' (West, 1972, p. 9).

The demographic history of Iceland can be seen in terms of the three conventional epochs of Icelandic history: from the founding of the society through the end of the Commonwealth (1262) when Iceland lost its independence and entered into a union with the king of Norway, the intermediate centuries when Iceland was a colony of Norway and later of Denmark (from 1380), and the modern period (from about 1830) (see table 1-1). This system is the commonly used, and commonly deplored, division of Icelandic history, but it does rather neatly fit the demographic history of the Icelanders.

The first four centuries of Iceland's history were filled with famines and natural calamities that took many lives, but the long-term trend of the population was for it to increase. Estimates and enumerations of the Icelandic and Norwegian populations from 965 to 1860, before the onset of large-scale emigration, are given in table 3-1. Most of the figures from before the middle of the seventeenth century are little more than educated guesses, but enumerations of all farms in Iceland were made for tax purposes in 1106 and 1311. Estimates of the size of the population can be made by multiplying the number of farms by estimates of average household size, but, of course, there have been differences of opinion on what that size was. Some of the worst years during these relatively beneficent early centuries were noted in the *Book of Settlements*. There we read, for example, that there was "a great famine-winter in Iceland in heathen days, the severest there has been in Iceland. Men ate ravens then and foxes, and many abominable things were eaten which ought not to be eaten, and some had the old and helpless killed and thrown over the cliffs" (Gwyn Jones, 1964, p. 139). Eighty years later, in 1057-1058, there was "another year of dearth." In 1118, "there was a great famine in Iceland." The next year was also a bad year, and, in June at the Althing, Saemund the Learned announced that "the men who had died of sickness could not be fewer in number than those who were then attending the Althing." In many of the sagas and in various historical accounts dating from the twelfth and thirteenth centuries, there are references to "bad years" and natural catastrophes. Let one example suffice for many. In *Njal's Saga* (chapter 47), it is noted that there "was a time of great famine in Iceland, and all over the country people were going short of hay and food"; this time has been determined to have been around 985.

The second phase of Icelandic history can be taken from the loss of Icelandic independence in 1262-1264 to some years after the 1783-1784 eruptions of Laki in south central Iceland, which involved "eruptions unparalleled on earth in historic times" (Jon Stefansson, 1902). The immediate result of this catastrophe was only the destruction of 37 farms, with some 400 people left without shelter. However, the volcanic ash ruined most of the grasslands with more tragic results; 9,336 persons died of famine and disease in 1784 and 1785, about a fifth of the total population. The loss of livestock was horrendous: 28,013 (or 77 percent) of all the horses in the country perished; so did 11,461 cattle (53 percent of the total) and 190,488 sheep (82 percent of the total) (Stephensen, 1808, p. 29). This was the third most catastrophic event in Icelandic history. The worst ravage occurred in 1402-1404, when the Black Death belatedly reached Iceland and killed an estimated two-thirds of the population—as great a toll as claimed in any country visited by the bubonic plague (see Ziegler, 1969). The second most terrible loss of life occurred as a result of the smallpox epidemic of 1707, when around 18,000 persons died, more than a third of the population. In 1708, the population of Iceland was reckoned to have declined to about 33,000, lower than at any time since the island had been settled (Finnsson, 1970, p. xxxiii).

This second period was a time of worsened climate and less fodder for animals, frequent famine, and a long-term but erratic decline in population (Utterström, 1955). The period 1270-1390, according to the investigations of Sigurður Thorarinsson (1955), was one of the worst epochs in Icelandic history, with a particularly high frequency of bad years and the Black Death that came just after the turn of the next century. The fifteenth and sixteenth centuries saw the continued decline and finally the termination of grain growing, which Thorarinsson takes as evidence of the deteriorating climate. The seventeenth was another bad century; the age structure of the 1703 census (table 3-10) indicates that there was a marked decline in the population during the latter part of that century. But the eighteenth century was unequivocally the worst of all the eleven centuries of Icelandic history. "During this century," wrote Magnús Stephensen (1808, pp. 15-16),

"Iceland experienced 43 years of distress due to cold winters, ice-floes, failures of fisheries, shipwrecks, inundations, volcanic eruptions, earthquakes, epidemics and contagious diseases among men and animals which often came separately, but often in connection with and as a result of one another." The two worst catastrophes in Icelandic history after the Black Death both occurred during the eighteenth century. The population of Iceland was reckoned by the Icelandic historian Jón Espólín (1821, p. 125) to have been 120,000 at the beginning of the fifteenth century, almost certainly too high an estimate (Steffensen, 1968), but for a total of about 25 years during the eighteenth century the population was fewer than 40,000.

In 1796, Hannes Finnsson (1970), the bishop of the Southern Diocese of Skálholt, wrote a remarkable book entitled *Mannfækkun af hallærum á Íslandi* (*Population Decline from the Bad Years in Iceland*), in which he chronicled the history and the consequences for humans and livestock of more than eight centuries of natural disasters, from the famine year of 975-976 through the aftermath of the Laki eruptions of 1783-1784. Toward the end of this meticulously documented demographic history, he posed this question (p. 158): "Is the decline in population from hunger so great . . . [that] after a few generations the country will be uninhabited?" In the final chapter, the bishop tries to give some grounds for hope about the future at that time of national depression. His strongest and first mentioned observation (p. 191) was that, while Iceland had had many bad years, "no other northern land is so fast to increase in population and livestock, and it is, therefore, not uninhabitable." The bishop was much impressed with the extraordinarily high fertility of the 1790s, some of which, however, was the result of the high fertility of the 1760s.

The third period of Icelandic history can be designated as beginning around 1830, when an improvement of living conditions began, the effects of natural disasters lessened, and the size of the population began an almost uninterrupted growth. Still, there were 10 years after 1830 when the number of deaths exceeded the number of births, the last two years being 1882 and 1883, when there was much ice off the coasts that lowered the temperature and resulted in famine and then cholera. (The last year during which the number of deaths exceeded the number of births in Norway was 1813 and in Sweden, 1809).

Many of those who traveled to Iceland before the last decades of the nineteenth century, however, commented on the bad diet and the poor health of the Icelanders. As late as 1856, Lord Dufferin 1910, p. 95) could write that "scurvy, leprosy, elephantitis, and all cutaneous disorders are very common." He also commented on the "frightful mortality of the babies," an observation confirmed by the

Table 3-4. Crude Birthrates for Iceland, Norway, and Sweden, 1735-1977

Years	Iceland	Norway	Difference between Iceland and Norway	Sweden
1735-1740	32.7	29.4	3.3	32.5*
1741-1750	34.4	29.6	4.8	33.9
1751-1760	28.3	33.4	−5.1	35.7
1761-1770	37.0	31.7	5.3	34.2
1771-1780	32.1	29.8	2.3	33.0
1781-1790	27.3	30.0	−2.7	32.0
1791-1800	41.4	32.7	8.7	33.3
1801-1810	32.2	27.9	4.3	30.9
1811-1820	24.6	30.2	−5.6	33.3
1821-1830	37.6	33.4	4.2	34.6
1831-1840	38.9	29.9	9.0	31.5
1841-1850	35.6	30.7	4.0	31.1
1851-1860	38.7	32.9	5.8	32.8
1861-1870	36.4	30.9	5.5	31.4
1871-1880	32.0	30.9	1.1	30.5
1881-1890	30.4	30.1	0.3	29.1
1891-1900	31.0	30.1	0.9	27.1
1901-1910	27.8	27.5	0.3	25.8
1911-1920	26.5	24.4	1.7	22.1
1921-1930	26.0	20.1	5.9	17.5
1931-1940	22.0	15.4	6.6	14.5
1941-1945	24.7	18.5	6.2	18.8
1946-1950	27.6	20.6	7.0	18.2
1951-1955	28.0	18.6	9.4	15.2
1956-1960	28.2	17.9	10.3	14.3
1961-1965	25.4	17.5	7.9	15.0
1966-1970	21.5	17.5	4.0	14.5
1971-1975	20.9	15.5	5.4	13.5
1976	19.5	13.3	6.2	12.0
1977	18.0	12.6	5.4	11.6

Sources: Same as for table 3-3.

Note: Figures are annual averages of births per 1,000 population.

*Data for years 1736-1740 only.

infant mortality statistics. His explanation was that mothers stopped nursing babies a few days after birth and put them on cows' milk (p. 95); this is an acceptable modern explanation (McKeown, 1976, p. 111). Many of the travelers paid particular attention to disease and health because much poorer standards of cleanliness and sanitation prevailed in Iceland than in the countries from which they came. A number comment on the high prevalence of leprosy, which probably persisted longer in Iceland than anywhere else in Europe; three Icelanders died from leprosy as recently as the years between 1926-1930 (Statistical Bureau of Iceland, 1933, p. 48). Standards of cleanliness and hygiene did not begin to approach western European standards until the end of the nineteenth century. Ida Pfeiffer (1852, p. 66) noted their "unparallelled filthiness" and found the floor of one farmhouse "actually slippery from the incessant expectorations" (p. 163). Lindroth (1937, pp. 112-18) claims that, until this century, people literally believed in the adage "clean is the tongue of a dog" and let their dogs lick their food boxes (from which they ate) and themselves, thus spreading disease from sheep.

During the last decade of the nineteenth century, the population began its rapid upward climb. Indeed, the population of Iceland fully tripled in the 83 years between 1890 and 1973, going from 70,927 to 213,070; and, during most of those years, there were more emigrants then immigrants. No European population has grown quite so rapidly for such a long period.[3] Deathrates declined rapidly during those years, and birthrates continued at a higher level (25-27 per 1,000 population) than elsewhere in western Europe from the 1920s until the mid-1960s. (See table 3-4.) In the four decades between the early 1920s and the

Table 3-5. Life Expectancies at Birth for Icelanders and Norwegians, 1851-1976

	Males			Females		
Years	Iceland	Norway	Difference between Iceland and Norway	Iceland	Norway	Difference between Iceland and Norway
1851-1860*	31.9	46.2	−14.3	37.9	49.0	−11.1
1891-1900†	44.4	50.4	− 6.0	51.4	54.1	− 2.7
1901-1910‡	48.3	54.8	− 6.5	53.1	57.7	− 4.6
1911-1920	52.7	55.6	− 2.9	58.0	58.7	− 0.7
1921-1930	56.2	61.0	− 4.8	61.0	63.8	− 2.8
1931-1940	60.9	64.1	− 3.2	65.6	67.6	− 2.0
1946-1955	69.4	70.2	− 0.8	73.5	73.7	− 0.2
1951-1960	70.7	71.2	− 0.5	75.0	75.1	− 0.1
1961-1965	70.8	71.0	− 0.2	76.2	76.0	0.2
1966-1970	70.7	71.1	− 0.4	76.3	76.8	− 0.5
1971-1975	71.6	71.4	0.2	77.5	77.7	− 0.2
1975-1976	73.0	71.9	1.1	79.2	78.1	1.1

Sources: Data for Iceland through 1960 are from Statistical Bureau of Iceland, 1967, p. 46; data for Norway through 1965 are from Norway, 1969, p. 57. The more recent life expectancies are from Nordic Council, 1979, p. 60.

*For Iceland, the period is 1850-1860.
†For Iceland, the period is 1890-1901.
‡For Iceland, the period is 1902-1910.

Table 3-6. Infant Deathrates for Iceland, Norway, and Sweden, 1838-1977

Years	Iceland	Norway	Difference between Iceland and Norway	Sweden
1838-1840	366.8	143.7	223.1	161.9
1841-1850	341.7	115.0	226.7	153.2
1851-1860	264.2	103.5	160.7	146.0
1861-1870	251.9	110.0	141.9	138.9
1871-1880	189.3	104.0	85.3	129.9
1881-1890	173.1	97.6	75.5	110.5
1891-1900	119.3	96.8	22.5	101.6
1901-1910	110.0	74.6	35.4	84.5
1911-1920	71.4	64.1	7.3	69.3
1921-1930	52.8	50.6	2.2	58.8
1931-1940	44.0	42.1	1.9	45.8
1941-1945	37.6	37.5	0.1	31.0
1946-1950	24.4	30.9	-6.5	24.0
1951-1955	21.6	22.7	-1.1	19.3
1956-1960	16.4	19.9	-3.5	16.9
1961-1965	17.2	17.1	0.1	14.8
1966-1970	13.2	13.9	-0.7	12.3
1971-1975	11.6	11.6	0.0	10.0
1976	7.7	10.5	-2.8	8.3
1977	9.5	9.2	0.3	8.0

Sources: Rates for Iceland are calculated from Statistical Bureau of Iceland, 1976, Table II-2, pp. 8-11. More recent rates are from Statistical Bureau of Iceland, *Hagtíðindi*, monthly Rates for Norway through 1965 were calculated from Norway, 1969, pp. 44-47; rates from 1966, from official statistics. Rates for Sweden through 1967 are from Sweden, 1969, pp. 88-99; rates from 1968, from official statistics.

Note: Figures are annual averages of deaths occuring per 1,000 live births.

early 1960s, mortality levels declined rapidly and average life expectancies reached the levels of Norway, Sweden, and the Netherlands — the highest in the world. (See table 3-5.) As early as the 1920s Iceland had one of the lowest levels of infant mortality at that time and has since continued to have one of the lowest levels. (See table 3-6).

The three periods of Icelandic demographic history are reflected by the mean heights of males. In the first period, during medieval times, the mean height of Icelandic males based on skeletal remains was just under 5 feet 8 inches (172 centimeters); by the eighteenth century, there had been a decline to less than 5 feet 6 inches (167 centimeters); by 1950, the mean height of males had increased to 5 feet 10 inches (176.8 centimeters) (Björn Thorsteinsson, 1966, p. 51). This is a greater mean height for males than was found among Norwegian (Norway, 1969, p. 69), Swedish (Sweden, 1969, p. 141), and Dutch (Netherlands,

1970, p. 29) military recruits in 1950. In all of these countries, mean height has increased over the past three decades, but I have found no more recent data for Icelanders; they may well be the tallest of all the European peoples.

THE COMPARATIVE DEVELOPMENT OF THE ICELANDIC POPULATION UNTIL 1860

The increase in population that occurred throughout Europe during the eighteenth century did not appear in Iceland (United Nations, 1953, pp. 9-15). Indeed, the population of Iceland saw no sustained growth from after the Black Death (1404) until the end of the 1820s. Table 3-1 lists estimates of the sizes of the populations of Iceland and Norway from the early Middle Ages until the eighteenth century and the results of census enumerations in Iceland from 1703 and in Norway from 1769. Norway is the most appropriate population for comparison with Iceland because the country is Iceland's mother country and, along with the Faroe Islands, is closest to Iceland in culture, topography, and economy.

The most striking comparative historical observation about the Icelandic and Norwegian populations is the change in their relative sizes. From the time that Iceland was fully settled in the tenth century until the time of the Black Death in 1402, the population of Norway was between two and five times that of Iceland, even if the estimates of the sizes of the medieval populations are way off. During the sixteenth and seventeenth centuries, the excess of births over deaths (the rate of natural increase) was so much greater in Norway that the population had become some ten times that of the Icelandic population by the time of the 1703 Icelandic census. This trend continued until around 1860, when Norway had a population 24 times that of Iceland, the greatest difference between the populations of the two countries since Iceland had been fully settled. The reasons for the enormous change in the relative sizes of the two populations were the natural calamities with their terrible mortality that continually afflicted Iceland, together with the relatively low mortality that characterized Norway, at least from the beginning of official death registration in 1735. Differences in fertility have not been a factor; from 1735 through 1860, Icelandic fertility was in fact slightly *higher* than Norwegian fertility.

Of particular note in comparisons of the history of the Icelandic population with other populations are the extremely sharp ups and downs in both mortality and fertility. Table 3-7 shows the alternating increases and decreases of the population from the census of 1703 through 1823, when the population once again approached its 1703 size. No such violent swings can be found in the eighteenth-century populations of the other Scandinavian countries. They offer no examples of rapid declines in population like the ones Iceland saw during the 1750s and 1780s, nor did their populations ever grow as rapidly as the Icelandic population did in the 15-year period 1787-1801, when the average annual rate of increase was 1.5 percent (Drake, 1969, pp. 41-74). Table 3-8 shows how much more extreme the high and low

Table 3-7. Changes in the Icelandic Population, 1703-1823

Years	Number of Years	Average Annual Rate of Change
1703-1734	32	-0.5
1735-1751	17	0.7
1752-1755	4	-0.3
1756-1759	4	-3.6
1760-1778	19	0.8
1779-1783	5	-0.4
1784-1786	3	-8.4
1787-1801	15	1.5
1802-1805	4	-0.9
1806-1811	6	0.9
1812-1816	5	-0.5
1817-1823	7	0.7

Source: Average annual rates of change were calculated from population figures for 1703-1823 given in Statistical Bureau of Iceland, 1960, p. 8.

Note: The population of Iceland in 1703 was 50,358; in 1823 it was 50,088.

Table 3-8. Highest and Lowest Recorded Deathrates and Birthrates for the Nordic Countries, 1735-1800

Country	Highest	Lowest	Difference
		Deathrates	
Iceland	134.0 (1785)	17.8 (1796)	116.2
Norway	52.2 (1742)	18.2 (1745)	34.0
Sweden	52.5 (1773)	21.7 (1780)	30.8
Denmark	39.7 (1763)	22.2 (1774)	17.5
		Birthrates	
Iceland	45.9 (1799)	14.4 (1785)	31.5
Norway	35.0 (1756)	23.4 (1773)	11.6
Sweden	38.7 (1751)	25.2 (1773)	13.2
Denmark	33.6 (1780)	27.8 (1772)	5.8

Sources: Same as for table 3-3.

Note: Figures are average annual rates based on 1,000 population.

points of mortality and fertility were in Iceland than in the other Scandinavian countries in the years between 1735 and 1800. Note that compact Denmark had, by far, the most stable mortality and fertility over this period.

I have emphasized that, while the eighteenth century was the most persistently calamitous time in Icelandic history, the fifteenth was almost as bad and the fourteenth and the seventeenth not far behind in the number and the severity of "bad years." The whole history of the Icelandic population through the 1820s, then, can be assumed to have shown the sharp alternations of increase and decrease that characterized the years 1703-1823.

GENERAL OBSERVATIONS ON NORDIC DEMOGRAPHY

Iceland and the other Nordic countries are particularly important in demographic history. They are the only countries in the world for which there are relatively reliable national population and vital statistics data for much of the eighteenth century (Gille, 1949-1950). For none of the five countries are the data as detailed and as reliable as those for Sweden, but Norway for the reasons previously stated is most comparable with Iceland.

There is continuity and similarity in many of the demographic patterns in the preindustrial societies in these countries. The patterns are characterized by comparatively low deathrates and birthrates, high median ages at marriage, low marriage rates, large proportions of the population remaining unmarried, and high rates of premarital conceptions and illegitimacy. Finland is the most deviant of the Nordic countries, particularly in its having had much higher fertility than the rest. An important source for these observations is Gustav Sundbärg's (1970) *Bevölkerungsstatistik Schwedens 1750-1900*, which compares Swedish and Nordic population phenomena (not including Iceland's) with those of the rest of Europe.

In all the Nordic countries, not excepting Iceland, deathrates during the preindustrial period were *lower* than in the rest of Europe. (See table 3-9.) For much of the eighteenth century, Iceland had deathrates at Norwegian levels, and in that century Norway had the lowest mortality among the Nordic countries, an annual average of 25.1 deaths per 1,000 population for the years 1735-1800 (substantially lower than the rate of 31.2 that Sundbärg calculated as being the average for Europe in the years 1801-1850). What made the *average* mortality of eighteenth-century Iceland so much higher than that of the other Nordic countries, an annual average of 31.6 deaths per 1,000 population

Table 3-9. Annual Deathrates and Birthrates in Scandinavia and
Other Parts of Europe, 1735-1850

Country	1735-1800	1801-1850
	Deathrates	
Iceland	31.6	28.6
Norway	25.1	20.9
Sweden	28.1	24.2
All Europe	. . .	31.2
Western Europe	. . .	27.5
Northwestern Europe	. . .	26.6
	Birthrates	
Iceland	33.3	33.8
Norway	31.0	30.4
Sweden	33.6	32.3
All Europe	. . .	38.7
Western Europe	. . .	34.6
Northwestern Europe	. . .	35.4

Sources: Same as table 3-3; and Sundbärg, 1970.

Note: Figures are annual averages based on 1,000 population.

for the years 1735-1780, were the natural catastrophes to which Iceland did not become immune until the end of the nineteenth century. In 23 of the 66 years in the period 1735-1800, Iceland had annual deathrates *lower* than the comparable Norwegian rates calculated by Drake (1969, pp. 192-95). In an additional 11 of these 66 years the Icelandic rates were only 0.1 to 3.0 points higher than the comparable Norwegian rates. Average annual birthrates in Iceland during the eighteenth and nineteenth centuries, as in Norway and Sweden, were in the low 30s; average annual rates for all of Europe during the first half of the nineteenth century, according to the calculations of Sundbärg, were 38.7 per thousand population.

THE CENSUS OF 1703

A general census of the whole population of Iceland was taken in 1703 (Statistical Bureau of Iceland, 1960), the first modern national census in the world.[4] It came about as a result of the terrible conditions in Iceland during the preceding years. The people appealed to the king of Denmark, who in 1702 commissioned two leading Icelanders, the collector of saga manuscripts Professor Árni Magnússon and Vice-Lawman Páll Vídalín, to travel throughout the country to see how conditions could be improved; one of the means for accomplishing this was to take a census. These census materials had been considered lost until they were discovered complete in the Danish National Archives in 1914. The entire census was published by the Statistical Bureau of Iceland during the years 1924-1947.

Each sheriff was ordered to compile a complete register of all persons in his district. For each farm—and virtually everyone lived on farms—every person was to be listed by name, age, and position in the household, whether they were present at the time of the census or not. Some information on the health of the population also was obtained. Particular concern was given to enumerating all of the paupers; those without fixed abodes were recorded at the places they spent the night before Easter 1703. The completeness of the enumeration and the reliability of the data are of a high order. Name-by-name checking of the census found that 497 persons were enumerated more than once, and corrections were made by the Statistical Bureau for these

Table 3-10. 1703 Icelandic Census

Age	Males	Females	Total
Under 1	217	216	433
1-4	1,609	1,686	3,295
5-9	2,251	2,360	4,611
10-14	2,453	2,648	5,101
15-19	2,529	2,843	5,372
20-24	2,288	2,551	4,839
25-29	1,648	1,837	3,485
30-34	1,741	1,987	3,728
35-39	1,596	2,096	3,692
40-44	1,691	2,219	3,910
45-49	1,353	1,684	3,037
50-54	1,168	1,534	2,702
55-59	852	1,223	2,075
60-64	503	862	1,365
65-69	306	539	845
70-74	225	440	665
75-79	131	266	397
80-84	83	191	274
85-90	45	78	123
90-94	11	25	36
95-99	5	11	16
Not reported	162	195	357
	22,867	27,491	50,358
Median age	24.0	27.6	25.7

Source: Statistical Bureau of Iceland, 1960, table 2, pp. 42-43.

errors. Most of those enumerated twice were paupers entitled to relief in more than one parish. Sex was completely reported. Age was unreported for only 357 individuals, 0.7 percent of the population of 50,358. I checked the degree of age heaping in the reporting of age and found the results to be similar to recent censuses in developed countries.[5]

One of the inadequacies of this census is that couples who were cohabiting, always a common practice in Iceland, are not enumerated as such. This presumption is based on the very low proportion of the population enumerated as married and on a partial census taken in 1729, which does give data on cohabitants and which substanitally raises the proportion of the population "married" (Statistical Bureau of Iceland, 1975b). Another inadequacy of the 1703 census is that some of the separated and widowed among the servants, farm workers, and paupers may have been misclassified as unmarried, probably because information on their marital status was not obtained. But it is important to note that, in traditional Icelandic society, marriage was not common among those who did not own or manage a farm.

Much information on the social structure of the Icelandic society of almost three centuries ago is revealed by this early modern census. Precise information on individuals' positions in the household and relation to head of household is given. It should be noted, however, that the census was taken during one of the many bad periods in the history of Iceland. More paupers and vagrant beggars were recorded (15.5 percent) than in any subsequent Icelandic census. The population was also declining. This is indicated by the age distribution of the population: a quarter more youth aged 10-19 were enumerated than were children aged 9 and younger. That this is not necessarily accounted for by the underenumeration of infants is indicated by the irregular age distribution of the population in other age categories. During other bad years, it seems reasonable to speculate, birth control in the form of coitus interruptus or abstinence was practiced. This speculation is probably an important part of the explanation for the irregular age distribution and the sharp annual fluctuations in the birthrate. Gustaf Utterström (1965, p. 530) in attempting to explain fertility differentials between eastern and western Sweden during the eighteenth century similarly observed that "it seems very probable that some form of birth control was practiced in Eastern Sweden at least as early as the eighteenth century." The Swedish and Finnish censuses of 1749 and the Danish and Norwegian censuses of 1769, however, do not show anything like the irregular age distribution that characterizes the 1703 Icelandic census.

SEX RATIO AND MARITAL STATUS

The sex ratio of the Icelandic population in 1703 was 832 (males to 1,000 females), an extraordinarily low ratio for a population involved in no wars and with negligible emigration and immigration. The first Swedish census of 1749 showed a sex ratio of 885 (table 3-12), but the country had been at war half the time during the preceding 60 years. The first Norwegian census in 1769 found a sex ratio of 903. Note from table 3-11 that there is a deficit of males in the 1703 census even in the age category 0-4 and that the sex ratio decreased sharply and without exception from ages 0-4 through 80 and over, from 960 to 472. What this indicates is that mortality fell much more heavily on males than females at all ages. After the great mortality resulting from the aftermath of the Laki eruptions of 1783-1784, the sex ratio dropped to 784 (table 3-12), indicating the enormously greater effect on males than on females of mortality from malnutrition and its sequalae. At least in Iceland, Norway, and Sweden there is a strong inverse correlation between the male/female sex ratio and the deathrate. A greater decline in relative male mortality is reflected in all of these countries in their achieving a sex ratio near unity by the 1940s.

The Icelandic population of 1703 was a population with a high proportion of people unmarried and with a very high age at marriage. In the age category 25-29 only 12.5 percent of males and 20.1 percent of females were married in 1703, compared with 60.6 and 71.8 percent, respectively, in 1978 (Statistical Bureau of Iceland, 1960, p. 50; *Hagtíðindi*, 1979, p. 18). Indeed, the Icelanders of 1703 were

Table 3-11. Sex Ratio of the Icelandic Population, 1703

Age	Number of Males to 1,000 Females
0-4	960
5-9	954
10-19	907
20-29	897
30-39	817
40-49	780
50-59	733
60-69	577
70-79	504
80 and over	472
Total	832

Source: Calculated from Statistical Bureal of Iceland, 1960, table 2, pp. 42-43.

Table 3-12. Sex Ratios for Icelandic, Norwegian, and Swedish Populations

Year	Iceland	Norway	Sweden
1703	832	. . .	. . .
1729	865*	. . .	. . .
1749	. . .	. . .	885
1769	843	903	911
1785	784	. . .	920
1801	839	918	914
1825	. . .	946	927
1835	. . .	961	935
1840	904	. . .	935
1845	. . .	965	937
1850	913	. . .	940
1855	. . .	960	941
1860	907	. . .	944
1865	. . .	966	947
1945	997	971	990
1973	1022	988	991
1977	1018	985	986

Sources: Calculated from official statistics of Iceland, Norway, and Sweden.

Note: Figures are numbers of males per 1,000 females in population.

*Figure for three counties only.

less married than in any subsequent census that inquired into marital status, and Icelanders were less married and did so at older ages than the Norwegians or the Swedes during the second half of the eighteenth century or at any time since. According to Sundbärg's comparative study of the demography of Europe in the nineteenth century, the Norwegians and Swedes were the most unmarried of all European people after the Irish. (Sundbärg did not deal with Iceland.) A check of the marital status of the Irish (Ireland, 1968, p. xii) from the first Irish census of 1841 shows that they were least married in the successive censuses of 1911, 1926, and 1936. In these censuses, Irish males were slightly less married at ages under 35 and over 60 than were the 1703 Icelandic males. Irish females were never as unmarried at any comparable age in any census from 1841 as were Icelandic females in 1703. (See table 3-13.) A fundamental difference between these two populations is that 1703 Iceland had a great excess of females while 1926 Ireland had a surplus of males, the respective sex ratios being 832 and 1029. As recently as 1940, Icelandic women were almost as unmarried as were Irish women in 1946, 35.8 percent of the former at ages 20 and over were enumerated as single in 1940 compared with 37.8 percent of the latter in 1946 (Statistical Bureau of Iceland, 1969, p. 30; Ireland, 1968, pp. 2-3). For males, the comparable percentages were 40.5 percent and 49.0 percent. Since that time, both populations, but particularly the Icelanders, have included more married people. Coterminous with the rapid modernization of Iceland since 1940 has been a remarkably swift decline in the proportion of the population aged 20 and over who had never married, reaching 29.1 percent for males and 21.3 percent for females in 1978 (Statistical Bureau of Iceland, *Hagtíðindi*, 1979, p. 18). Still, the Icelanders remain the most unmarried of all the Scandinavians.

To my knowledge, the only demographer who has commented on these 1703 Icelandic marriage data is John Hajnal (1965). He made the observation (p. 137) that "they are staggeringly low even for a European population," and he claimed that they "are quite unlike any data recorded at other times in Iceland or indeed anywhere else, except by obvious misclassification of the data." I examined the text and tables of the 1703 census report and could find no "obvious misclassification" except for the suspiciously high percentages of unmarried people over age 60. I suspect that some widowed and separated people were classified as unmarried. Otherwise, the tables that give data for the unmarried, married, and widowed seem to be internally consistent on the basis of age and household status. What is striking is

Table 3-13. Percentages Enumerated as Never Married, by Age and Sex:
Iceland 1703 and Ireland 1926

Age	Males		Females	
	Iceland, 1703	Ireland, 1926	Iceland, 1703	Ireland, 1926
15-19	100.0*	99.9	99.9	99.3
20-24	99.0	96.0	95.2	87.0
25-29	87.1	79.8	79.3	61.8
30-34	64.4	62.4	59.1	41.6
35-39	41.5	49.6	48.5	32.5
40-44	30.4	40.2	41.4	26.4
45-49	26.6	33.5	42.7	24.2
50-54	23.5	29.3	41.9	23.7
55-59	24.2	26.3	44.3	23.2
60-64	29.6	25.8	48.0	24.0
65-69	29.7	23.4	43.8	21.9
70-74	30.7	21.2	41.8	20.7
75-79	42.0	18.2	45.1	18.4
80-84	34.8	15.3	45.0	16.0
85 and over	50.8	11.7	58.8	13.5

Sources: Percentages for Iceland are calculated from Statistical Bureau of Iceland, 1960, table 5, pp. 48-50; percentages for Ireland are calculated from Ireland, 1968, pp. 2-3.

*There was one Icelandic male under age 20 enumerated as married in Iceland in 1703.

that at that time 9,669 individuals were classified as servants, almost a fifth of the total population or more than a quarter of the population aged 15 and over. The pattern in Iceland, probably from the beginning, has been for servants and farm workers to be young and unmarried (their modal age is 20-24 in 1703 and 2.2 percent of the total enumerated as married or widowed). Another 6,789 persons, or 13.5 percent of the population were classified as paupers apportioned to households by the parishes; of these, only 3.3 percent were recorded as married or widowed. Almost half of the paupers were under age 20 and the number of females was twice that of males. Thorstein Thorsteinsson, past director of the Statistical Bureau of Iceland and author of the report on the 1703 census (1960), shows an awareness of the extraordinarily low proportion of the population who are reported as married. As he stated (p. 29), "This fact certainly must be ascribed to the great number of servants. It is, however, possible that the number of married people is somewhat understated, because the marital status may not have been given for married people who had separated and passed into the classes of servants and paupers."

In 1729, there was a census of three counties of Iceland (Statistical Bureau of Iceland, 1975b, p. 18) (the tabulations of which were not published until 1975), which provides some insight into the marriage data in the 1703 census. This 1729 enumeration of about 20 percent of the total population obtained data on cohabitation in addition to data on marriage. A distinction was made between those "explicitly" and those "implicitly" registered as married. From table 3-14, one can note that more than a third as many couples were cohabiting as were "explicitly" registered as married. The marital status of the 8,177 heads of households in the 1703 census shows that a fifth of the males ($N = 7,046$) and *all* of the female heads of household ($N = 1,131$) are reported as single or widowed. It is tempting and reasonable to assume that a sizable proportion of these were in "implicit" marriages in the meaning of the 1729 census. Unfortunately, the 1729 census does not give sufficient data on positions in the households to make direct comparisons with the 1703 census.

Another marriage pattern apparent from the 1703 census is the disparity in age between the spouses. In only 60.6 percent of the marriages was the husband older than the wife, in 6.4 percent of the cases husband and wife were born the same year, and in 33.1 percent the wife is older. Indeed, in 17.9 percent of marriages the wife was five or more years older than the husband. The frequent disparity in age between spouses and the fact that a third of the wives were older than their husbands are consequences of the need for having a man and a woman to run a farm. Some young Icelandic farmhands, and many

Table 3-14. Percentage of Icelanders in Three Counties Married and Living with Spouse and Percentage Not Married but Cohabiting, 1729

Age	Males			Females		
	Married	Cohabiting	Total	Married	Cohabiting	Total
15-19	0.3	0.3	0.6	1.2	. . .	1.2
20-24	5.7	1.1	6.8	10.0	3.7	13.7
25-29	26.6	12.2	38.9	32.6	13.2	45.8
30-34	38.3	21.2	59.5	38.3	20.1	58.4
35-39	51.0	26.0	77.1	43.3	19.3	62.7
40-44	63.4	14.9	78.4	45.8	23.3	69.2
45-49	52.6	25.4	78.0	50.0	18.4	68.4
50-54	60.3	25.6	86.0	41.7	13.4	55.1
55-59	62.1	17.9	80.0	43.9	14.4	58.3
60-64	59.2	19.2	78.3	33.7	9.3	43.0
65-69	45.2	13.9	59.1	28.7	5.6	36.3
70-74	40.4	9.6	50.0	17.9	3.2	21.2
75 and over	33.1	8.5	41.5	9.4	1.4	10.8
Total 15 and over	34.3	13.1	47.4	27.7	10.6	38.4

Source: Calculated from Statistical Bureau of Iceland, 1975b, tables 1 and 2, pp. 14-18.

not so young, married widows older than themselves in order to become independent farmers. Some housekeepers and servant girls—although not as high a proportion as among the farmhands because of the much higher rate of male mortality—married widowed farmers. The distribution of the ages of the spouses is not unique. Note from

Table 3-15. Age Gaps between Spouses, Iceland in 1703 and Norway in 1801 (In Percentages)

	Age Gap in Years					
	0	1-4	5-9	10-14	15+	Total
Iceland, 1703	6.4	37.3	31.2	15.4	9.7	100.0
Norway, 1801	5.9	37.0	29.5	16.7	10.9	100.0
	Husband Older					
Iceland, 1703		22.2	20.4	10.6	7.4	60.6
Norway, 1801		21.3	19.4	11.2	7.1	59.0
	Wife Older					
Iceland, 1703		15.2	10.8	4.8	2.3	33.1
Norway, 1801		15.7	10.1	5.5	3.8	35.1

Sources: Icelandic percentages are calculated from Statistical Bureau of Iceland, 1960, pp. 16-17, N = 5,791 marriages. Norwegian data are for five different parts of Norway and are taken from Drake, 1969, pp. 126-27, 223-24, N = 7,069 marriages.

table 3-15 that precisely the same pattern of age disparities was found by Michael Drake for Norway in 1801.

In traditional rural Iceland, the polar opposite of rural Ireland in relations between the sexes (see Arensberg and Kimball, 1968, chapter 11), many farm couples lived in de facto unions, and so did many of the servants. And so, too, did many of the Lutheran clergy who were also nearly always farmers. It would be an enormous error, then, to conclude from these 1703 marriage data and similar, although not so extreme, data from later censuses that so large a proportion of the population lived celibate or even childless lives as were classified as unmarried. In sharp contrast to their North Atlantic neighbors, the Irish, and to a greater extent than their Scandinavian cousins, the Icelanders never fully accepted Christian conceptions of marriage and sexual relations, either in its Catholic or its Lutheran form. In the next chapter, I will show from historical records, genealogies, and travelers' accounts that a high incidence of illegitimacy and liberality in sexual matters have been persistent characteristics of Icelandic society from the beginning. None of the other Scandinavian peoples has approached the amount of de jure illegitimacy of the Icelanders or the tolerance of it. Marriage in rural Icelandic society was an arrangement generally entered into only when a couple had access to a farm. But, even when they had acquired a farm, some couples still never formally married.

While it would be impossible to quantify the social reality from detailed study of the household units enumerated in 1703 (and in successive censuses), it is clear that many (most?) rural Icelandic adults have lived in de facto sexual unions for some period in their lives, just as many Icelanders do today. (In the 1950 and 1960 censuses and in vital statistics, there is the official category "in unmarried de facto union.") Whether rural couples married depended on whether they had access to a farm, either through ownership or tenantship. In 1703, only 42.2 percent of the men and 32.9 percent of the women aged 20 and over were enumerated as married, but it seems, because of the higher proportion of unmarried people over age 60, that in the latter decades of the seventeenth century when the population was larger that a still *smaller* proportion of the population was married. Similarly, in the census of 1801, after the great loss of life following the Laki eruptions of 1783-1784 and when the population was smaller than it had been in 1703, the proportion of males aged 20 and over who were married reached 63.7 percent. This is slightly higher than the percentage for 1960 (63.2 percent) and was not surpassed until the early 1960s. The high proportion of married males at the beginning of the nineteenth century can be explained by the observation that there were few times in Icelandic history when there were so few males aged 20

Table 3-16. Annual Average Numbers of Illegitimate Births and Marriages
in Iceland, 1827-1977

Years	Illegitimate Births	Marriages	Ratio*
1827-1830	339	393	0.86
1831-1840	310	393	0.79
1841-1850	303	422	0.72
1851-1860	367	458	0.80
1861-1870	400	412	0.97
1871-1880	465	441	1.05
1881-1890	461	486	0.95
1891-1900	402	520	0.77
1901-1910	315	490	0.64
1911-1920	322	558	0.58
1921-1930	375	631	0.59
1931-1940	539	708	0.76
1941-1950	899	1,073	0.84
1951-1955	1,127	1,253	0.90
1956-1960	1,198	1,327	0.90
1961-1965	1,214	1,458	0.83
1966-1970	1,278	1,650	0.77
1971-1975	1,458	1,730	0.84
1976	1,469	1,645	0.89
1977	1,437	1,568	0.92

Source: Calculated from official statistics of Iceland.

*Ratios computed by dividing number of illegitimate births by number of marriages.

and over and when the relative availability of farms was so great. By contrast, during the 1870s after a steady increase in population from 56,094 in 1840 to 69,763 in 1870 that resulted in a decline in the availability of farms, there was a decline in the marriage rate from 7.2 per 1,000 population in the decade 1841-1850 to 6.2 per 1,000 in 1871-1880 (Statistical Bureau of Iceland, 1967, pp. 36-39). In 1880, 43.6 percent of all men aged 20 and over were enumerated as unmarried, the highest percentage from at least 1801 to the present. Related to this was the increase in the illegitimacy ratio, from 14.1 to 19.8 percent of all births between the 1840s and the 1870s. In fact, during the 1871-1880 decade, the annual average number of illegitimate births was *higher* than the annual average number of marriages. (See table 3-16.)

HOUSEHOLD COMPOSITION

In table 3-17 are listed data on household composition in 1703. Unfortunately, these data tell less than they seem to on the surface. Certainly, some of the servants were partners in de facto unions with each other, with members of the family, and perhaps even with the parish paupers. All that we know about the relations between the sexes in Iceland suggests this. Some of the children in the households were probably the children of the servants—there must have been some even if the great majority of the servants were unmarried. The extent of this could be determined by the patronymics of the children of the household since everyone in the census is listed by given name and patronymic. Some of the foster children, too, may have been the children of servants, for there is a tradition of fostering children in Iceland that goes back to saga times. It was considered a mark of respect and devotion to give one's child to a more distinguished family to bring up.

The precise relationships of the relatives and the dependents to the heads of household have been tabulated. Most of the males were brothers (349) and brothers-in-law (113), relatively few were fathers (80) of the heads of households (Statistical Bureau of Iceland, 1960, pp. 54-55). Among the females, mothers (556) and mothers-in-law (178) and sisters (772) and sisters-in-law (242) predominated. Note the

Table 3-17. Icelandic Population by Position in Household, 1703
(In Absolute Numbers)

	Males	Females	Totals
Family			
Heads of household	7,046	1,131	8,177
Housewives		5,670	5,670
Children at home			
Under 15	4,895	4,995	9,890
15 and over	2,850	2,886	5,736
Foster children	437	474	911
Relatives and dependents	895	2,227	3,122
	16,123	17,383	33,506
Servants			
Managers and housekeepers	32	293	325
Work people in service	3,847	5,106	8,953
Work people not in service	372	19	391
	4,251	5,418	9,669
Paupers			
Paupers apportioned to households	2,273	4,516	6,789
Vagrant beggars	220	174	394
	2,493	4,690	7,183
Total population	33,867	27,491	50,358

Source: Statistical Bureau of Iceland, 1960, table 7, p. 19.

great preponderance of females classified as relatives and dependents, servants, and paupers. Work people not in service, however, were overwhelmingly male. My guess is that they were boarders who worked on neighboring farms; their modal age was 30-39. There was also an excess of males among the vagrant beggars.

The total number of households enumerated in 1703 was 8,191, with an average of 6.1 persons each. Of the total, 567 were one-person households and 2 were the bishoprics of Skálholt and Hólar with 70 and 80 people. Eliminating these, we are left with an average of 6.5 persons. If we eliminate further the paupers and vagrant beggars from our figures, we come to an average family household size of 5.6 persons. The average household size remained relatively constant (between 6 and 7 persons) down to the 1901 census, when it was 6.2 (Statistical Bureau of Iceland, 1969, p. 51). This size since has declined; it was 3.8 in 1950 and 3.9 in 1960.

THE CURRENT DEMOGRAPHIC SITUATION

Iceland as a demographically modern society is a recent phenomenon and it came about with extraordinary rapidity; the large majority of the Icelandic population participated in the traditional rural culture of Iceland until well into this century. By 1977, 86.3 percent of the population lived in places of 300 or more inhabitants, compared with 11.1 percent in 1890 and 42.7 percent in 1920 (table 3-5). More than half of the population has lived in the Reykjavík metropolitan area since the mid-1960s.[6] Modernization in the sense of achieving a standard of living comparable to the other Scandinavian countries did not begin until after the Second World War, but it was achieved by the 1950s.

Iceland was the first country to take a modern census; it also was the first country to give up census taking. The 1960 census was the last one, and the Statistical Bureau of Iceland did not even get around to publishing the results of it until 1969. Reliance is placed now entirely on the National Population Register (þjóðskrá). This is the reason that certain data (for example, average household size and detailed data on occupational distribution) do not exist for the years after 1960.

Mortality. As can be seen in tables 3-3, 3-4, and 3-5, Iceland underwent a rapid drop in mortality that began in the closing decades of the nineteenth century and accelerated in this century until the 1950s, since which time the decline has been slower. For a number of decades, Iceland has had infant and age-specific deathrates and expectations of life at or close to Norwegian, Swedish, and Dutch levels—

the European populations with the best recorded mortality experience since the early 1920s (see Dublin, Lotka, and Spiegelman, 1949, pp. 346-51). Iceland, Sweden, and Norway are the only countries in the world to have recorded infant deathrates of under 10 (Iceland in 1973, 1976, and 1977; Sweden since 1973; and Norway in 1977). Icelandic men in recent years have had age-specific deathrates at ages 60 and over lower than their Scandinavian agemates, and these rates may well be the lowest in the world. For 1961-1965, Icelandic women had the highest life expectancy at birth in the world, and since then they have had about the same life expectancy as Norwegian and Swedish women.

Fertility. Iceland until the early 1960s had the highest crude birth-rate of all the developed nations; since then, it has been exceeded only by Ireland. Between 1956-1960 and 1970, the Icelandic birthrate declined from 28.2 to 19.7 per 1,000 population, not falling below this level until 1976, when it declined to 19.5 and in 1977 to 18.0. (See table 3-4.) Yet, Icelandic fertility remains substantially higher than that of the other Nordic countries at *all* ages, with age-specific rates most commonly 20 to 100 percent higher. Table 3-18 lists these rates for 1977 for Iceland and the other Nordic countries.

Illegitimacy. The rate of illegitimacy continues to be higher in Iceland than in any modern society in the world. More than a third of all births (36.7 percent in 1978) and three-fourths of first births

Table 3-18. Age-Specific Birthrates for the Nordic Countries 1977

Age	Iceland	Denmark	Finland	Norway	Sweden
15-19*	56.2	22.1	24.2	32.3	22.1
20-24	138.3	115.2	99.2	116.0	103.6
25-29	129.8	120.6	115.2	117.5	117.9
30-34	81.7	54.8	67.8	60.6	61.5
35-39	44.8	16.4	25.6	20.9	20.7
40-44	12.1	2.8	5.9	4.4	3.6
45-49	0.9	0.1	0.4	0.2	0.2
Total fertility rate[†]	2,320	1,660	1,692	1,752	1,648
Crude birthrate	18.0	12.2	13.9	12.6	11.6

Source: Nordic Council, 1979, pp. 48, 50.

Note: Figures are numbers of live births per 1,000 women.

*Children born to women under age 20 per 1,000 women aged 15-19.

[†]Number of live-born children per 1,000 women who survive the child-bearing period, calculated according to the fertility rates of the current period.

occur outside of legal wedlock. Much of this illegitimacy, however, is only de jure illegitimacy in the sense that there is a man present in the household. This topic will be dealt with in detail in the next chapter.

Marriage. By the mid-1970s, the median age at first marriage in Iceland had become the lowest among the Nordic countries, 24.9 years for males and 22.7 years for females in 1977; for Sweden, the highest, median ages at first marriage for 1977 were 28.1 and 25.5, respectively. (See table 3-19.) Yet, the Icelanders continue to be the most unmarried of all the Scandinavians; 34.7 percent at ages 15 and over have never married. The Norwegians and the Danes are the most married with 26.9 percent of those 15 and over having never married in both countries. The Swedes (30.2 percent) and the Finns (30.9 percent) fall in between. The Icelanders in 1977 are even more unmarried than the Irish in the census of 1966, which reported 34.1 percent of those 15 and over never married. Unlike the Irish, however, a sizable proportion of Icelanders continue to cohabit in relationships of varying duration and stability, as they have for centuries. Again, this is a topic that will be dealt with in detail in the next chapter.

Table 3-19. Median Age at First Marriage in the Nordic Countries, 1977

	Iceland	Denmark	Finland	Norway	Sweden
Males	24.9	26.7	25.8	25.7	28.1
Females	22.7	24.0	23.9	23.1	25.5

Source: Nordic Council, 1979, p. 63.

Divorce. According to all measures of the incidence of divorce, Iceland is well ahead of Norway, a little behind Finland, and far behind Denmark and Sweden. While the frequency of divorce has increased substantially in all of the Nordic countries over the past few decades, the relative ranking of Iceland—well ahead of Norway and slightly behind Finland—has been constant since the 1930s. In terms of the number of divorces per 1,000 married women in 1977, the rates for the five Nordic countries are these:

Denmark 11.32
Sweden 11.11
Finland 9.57
Iceland 9.12
Norway 6.40

Migration. In 8 of the 10 years in the decade 1968-1977, Iceland has recorded an excess of emigrants over immigrants. During the decade a total of 16,378 persons left the country and 11,019 moved to it, giving an excess of emigration over immigration of 5,359 or an average net emigration of 536 persons per year (Statistical Bureau of Iceland, *Hagtíðindi*, 1978, pp. 38-39). Internal migration between communities is also of modest proportions involving 5.1 percent of the population in 1977.

Population Growth. As a combined result of high fertility (for a modern society), a young population, low mortality levels, and only a slight excess of emigration over immigration, the Icelandic population is expected to increase rapidly in the years ahead. The official projection is for a 28 percent increase in the period 1976-2000, from 221,000 to 283,100. All of the other Nordic populations are projected to increase by less than 5 percent over this same period.

CHAPTER 4

Men, Women, and Kinship

We have been bad pagans for a century and bad Christians for ten.

Sigurður Nordal (1971)

No, it was rather that we became better pagans after we became Christians.

Thor Vilhjálmsson (1971)

Relations between the sexes and family structure in Iceland show a remarkable continuity from the ancient Scandinavians to the present. Any schema of traditional to modern family systems does not fit Iceland as it might other societies. Some of the ancient patterns appear remarkably modern; some of the contemporary patterns, strongly traditional. In this chapter, I will discuss the institution of marriage, focusing on the legitimacy of children, the status of women, and the patterns of kinship.

MARRIAGE AND THE LEGITIMACY OF CHILDREN

Nowhere in the North has such long-term continuity been maintained in the area of marriage and sexual relations as in Iceland. Neither Latin Catholicism nor Lutheran, pietistic, or evangelical Protestantism ever overwhelmed the secular and egalitarian Germanic conceptions of the relations between the sexes that have remained tenaciously embedded in the folk culture of Iceland. As Björn Björnsson (1971, chapter 2), an Icelandic theologian and sociologist, has made so clear, all through the 1,100 years since Iceland was settled—through heathen, Catholic, and Lutheran times—marriage has been popularly conceived as coming about through the betrothal ceremony, a civil and not a religious con-

86

ception of marriage. Along with this has gone a remarkably tolerant view toward sexual relations that seems to be related to the traditional equality that has prevailed between the sexes combined with the *general* tolerance that characterizes Icelanders in moral and religious matters. The whole history of Iceland from the pragmatic conversion to Christianity in A.D. 999 or 1000 to the modern indifferentism supports this contention.

During the Catholic centuries, the Church was forced to sanction a civil conception of marriage which stemmed out of heathen Iceland. The Church was subservient to the Icelandic Althing and had only modest influence on the heathen culture and social structure until well into the thirteenth century, when in 1262 Iceland lost its independence to Norway with its stronger church. After the Danish-enforced Reformation in Iceland, the Lutheran Church attempted to establish an exclusively ecclesiastical conception of marriage, but it achieved little success.

The sagas of the Icelanders and the oldest codification of Icelandic law, *Grey Goose* (*Grágás*, 1190), give a clear idea of the nature of the marriage process, relations between the sexes, and kinship in medieval Iceland. Marriage was not so much, at least at first, a relationship between a man and a woman as it was a relationship between two kin groups. Marriage was largely a process of striking a bargain by the most influential person closest to each of the principals, most often the two fathers. The wishes of the prospective mates, however, often seem to have been considered (for example, in *Njal's Saga*, chapter 97, and *Laxdaela Saga*, chapters 7, 23). The marriage process involved three steps: first, a marriage proposal was made that was followed by formal negotiations together with assertions of the virtues of the individuals involved; second, the ceremonial betrothal took place in the presence of the bridegroom and witnesses; and, third, a wedding feast for both kin groups took place within a year after the betrothal; most commonly it was given by the bride's father.

A typical example of the three steps is the marriage of Hrut Herjolfsson, whose marriage is negotiated for him by his older half-brother, Hoskuld Dala-Kollsson, at the Althing (circa 960). *Njal's Saga* (chapter 2) describes the marriage process as follows:

> Hoskuld said to Hrut, "I would like you to look to your future, brother, and find yourself a wife."
>
> "I have been of two minds about it for a long tim," replied Hrut. "But now I will do as you wish. Where should we turn our attention?"
>
> "There are many chieftains here at the Althing," said Hoskuld, "and we have a wide choice. But I have already decided on a match for you, a woman called Unn; she is the daughter of Mord Fiddle, a very wise man. He is here at the Althing now and his daughter is with him, so you can see her if you wish."

Next day, as people were making their way to the Court of Legislature, the brothers saw a group of well-dressed women outside the Rangriver booth.

"There is Unn now," said Hoskuld, "the woman I was telling you about. What do you think of her?"

"I like the look of her," replied Hrut. . . .

They walked on towards the court. Mord Fiddle was interpreting the law there as usual, and afterwards he went back to his booth. Hoskuld and Hrut rose and followed him. They entered the booth and greeted Mord who was seated at the far end; he rose to meet them, took Hoskuld by the hand, and gave him the seat beside his own. Hrut sat down beside Hoskuld.

They talked about a number of things. Eventually Hoskuld said, "I want to discuss a marriage-deal with you. Hrut wants to make an offer for your daughter's hand and become your son-in-law, and I shall not be sparing in my support."

"I know you are a great chieftain," said Mord, "but of your brother I know nothing."

"He is a better man than I," replied Hoskuld.

"You would have to settle a very large sum on him," said Mord, "for Unn will inherit everything I own."

"I shall not keep you waiting long for my offer," said Hoskuld. "Hrut is to have Kambsness and Hrutstead [two farms] and all the land up to Thrand-argill; and in addition he owns a trading-ship which is out at sea just now."

Hrut intervened. "You must realize," he said to Mord, "that brotherly love makes Hoskuld exaggerate my virtues. But if you are prepared to consider the matter at all, I would like you to name the terms yourself."

"I have already decided on my terms," said Mord. "Unn's dowry from me will be sixty hundreds [of woolen cloth, the equivalent of eighty cows], which you are to increase by half; and if you have heirs, the whole estate is to be divided equally between the two of you."

"I accept these terms," said Hrut. "Let us now call in witnesses."

They stood up and shook hands, and Mord betrothed his daughter Unn to Hrut, the wedding [feast] to take place at Mord's home a fortnight after midsummer.

Apparently, couples at this time did not live together until after the wedding feast, but it was the second step—the betrothal—that had marriage-creating significance. And betrothal, or engagement, has continued to have this significance in the popular consciousness to the present, although in a less formal way. No ceremony is known to have occurred at the wedding feast.

Legal polygamy never existed in Iceland, although it may have elsewhere in Scandinavia during the Viking era (Adam, 1959, p. 203). However, maintaining concubines was legally and socially acceptable in ancient Iceland, but it probably could be afforded only by the richest farmers (for example, see *Laxdaela Saga*, chapter 12, and *Njal's Saga*, chapter 25).

The acceptance of Christianity by the Althing in 999 or 1000 does not seem to have affected the pre-Christian marital process much. As a matter of fact, the sagas, written mostly during the thirteenth century, may better describe the practices of that time than those of the tenth century. Not until 1275, after Iceland had fallen under the hegemony of the king of Norway and a stronger church, was a law promulgated by the Althing that gave the Church complete jurisdiction over the institution of marriage. The Althing thereby acknowledged one of the universal claims of the Church. Yet, the new law reflected the three established steps in the pre-Christian process of marriage (Björn Björnsson, 1971, pp. 43-45). First was the *contract for a future marriage*, which corresponded to the marriage proposal, the subsequent negotiations, and the final agreement on conditions. Second was the *ceremonial betrothal*, which took place before witnesses and which the bridegroom concluded by saying "from now on you are my legal wife." The consent of the bride to this statement had to be heard by the witnesses. Third was the *wedding ceremony*. What is significant is that it was the betrothal ceremony that had marriage-creating significance. Children born to a betrothed couple were to be considered legitimate, and the betrothal had the same binding consequences for the couple as the wedding ceremony proper. Only the last step, the wedding ceremony, required the auspices of the Church. The pagan ceremony, in effect, was placed within the legal framework of the Church.

Subsequently, the Church attempted to require that the betrothal and the wedding ceremony occur on the same day to give the impression of their being one element. The Church was not always successful in accomplishing this, but it did have some effect (Björn Björnsson, 1971, p. 46). With the coming of the Protestant Reformation and a new religious consciousness, Frederik II of Denmark wrote to the two bishops of Iceland in 1560 about the "great immorality among our subjects in our land, Iceland" (p. 52). But it was not until 1567 that Frederik had a marital code in Iceland drawn up, based on similar legislation introduced into Denmark and Norway five years earlier. These *Articles on Marriage* remained in force until 1824.

The articles begin with another reference to the fact (cohabitation) that "in this land of ours, Iceland, there is to be found great immorality with regard to marriage" (quoted by Björn Björnsson, 1971, p. 55). The intent of this legislation was to oppose any civil conception of marriage and to replace the traditional betrothal ceremony with a new engagement ceremony. The net result was that the people and some of the clergy did not distinguish the new engagement ceremony before a pastor and several witnesses from the old betrothal ceremony, except that the former was taken to be *not as binding* and was dissolvable at will. The Church reacted against this intolerable practice by stressing that engagement was the beginning of marriage and could be dissolved only in rare instances, and "by so doing the Chruch did in fact play right into the hands of the traditional interpretation, which justified the married way of life for engaged persons" (Troels-Lund, quoted by Björn Björnsson, 1971, p. 37).

Children of betrothed couples continued to be regarded in Icelandic law as legitimate *"whether they are born before betrothal or after"* (Björn Björnsson, 1971, p. 62, italics his). This was in agreement with the old legal principle that all the children of a couple become legitimate when a couple was betrothed. The *Articles on Marriage* had remarkably little effect on the traditional significance of the betrothal ceremony so deeply embedded in the popular consciousness.

An additional regulation was promulgated in 1746 specifically to outlaw the betrothal ceremony and to prohibit cohabitation, but again it had little effect. A case from 1762 demonstrates the lack of agreement on premarital sexual relations that existed even at the official level (Björn Björnsson, 1971, pp. 66-67). A sheriff demanded fines from a woman who gave birth to a child 12 weeks after her marriage. A royal letter, in answer to the sheriff, held that the woman should not be fined because the marriage had taken place before the birth of the child.

The failure of the Lutheran engagement ceremony to replace the traditional betrothal ceremony is indicated by the fact that the engagement ceremony was abolished by royal order in 1799. At that time, it was stipulated that any couple who wished to enter the state of matrimony must be married in Church without a preceding engagement. There is no indication in the later data on illegitimacy that this legislation had any effect.

In 1821 Magnús Stephensen, the supreme judge of the Icelandic High Court and so the most authoritative spokesman of the civil authorities in the land, wrote a small book that dealt with marital offenses and fornication. Stephensen showed great respect for Icelandic legal practices and assumed that an engaged couple had sexual relations. He (quoted in Björn Björnsson, 1971, pp. 71-72, italics his) wrote:

> The Law of Nature demands for a natural and valid marriage only, that a man and woman agree to live together as man and wife for life and to bring up properly the children they will have. Formal announcements preceding the marriage, or a wedding ceremony performed by a minister of the Church, are not necessary according to this Law. For many centuries, the Law did not prescribe these ceremonies, either. . . . Later, however, the civil law found it necessary to demand the ceremonial announcement of marriage and

its formal constitution, in order to restrain the uncertain nature of love. *Priests, however, were not required to wed couples, until the introduction of canon law, when the papacy had turned marriage into a sacrament.* . . . Even so, men continued to betroth women to themselves with the consent of the due parties according to the prescribed form and in the manner of *Jónsbók* [the old Icelandic lawbook] The Augsburg Confession from 1530 leaves no prescriptions on this matter . . . but first at the Council of Trent in 1563 it was so ordered, that marriages not performed by a priest should be considered as of no legal force. . . . As to fines, however, these general laws were never accepted for Iceland, the specific law of which dealing with fornication never set down any fines against premarital relationships. . . . ; and adding to this the fact, that children, born before the wedding, are considered to be legitimate, which always is done when their parents later get married. . . *it is hard to punish premarital relationships.*

Stephensen's statement on marriage was written two decades after the ecclesiastical engagements were abolished. That Stephensen was reflecting the dominant view, a view that was even shared by many (most?) of the clergy, seems reasonable. The earliest Icelandic statistics on illegitimacy date from 1827. Table 4-1 shows that 15.8 percent of all births during the years 1827-1830 were illegitimate. During the 1820s, there were almost as many illegitimate births recorded as there were marriages, and, in 1830, there were more—423 illegitimate births and 393 marriages (Statistical Bureau of Iceland, 1976, p. 8). The observation that 42.7 percent of all Icelandic clergy born in the years 1811-1850 themselves had an illegitimate first child or one born less than nine months after marriage (table 4-3) strongly suggests that they, too, held tolerant views toward premarital sexual relations.

After the abolition of the public engagement ceremony in 1799, it became clear that new marriage legislation was required, but such was not promulgated until 1824. The 1824 legislation was highly ecclesiastical and regulatory and served with some modifications until the contemporary legislation was passed by the Althing in 1921. As with the earlier legislation, that of 1824 never succeeded in disestablishing the old cohabitation patterns. Indeed, until the end of the nineteenth century, there was a steady increase in illegitimacy. The old view that a child is legitimated upon the marriage of the parents continues to be law in Iceland. The discussion of legitimacy in the Icelandic *Legal Handbook* states: "Finally, if a man and woman marry, who had had an illegitimate child together, then this child is to be regarded as legitimate" (Schram, 1970, p. 104).

So far I have dealt only with how the traditional betrothal ceremony of the folk culture triumphed over the established practices of international Christianity, both Catholic and Lutheran, based largely on

Björn Björnsson's account. Of even greater importance in an understanding of the premarital sexual permissiveness that prevails in modern Iceland is realizing that sexual permissiveness also has been characteristic of the folk culture from the beginning. All through Icelandic history, there appears to have been a high degree of sexual freedom for both men and women, combined with high levels of illegitimacy and a pervasive tolerance of it.

Table 4-1. Illegitimate Births in the Nordic Countries, 1749-1977

Years	Iceland	Sweden	Denmark*	Norway	Finland
1749-1750	. . .	2.1	. . .	. . .	. . .
1751-1760	. . .	2.4	. . .	. . .	1.4
1761-1770	. . .	2.6	. . .	3.6†	1.7
1771-1780	. . .	2.9	. . .	4.2	2.4
1781-1790	. . .	3.9	. . .	4.8‡	3.1
1791-1800	. . .	5.0	. . .	. . .	4.5
1801-1810	. . .	6.1	1.4	6.3	5.7
1811-1820	. . .	6.8	8.7	7.4	6.3
1821-1830	15.8§	6.6	8.6	7.2	6.3
1831-1840	13.8	6.7	9.8	6.8	5.9
1841-1850	14.1	8.6	11.5	8.2	7.2
1851-1860	14.3	9.0	11.1	8.7	7.0
1861-1870	15.6	9.6	11.1	8.1	7.3
1871-1880	19.8	10.7	10.7	8.7	7.9
1881-1890	20.4	10.2	9.9	7.8	6.8
1891-1900	16.9	10.9	9.6	7.3	6.6
1901-1910	13.5	12.7	10.7	6.9	6.8
1911-1920	13.2	15.0	11.4	7.0	6.8
1921-1930	14.0	15.4	10.8	6.9	8.4
1931-1940	20.9	13.9	9.4	6.6	7.6
1941-1950	25.6	9.5	8.4	6.1	6.1
1951-1955	26.6	9.9	6.8	3.7	4.5
1956-1960	25.3	10.5	7.2	3.6	4.1
1961-1965	25.7	12.8	8.9	4.0	4.3
1966-1970	29.6	16.0	11.0	5.7	5.3
1971-1975	32.8	27.6	16.4	9.0	7.9
1976	34.3	33.2	24.0	10.9	10.9
1977	36.0	34.7	25.9	11.6	11.1

Sources: Percentages are from the official statistics of the countries or were calculated from them.

Note: Figures are annual averages in percentages of all live births.

*Data for 1801-1900 include stillbirths; for the nineteenth century, the rates are for 1801-1809, 1810-1819, 1820-1829, 1830-1839, 1840-1849, 1850-1859, 1860-1869, 1870-1879, 1880-1889, and 1890-1900.

†Figure is for 1770 only.

‡Figure is for 1781-1783 only.

§Figure is for 1827-1830 only.

Indeed, no modern Western society, except Sweden, has approached Iceland's level of illegitimacy since the advent of modern vital statistics, dating from the first half of the nineteenth century for most European countries. The proportions of illegitimate births for the five Nordic countries are listed in table 4-1. In 1977, 36.0 percent of all births in Iceland were illegitimate. Only Sweden has a comparable percentage of births outside of formal wedlock. In Sweden, the explanation of the extraordinary rise in illegitimacy since the late 1960s is the equally extraordinary decline in the proportion of couples who legally marry. Between 1961-1965 and 1973, the first-marriage rate per, 1,000 single Swedish males ages 20-49 fell from 104.0 to 53.3; for single females ages 20-44, the rate dropped from 192.4 to 90.0 per 1,000. From this 1973 low, the Swedish marriage rates have moved up a little. This trend also has been apparent in Denmark, but the trend is evident only slightly if at all in Iceland, Norway, and Finland. Most of the illegitimacy in Sweden is only de jure since the father is present in the household. But the pattern of couples deliberately electing not to be formally married has become a pervasive one (see Prioux-Marchal, 1974).

Iceland, by contrast, has seen no such sharp decline in the marriage rate, and the patterns of illegitimacy are quite different than Sweden's. In fact, Iceland in recent years has had the highest marriage rate and the youngest age at marriage of the five Nordic countries, with 7.07 marriages per 1,000 population and median ages at marriage of 24.9 years for males and 22.7 for females in 1977 (Nordic Council, 1979, pp. 62-63). Yet, in the period 1971-1973, 65 percent of the parents of illegitimate children in Iceland lived separately, an increase from 48 percent in the years 1961-1965 (Statistical Bureau of Iceland, 1976, p. 49). But it is important to note, many of those parents who live apart eventually establish a home together and some are formally engaged but are still under age 20 and are living with their parents. And some women later marry, cohabit with, and/or become engaged to men not the natural fathers of their children, but who become the children's functional fathers. Thus, the common distinction between de facto and de jure illegitimacy is not very useful for Iceland if we define the former as the absence in the mother's place of residence of a social father, a common definition of "social problem" illegitimacy. In Iceland, a social father *is* frequently absent but often only during the early life of the child. Yet, the maternal grandfather frequently assumes a role analogous to that of the social father during the early years of a child born out of wedlock.

Some general statistical observations about the distribution of illegitimacy in present-day Iceland include the following:

1. Increasingly, illegitimate births in Iceland are first births, 75.0 percent in the period 1971-1973 compared with 63.5 percent in 1961-1965 (Statistical Bureau of Iceland, 1976, p. 47). This reflects a decline in the pattern of long-term cohabitation with more than one child, a trend first pointed out by Björn Björnsson (1971, p. 137). What proportion of mothers with illegitimate children eventually marry the biological fathers is not known. It may be a majority. An increasingly common and unique pattern in Iceland is for a couple to follow the marriage ceremony immediately with the baptism of their first child.

2. The mothers of illegitimate children in Iceland, as elswhere in the world, are young; 43.2 percent of all illegitimate births in 1971-1973 were to mothers under age 20, compared with only 3.5 percent of births to mothers of legitimate babies. Table 4-2 shows the age distribution of the mothers of legitimate and illegitimate babies in the years 1971-1973, compared with a century earlier (1871-1880) when the illegitimacy rate was almost as high as at present—7.0 illegitimate births per 1,000 population in 1971-1973 compared with 6.6 a century ago.

Table 4-2. Ages of Mothers Giving Birth in Iceland in 1871-1880 and 1971-1973
(In Percentages)

Age	1871-1880			1971-1973		
	All	Legitimate	Illegitimate	All	Legitimate	Illegitimate
Under 20	1.1	0.7	2.7	16.4	3.5	43.2
20-24	11.6	9.3	21.1	36.3	34.7	39.8
25-29	25.3	24.0	30.9	24.8	32.0	9.8
30-34	26.1	26.8	23.1	13.1	17.4	4.0
35-39	22.6	24.3	15.4	7.0	9.2	2.4
40-44	11.8	13.3	5.7	2.3	3.0	0.8
45 and over	1.5	1.6	1.1	0.1	0.2	0.0
	100.0	100.0	100.0	100.0	100.0	100.0
Birthrate per 1,000 population	(32.0)	(25.4)	(6.6)	(21.8)	(14.8)	(7.0)

Source: Statistical Bureau of Iceland, 1976, p. 45; rates were calculated from data on pp. 8-11.

3. Illegitimacy is fairly evenly distributed through the country. For the years 1966-1970, national illegitimacy was 29.6 percent of all births. In the fourteen towns of Iceland, where over two-thirds of the population lived, 29.2 percent of all births were illegitimate; among the remaining one-third of the population, the villages and farm areas, 31.0 percent of all births were illegitimate. During the 1920s, when

only a third of the population lived in towns, illegitimacy was slightly higher in the towns. Still, the relatively enormous illegitimacy in Iceland has its roots in the traditional rural culture, and it has consistently been highest in the north, where the oldest cultural patterns and practices have persisted most vigorously.

4. It is clear that illegitimacy is lower in the educated sectors of the population, coterminous in Iceland with the higher status groups, than in the general population. But the data in tables 4-3 and 4-4 show a level of illegitimacy among those in the professions that is substantial and undoubtedly higher than in any other modern society, and probably unsurpassed anywhere. Note that 18.0 percent of the first children of the Lutheran clergy born in the first half of the nineteenth century were illegitimate, compared with 10.5 percent for those born in this century. Note also that one-third of the first children of male physicians born during the 1920s were illegitimate and that almost one-third of those of male lawyers born in the 1930s were illegitimate.

Table 4-3. Status of Firstborn Children of Icelandic Clergymen
Born 1811-1931
(In Percentages)

Status of Children	1811-1850	1851-1900	1901-1931
Born illegitimate	18.0	15.6	10.5
Born 0 to 8 months after father's marriage	24.7	16.1	30.5
Born 9 or more months after father's marriage	57.3	68.3	59.0
	100.0	100.0	100.0
Number of clergymen with children	(89)	(180)	(95)
Number of clergymen without children	(18)	(40)	(36)

Source: Calculated from data in Björn Magnússon, 1957.

There has been some research into family, marriage, and illegitimacy in Iceland since the mid-1960s. The first such study was probably that of Björn Björnsson done in 1965 as a part of a dissertation at the University of Edinburgh in both social anthropology and theology, which later was published under the title *The Lutheran Doctrine of Marriage in Modern Icelandic Society* (1971). His study grew out of "an awareness of somewhat unusual patterns of family organization in this particular society" (p. v). As part of his dissertation, Björnsson interviewed 56 randomly selected couples in Akranes, a town of just over 4,000 people, 20 miles across Faxi Bay from Reykjavík (but much farther by road), but not a suburb of the capital city. At the outset

Table 4-4. Status of Firstborn Children of Icelandic Male Physicians Born 1601-1938 and Male Lawyers Born 1701-1937 (In Percentages)

Status of Children	Physicians						
	1601-1800	1801-1850	1851-1900	1901-1910	1911-1920	1921-1930	1931-1938
Born illegitimate	57.1	17.2	16.9	10.0	19.1	32.3	21.7
Born 0 to 8 months after father's marriage	9.5	13.7	16.3	22.9	32.4	36.2	41.3
Born 9 or more months after father's marriage	33.3	69.0	66.6	67.1	48.5	31.5	37.0
	99.9	99.9	99.9	100.0	100.0	100.0	100.0
Number of physicians with children	(21)	(29)	(153)	(70)	(68)	(130)	(92)
Number of physicians without children	(9)	(13)	(26)	(10)	(6)	(12)	(10)
Insufficient data	(2)	(–)	(2)	(–)	(–)	(1)	(–)

Status of Children	Lawyers						
	1701-1800	1801-1850	1851-1900	1901-1910	1911-1920	1921-1930	1931-1937
Born illegitimate	25.0	20.0	14.3	9.1	14.7	21.1	29.4
Born 0 to 8 months after father's marriage	6.8	10.0	17.9	29.1	27.4	38.2	31.8
Born 9 or more months after father's marriage	68.2	70.0	67.9	61.8	57.9	40.7	38.6
	100.0	100.0	100.1	100.0	100.0	100.0	99.9
Number of lawyers with children	(44)	(30)	(112)	(55)	(95)	(123)	(44)
Number of lawyers without children	(10)	(8)	(28)	(10)	(15)	(31)	(24)
Insufficient data	(9)	(–)	(–)	(–)	(–)	(–)	(–)

Sources: Data on physicians calculated from Blöndal and Jónsson, 1970; data on lawyers from Agnar Kl. Jónsson, 1963.

he was "hesitant" about inquiring into the premarital relations of his respondents and hesitated to ask questions about whether or not they had lived together before their marriage. His reluctance soon lessened (pp. 144-45):

> But I very soon discovered . . . I was only asking about the most natural things as far as my respondents were concerned, namely how long they had been living together as engaged before they got married, etc. . . . . The persons in question did not look upon their behavior as deviating in any sense nor did they see others in similar positions, e.g., their sons and/or daughters, as being wrong.

Björn Björnsson discusses (pp. 144-76) three types of family organization existing in modern-day Iceland: (1) The *engagement family* is that type in which the couple is formally betrothed. Increasingly, a couple of this type later marry, frequently at the time of the baptism of their first child. (2) The *cohabitation family* is the type in which the couple has never been formally engaged, a form Björnsson believes is declining. And (3) the *marriage family* in which the couple has had either a civil or a church wedding. Most of those in the third category had previously been engagement or cohabitation families.

In the summer of 1967, Pétur Guðjónsson, an Icelander then in the undergraduate program in social science at Harvard, interviewed a random sample of 132 Reykjavíkans over age 21 on their "attitudes toward premarital sexual relations, unwed motherhood, and illegitimacy" (1967, p. 20). He chose these topics "because Iceland's view of them is unique compared to the views of other western countries" (p. 20). He found, to his surprise, that "the sex questions did not cause as much hesitation as those pertaining to economic matters" (p. 21). Guðjónsson put forth 49 propositions that he modestly called "only hypotheses." Based on Björnsson's more formal and less freewheeling interviews and my 100 interviews with Icelanders (although I asked no specific questions about marriage and premarital relations), I think Guðjónsson's observations (pp. 22-24) are very much on target. Here I quote at length from his "hypotheses."

> Reykjavíkans over age 30 became engaged as a result of infatuation or love, whereas those under 30 became engaged because (a) it is fashionable, and (b) the other partner was infatuated.
>
> Reykjavíkans got married for the following reasons, and in that order: (1) to have their own home, (2) to beget children, (3) pregnancy, (4) status symbol, (5) infatuation or love for mate.
>
> The time of marriage is determined by (a) a place of their own to live in, (b) the first child's baptism, (c) if the future couple lives with either's parents and there is a younger brother or sister who wants to have his or her fiancé move in, the parents "pressure" the couple to get out, as the time has come

for the younger ones to get better acquainted and cohabit where the future couple now live.

Most Reykjavíkans met their mates at a dance or a party.

Reykjavíkans prefer to get married by a minister at his home for two reasons: (a) they are reluctant to have any "fuss" around their marriage, and (b) the woman is usually pregnant when she gets married or has a child beforehand, and hence she is "ashamed" at being married in church. . . . They do not get married by a minister for any religious reason, but because it is the custom, and it seems to them to be more beautiful.

It doesn't matter whether someone is illegitimately born or not. Unwed mothers are not looked down on, only considered unfortunate, nor is a man stigmatized for fathering illegitimate children. Nevertheless, there is a stigma on one brought up as an only child vs. one who has been brought up with other siblings.

Reykjavíkans do not accept abortions and also frown upon giving away children, although most people would take a child. Neither do they think it wise for a girl to get married or engaged just because she is pregnant.

The younger generation is apparently going to bring up its children more strictly then the older has done. They, for instance, would not allow their daughter to go camping alone with a boy if she weren't engaged, though the older generation would allow her to.

Most if not all Reykjavík men have sexual intercourse with a girl for the first time for the sense of adventure. About one-third of the women reported that their first man was someone they loved, but two-thirds felt only curiosity and adventure. Most men had known their first "woman" only a day or two.

In spite of much talk, adultery does not appear to be very common. Nevertheless, it appears that people associated with commerce are more likely to commit adultery than those who are not.

Teenagers begin to copulate at 15 or 16.

Young Reykjavíkans become entirely independent at 15-17.

Most Reykjavík husbands kiss their wives daily, but most said it was habit, not love.

Most marriages in Reykjavík are "reasonably happy" with no tremendous love, no hatred, but a 50-50 existence.

Although most Reykjavíkans feel publicly engaged couples should not cohabit constantly before marriage, most of them have actually lived together.

Most Reykjavíkans feel that young people should not have sexual relations before engagement. Most of them have, however, copulated before becoming engaged and also before they met their marriage partners.

Since there is no stigma against unwed mothers and a girl can always rely on her mother to take care of her child, Icelandic girls do not "need" to worry about contraceptives. (The researcher visited several families where the mother had little children of her own but joyfully took care of her daughter's child also and said she would be happy to care for any further illegitimate children of her daughter.)

A child is nearly always welcome no matter what the surroundings into which it is born.

Although the engaged couple is viewed as one irrevocable unit, e.g., they usually receive common gifts for their future home even when they are engaged, and although most Reykjavíkans have been publicly engaged, the majority of them view engagement as an unnecessary institution. . . .

Most people feel that one adulterous side-step is natural and forgiveable.

Let me offer a typical example of the matter-of-fact attitude toward illegitimacy of Icelanders from the kind of published genealogies of which there are so many. This one translates as *Strong Trunks* (Björn Árnason, 1960) and gives descriptive genealogical accounts of individuals in one of the northern fjords. My example—almost taken at random—is that of Jón Stefánsson (1859-1935), a farmer and boatbuilder respected by the genealogy's author (pp. 45-52). Jón was a "natural child" of his father who, like his son, was admired by the author. After the death of his father's first wife, who was not Jón's natural mother, his father "lived for several years" with Snjólaug Jónsdóttir "by whom he had several children." Jón himself married Rósa Thorsteinsdóttir who was the foster daughter of the Reverend Páll Jónsson and his first wife, who had an academic background—probably the family of the highest status in the northern fjord. The writer informs us that Rósa had a daughter, María Edvaldsdóttir, "before she married him" and that Jón treated her "as one of his own children." As is customary, María was known throughout her life as Edvaldsdóttir and never as Jónsdóttir, even though Jón was her functional father and she may well have had no contact with Edvald, her natural father. Such arrangements are so common everywhere in Iceland that they hardly bring forth comment.

It is perhaps not appropriate here to mention leading Icelanders who are themselves illegitimate or who are the parents of illegitimate children. Yet, this information is readily available in a number of directories. Even children conceived extramaritally are listed in the directories of the clergy, the lawyers, and the physicians. The two-volume *Physicians in Iceland* (Blöndal and Jónsson, 1970) illustrates the enormous emphasis placed on genealogy by the Icelanders, a concern that makes lineage on the male side somewhat more certain than it might otherwise be. Not only does this directory list the children born in and out of wedlock to Icelandic physicians, both living and dead, but there was an attempt by the compilers to list the parentage of all of the adopted and foster children of the physicians. A court case brought by a group of physicians to prevent the listing of this information held up the publication of the directory for two years and forced the compilers to desist from listing the natural parents of the adopted and foster children (introduction, volume 1). Instead, they left blank spaces set off by parentheses where the names would have been.

That a tolerant and accepting view of sexual behavior and its fruits is no recent phenomenon and goes back to medieval times, and probably earlier, is quite unambiguously clear. The sagas of the Icelanders show a matter-of-fact attitude toward illegitimacy. Let one example suffice for many. In *Njal's Saga*, written about 1280, Njal—the wisest man of his time (circa 980-1010)—is reported to have an illegitimate son (chapter 25): "Njal had a fourth son, called Hoskuld, who was illegitimate; his mother was Hrodny, the sister of Ingjald Hoskuldsson of Keldur." Yet, Hoskuld was Njal's favorite son, and Bergthora, his devoted wife, considered him as much Njal's son as the three she had with him. Nowhere in the chaste sagas is celibacy, virginity, or continence dealt with, much less celebrated. Nowhere is illegitimacy condemned.

During Catholic times, the clergy refused to remain celibate. This was not unusual in medieval Catholicism, but the extent, persistence, and general acceptance of it that prevailed in Iceland was. The case of the priest Jón Loftsson (1124-1197) is an illustration of the failure of Catholic attitudes to take hold in Iceland as late as the twelfth century. Jón was the most admired, learned, and powerful chieftain of his time. He was also a leader in the Church, even though he never became a bishop. In a thirteenth-century historical account (*Thorlak's Saga*, chapter 2, quoted in Simpson, 1965, p. 77), it is written most objectively that he

> was very well suited to the love of women, and by various women he had had many other sons: Thorstein and Halldór, Sigurd and Einar. But his sons Páll (who later became bishop) and Orm (who later lived at Breidabolstad) were the sons he had by Ragnheid Thorshallsdóttir, the sister of Bishop Thorlak. She and Jón had loved each other since childhood. Nevertheless she had children by other men too.

Apparently, the majority of the people found no fault with Jón's sexual activity. Jón and Ragnheid's illegitimate son Páll became the bishop of the southern diocese at the death of Bishop Thorlak; he married at an early age but lived an ascetic life. His brother Orm never married but had four children by two mistresses. Saemund, the only legitimate son of Jón, had ten children by four mistresses (Hermannsson, 1932).

Another example is Snorri Sturluson (1178-1241), the greatest Icelander of his time and perhaps the greatest of all medieval historians, who had a number of recognized and fully accepted illegitimate children (*Sturlunga Saga*, chapter 16). Snorri fathered these children while he was separated from his wife Herdis whom he never divorced.

The Norwegian author Sigrid Undset, whose major novels were based on saga materials, understood the situation well. In *Kristin Lavransdatter*, which is set in fourteenth-century Norway but which could just as well have been set in Iceland, she wrote (1937, chapter 7) about the tolerance toward Father Eirik's illegitimate children:

> In these far-away country parishes folk held it was not reason [sic] that priests should live like monks, for they must at least have women to help on their farms, and they might well need a woman to look after things for them, seeing what long and toilsome journeys they must make round the parishes, and that too in all kinds of weather; besides folk had not forgotten that it was not so very long since priests in Norway had been married men. Thus, no one had blamed Sira Eirik overmuch that he had had three children by the woman who tended his house, while he was yet young.

Jónas Jónasson, an Icelandic clergyman who wrote the only ethnography of Icelandic culture, claimed (1961, p. 383) that "many of the Catholic bishops and most of the priests" had concubines. A record of some sort, he noted, is that of Séra Barna-Sveinbjörn (who died in 1489), who in his 27 years of service as a priest in Múla recognized 50 children as his and partially acknowledged some others. The Englishman Andrew Boorde, who visited Iceland shortly before the Reformation, noted: "There be som prestes, the whych be beggars, yet they wyll have concubynes" (quoted by Seaton, 1935, pp. 13-14). A final example of the failure of orthodox Catholic views to subdue a certain old Norse "looseness" in things sexual as late as the sixteenth century is the case of Bishop Jón Arason (1484-1550), to whom virtually all Icelanders can validly claim direct descent. Jón was the last Catholic bishop of Iceland; he was beheaded by the Protestants for refusing to accept the "new faith." He had nine children with his concubine Helga Sigurðardóttir (Ólason, 1944, p. 63).

In Lutheran times, up to this century, the clergy produced a not insignificant number of "natural children," with their paternity fully acknowledged and entered into the genealogical records. And the illegetimacy seems to have been at least generally tolerated, although up to the second half of the nineteenth century it was not uncommon for clergymen to lose their posts for fathering illegitimate children too abundantly or for committing adultery too blatantly.[1] Table 4-3 shows the percentages of first children who were illegitimate among the graduates of the theology faculty of the University of Iceland born between 1811 and 1931. These unique data are from the *Directory of Icelandic Clergy* (Björn Magnússon, 1957), which, like similar Icelandic professional directories, attempts to give full genealogical data. While the proportion of first children that were illegitimate has declined since the first half of the nineteenth century, the percentage of first babies fathered premaritally by members of the clergy has increased; among the clergy in the twentieth century, 30.5 percent of first children were born less than eight months after the clergymen were married.

Table 4-4 provides data from similar professional directories on the illegitimacy and birth status of the first children of doctors and lawyers. These professionals sired more illegitimate children than did the members of the clergy, particularly in this century. One observation warranted by these data is that while there are ups and downs in the proportions of illegitimate first children among those born prior to the nineteenth century, the proportions are *at least* as high as those born in our century.

Some of the travelers who wrote about Iceland observed the sexual permissiveness and the high degree of concubinage that prevailed on the island. At least two travelers from the sixteenth century in addition to Boorde made such observations.[2] The first was a German merchant from Hamburg, Gories Peerse, who allegedly came to Iceland in 1561. On the subject of sexual relations, he wrote: "Whoring and concubinage are very common here, and men engage in these activities more than in other places" (Sigurður Grímsson, 1946, p. 25). Peerse went on to qualify this by saying that they could not, however, be regarded as morally loose "although they cheat the Germans liberally." (Here he is referring to merchants like himself.)

In 1563, two years after Peerse's visit, a Hollander by the name of Dithmar Blefken claimed to have traveled to Iceland. There is evidence, however, that he never visited the country and that his account was based on seamen's tales (Jakob Benediktsson, 1943, p. xvii). In any case, the tone of his book *Islandia* is hostile and he tends to be very gullible. He wrote, for example, that many Icelanders lived to be "150 years old, and I saw one oldster who was said to be 200" (Sigurður Grímsson, 1946, p. 38). Still, the book was translated into a number of languages and was the most read travellers' account of Iceland until the middle of the eighteenth century. About sexual permissiveness Blefken (Sigurður Grímsson, 1946, p. 39) wrote:

> When Icelanders come into town, they have their daughters with them, those who are of marriageable age. When the merchants report that they have left their wives at home, they [the parents] offer their daughter to spend a night for bread, bisquits, or other small things. Sometimes parents give their daughter gratis, even for a month's time or as long as the merchant lives in Iceland. If it happens that sometimes they become pregnant in this relationship, the parents bestow even more love on them. When the child is born, they raise it for several years, until the father should return or they give the child to their future son-in-law as a dowry with their daugh-

ter. They scorn him not at all because German blood runs in these veins. If any girl associates with a German, she receives much respect and gets more wooers than before. Such was it at the time that whoredom was thought to be no disgrace, if there were no criminal connection involved. To be sure, the priests rage against whoredom, and the culprits are heavily punished [by the Danes], but the natives have little to say about it.

George Steuart MacKenzie (1811, p. 93), at the beginning of the nineteenth century, made the euphemistic observation that house-keepers were "on a very familiar footing with their employers." He also noted (p. 95) a certain looseness in marriage in Iceland: "I was informed that when a couple are dissatisfied with each other, or when a lady chuses to change her helpmate, the separation is sanctioned without any inquiry into the cause, and new bonds solemnly unite those who have most openly slighted their former engagements." Richard F. Burton (1875, volume 1, p. 151) later in the century observed that the marriage tie was "held rather lightly."

Others have come to the same conclusion as I about the persistence in Icelandic culture of a high degree of permissiveness and tolerance in relations between the sexes. Most notable is Hjalmar Lindroth (1937, p. 101) who, in writing about the persistence of pre-Christian conceptions of life, observed:

> that this condition obtains to some extent in married life and in the relation between the sexes. In pagan times such matters were hardly *moral* questions at all, and still less religious in our sense, but social; or, it was regarded as a purely personal and family affair. Therefore a marked liberality and freedom from prejudice has always prevailed in such things in Iceland.

Jónas Jónasson, the Icelandic ethnographer-clergyman referred to earlier, did not deal much with the persistence of Icelandic sexual permissiveness, but he did say: "It is certain that there has been a dulling of the moral consciousness in this area, and that it goes far back in time" (1961, p. 279). The late Sigurður Nordal (1886-1974), generally acknowledged to have been the greatest scholar of Icelandic literature and culture of his time and who took as his domain the whole of Icelandic literature from the beginning, made the comment that heads this chapter with a twinkle in his eye in response to my question on his opinion of the continuity of Icelandic sexual permissiveness.

That premarital sexual permissiveness was also conventional in rural Norwegian society and has the same roots there as in Iceland is suggested by the observations of Thomas Malthus (James, 1966), who visited Norway during the summer of 1799. In his diary entry for July 14, he noted: "I have understood from two or three authorities that the country girls generally have sweethearts for a considerable time before they marry. A marriage seldom takes place but when a child is about to appear" (p. 35). On July 21, he wrote: "I understood from Count Moltke and another gentleman, that much irregularity prevails among the common people before marriage, and that in some districts, it is even approved of and sanctioned by the parents. In general, however, it is not thought creditable to have more than one sweetheart at a time" (p. 172). Eilert Sundt (1817-1875), the first Norwegian family sociologist, wrote about marriage and relations between the sexes from first-hand observation during the middle decades of the nineteenth century (Allwood, 1957). Most significant in this context is his graphic description of Norwegian night courtship patterns in which couples had sexual relations; but, when pregnancy occurred, unlike in Iceland, marriage almost always followed. Such courting, however, took place with social control being exerted by family and peer group. Night courtship apparently also was common among the Swedes (Myrdal, 1945, pp. 42-47), but it was unknown among the Icelanders. This indicates that such patterns developed in Scandinavia after Viking times (Björn Björnsson, 1971, p. 178).

Elsewhere (1976a, pp. 265-68) I argue that the variations in the frequency of illegitimacy in the Nordic countries are related to the differential impact of evangelical and moralistic Protestantism during the eighteenth and nineteenth centuries. It is those areas in the Nordic countries most culturally isolated in the past and least touched by this sort of Protestantism where illegitimacy has been so high: in Iceland, the rural north of Norway (Nordland, Troms, and Finnmark), and inner central Sweden (Jämtland, Gävleborg, and Västernorrland). By contrast, those areas heavily affected by various forms of evangelical Protestant enthusiasm have much lower rates of illegitimacy. Moralistic Protestantism in the Nordic countries seems to have created strong sanctions against illegitimacy while having relatively little effect on the traditionally liberal attitudes toward premarital sexual relations. This attitudinal complex is particularly notable among the Norwegians (Simonson and Geis, 1956). Iceland, unlike Norway and Sweden, has been little affected by any form of evangelical Protestantism. In 1829, the Icelandic historian Jón Espólín wrote that the Icelanders are a "cool-tempered people," that they are "generally not pious," and that "one can hardly find a religious fanatic in the whole country" (quoted by Finnbogason, 1933, p. 305). Other observers have made similar observations (for example, Lindroth, 1937, p. 98; Leaf, 1949, p. 32). The west and south of Norway, strongly affected by pietism in the eighteenth century and by Haugeanism (an evangelical movement within the state church) in the early nineteenth century, are the areas with the lowest illegitimacy ratios in the country—

generally below 5 percent (Norway, 1971, p. 22). In rural Rogaland in the southwest of Norway, only 1.8 percent of all live births were illegitimate in 1970; this level is comparable to that of Ireland, Spain, and the Netherlands, the lowest in Europe. Similarly, the south and west of Sweden affected by Schartauism (Gustafsson, 1965), a pietistic movement within the state church, and the free church movement in the nineteenth century (particularly affecting Jönköping, Halland, and Kronoberg) have had the lowest illegitimacy ratios in Sweden for many decades. In Norway and Sweden, there are negative correlations between the illegitimacy ratios by county and the share of the vote going to the liberal political parties (including in Norway the Christian People's Party), the affiliations of those segments of the population historically most affected by moralistic Protestantism.

An important sociological question regarding the very high proportion of out-of-wedlock births that occurs everywhere in Iceland and in parts of the other Nordic countries is whether these societies are an exception to Malinowski's Principle of Legitimacy (1962, pp. 62-64), which holds that all societies have a norm that every child should have a social father. William Goode (1960, 1961) has vigorously upheld the universality of this principle, although he sees that its function is more to insure social placement in society than to provide paternal protection. High illegitimacy, then, is to be interpreted as a manifestation of the breakdown of a cultural system with a consequent high degree of social disorganization. Insofar as the Nordic countries are concerned, Goode has argued that "though some children may be born outside of wedlock, they are likely to be only technically and temporarily illegitimate, not socially illegitimate" (1961, p. 925). This is true only insofar as there is little of the kind of illegitimacy that grows out of social disorganization, what he calls "social illegitimacy."

Goode has not satisfactorily reconciled the situation in the Nordic countries with Malinowski's principle. To do so would require much modification of it. Grandparents or members of an extended family frequently fulfilled the role of parents in the past and often still do in Iceland. There are many unwed mothers in Iceland without functional fathers for their children who have never faced any social opprobrium and who lead conventional lives. The best explanation, although it is not a functional one, of the high illegitimacy ratios that have prevailed in the northern European countries and of the marked regional variations within them is the effects of the differential penetration of Christian mores of marriage into the traditional folk cultures. The older permissive pattern persisted in those areas where the influence of Christian conceptions of marriage was weakest. In the words of Alva Myrdal, who was writing about Sweden, this older permissiveness was then "paralleled by more modern patterns [of permissiveness] and thus strengthened before its ultimate decline" (1945, p. 45).

THE STATUS OF WOMEN

One of the notable characteristics of ancient Scandinavian culture was the high status of women and the independence accorded them. The role of women, particularly among the old Icelanders, was distinctly different from any that ever prevailed among the ancient Hebrews, Greeks, and Romans (see, for example, Finley, 1967; O'Faolain and Martines, 1973). Women in old Norse culture had a high degree of equality in marriage and could divorce their husbands by declaration. Marriage, divorce, and, presumably, sexual relations were private matters to be settled by the individuals directly concerned and by their kin; they were not seen as moral, religious, or societal questions, as they were in Christian societies. Such attitudes generally appear to be concomitants of a high degree of equality between the sexes (Tomasson, 1970, pp. 165-84).

Jacobsen (1978, p. 171) has compared the position of women in the Scandinavian countries during the Viking period and concluded about Iceland that

> the Iceland law, the *Landnámabók* [*Book of Settlements*], and the family sagas were found to be in agreement concerning the position of women in Iceland. The Icelandic woman enjoyed a great measure of independence whether she was single, married, or widowed. She had economic power as she could control her own property and she was also entitled to act as a trustee . . . for the property of minors. . . . With her independence followed civic responsibilities, and she was clearly considered an important member of the Icelandic society.

Jacobsen also has observed that the divorce laws in ancient Iceland were "extraordinarily liberal compared with those in the other extant Scandinavian laws" (p. 53). Just to enter into divorce proceedings under the old Icelandic laws could make a woman independent; "as soon as divorce procedures were begun the wife could demand that all her property be handed over to her whatever the outcome of the proceedings" (p. 53).

Even some of the Vikings were women. Women made trips to America, and at least one expedition was led by a woman, the bloody Freydis, sister of Leifur Eiríksson. The sagas support and illustrate what is known from early Scandinavian law and modern research about the high status of women. Strong and admirable women, as well as nasty and goading ones, play in this literature a central role unparalleled in any other classical literature. Again, let one example from the sagas (*Laxdaela Saga*, chapter 5) suffice for many. Here is how Aud the Deep-minded, a strong-willed settler old enough to have a married grandaughter, is matter-of-factly described as "taking land" in Iceland:

> Aud now prepared her departure from the Faroe Islands and announced to her companions that she was going to Iceland. She had with her Olaf Feilan, Thorstein the Red's son, and those of Thorstein's daughters who were still unmarried. She put out to sea and had a good voyage. . . . [Later] Aud went round all the Breidafjord Dales and took possession of as much land as she pleased. Then she sailed right up to the head of the fjord, and there her high-seat pillars had been washed ashore. . . . She had a farm built at this place, which has been known as Hvamm ever since, and there she settled.

The case of Aud is not particularly unusual; women all through Icelandic history have managed farms. During the Viking period, it was the practice to give a farm the name of its chief occupant, the head of the household in modern census terminology. Barði Guðmundsson (1967, p. 40) has shown that during the tenth and eleventh centuries about 11 percent of the Icelandic farms were named after women, compared with less than 1 percent of farms at the same time in Norway. At the time of the 1703 census, 13.8 percent of all farms in the country were managed by women (table 3-17).

Guðmundsson (1967, p. 27) also has observed that in an enumeration of poets in the early centuries that of the "more than a hundred," ten are named after their mothers. Among the court poets—all those in Norway and Denmark were Icelanders—one in six carried the name of his mother (p. 28). All told, Guðmundsson (p. 29) found 34 women up to the middle of the eleventh century who "share the honorable distinction that their sons bear their mother's name as though they were patronymics." Yet, it has always been extremely rare in Iceland, and in most periods unknown, for anyone to bear the name of his or her mother. Guðmundsson's theory, although not crucial to the argument that women in ancient Iceland had a uniquely high status, is that Iceland was settled by a distinct Scandinavian ethnic group among whom women enjoyed particularly high (equal?) status. The settlers of Iceland were "*fertility worshippers who venerated female divinities*" (p. 60, italics his). Women had an important role in the worship of these female gods, particularly Freya, with whom the old Norse poetic tradition was intimately involved, and this is why so many of the skaldic poets, and almost no one else, bore the names of their mothers.

The Icelandic anthropologist Jón Steffensen has been concerned with the empirical study of the role of women in heathen and early

Christian times. He agrees that women in heathen times enjoyed high status and much influence and has observed (1967-1968, p. 182), for example, that "a good number of the women's nicknames from the pagan period are laudatory and testify to a mental capacity fully comparable with what is witnessed of menfolk in their nicknames." He also observed (p. 183), perhaps making his point too strongly, "a complete change in the situation of women in society and in the attitude toward them" after the coming of Christianity. First, he noted (p. 182) the evidence in the "mere numbers" of women recorded in the two old Icelandic works with the greatest number of personal names, the *Book of Settlements* (the pre-Christian source) and *Sturlunga Saga* (a contemporary work from the second half of the thirteenth century and the Christian source): women comprise 24.3 percent of the total number of names in the source from the pre-Christian period but only 18.3 percent in the source from the Christian period. He also noted that nicknames, although more common during the heathen period than during the Christian period, are relatively more negative toward women in the Christian period. Although Steffensen makes no mention of Guðmundsson in his study, he agrees with him that the high status of women in pre-Christian Iceland was related to their special religious role. He concluded his discussion (p. 191) of the role of women in religious and magical matters as follows:

> An important part of the heathen cult practices took part within her domain, in the home itself, and it is understandable that she played an important role in them, just as the recorded nicknames would lead us to suppose. With the Conversion the major part of religious activity shifted from the home to the church, and more important still, women were forbidden any kind of role in connection with divine service.

Once we leave the world of the old Icelanders, we could speak of the silent women of Iceland, as Finley (1967) does of the women of ancient Rome. The absence of women from written Icelandic history before the twentieth century is remarkable in its near totality; women apparently were only wives and mothers, concubines and mistresses, housekeepers and doers of all sorts of work. The multivolume *Saga Íslendinga* mentions women only in their relationships to men. When I asked my 100 Icelanders to name the two deceased and the two living Icelanders whom they most admired, *not a single woman's name was mentioned* (see chapter 5).

Literature is the field where there are more notable Icelanders—by far—than any other, yet it is an area almost totally bereft of women until this century. In Stefán Einarsson's (1957) *History of Icelandic Literature*, which contains hundreds of names, only two women authors who wrote before this century were noted: Steinunn Finnsdóttir (1641-?), a poet, and Torfhildur Thorsteinsdóttir Hólm (1845-1918), an author of historical novels. In the two most authoritative anthologies of Icelandic literature, which contain examples of the work of scores of Icelandic poets and authors, one dealing with the period 1400-1750 (Siguður Nordal et al., 1953) and the other the period 1750-1930 (Siguður Nordal, 1970), only one woman is represented, a poet using the pen name Hulda (1881-1946). When I asked my 100 respondents to name five deceased Icelandic writers, only 3 of 462 names given were those of women (see chapter 5). However, when the respondents were asked to name five living authors, 50 of 473 names given were those of women.

From this absence of publicly known women are we to conclude that women have been unequal and repressed throughout the centuries in Iceland? I think not. It is crucial to make a distinction between the demands of a rural and of a developed society, between traditional equality and modern equality. In rural societies — especially one such as Iceland was until this century — on the verge of survival, a high degree of sex role differentiation can be considered almost a societal imperative. As Burton (1875, volume 2, p. 6) noted more than a century ago, this was "a country where all domestic comfort and worldly prosperity [depended] upon the 'gudewife.'" Only with modernization can we expect to see much diminution of sex role differentiation. There *was* a high degree of traditional equality in the Icelandic rural society. Women always had a great deal of independence and were admired for the same mental qualities that men were. They have always had a high degree of sexual freedom, not much less than that of men; virginity has never been any kind of an ideal. Women have always had an important, perhaps I might even say equal, role in family decision making; the husband-father as patriarch is a role utterly absent from Icelandic literature and autobiography. On the other hand, girls were slighted in education even though most of them were taught to read since the sixteenth century (Ólason, 1942, p. 212), and they probably always worked harder on the farms than the men did. The women helped in haying and other outside work, but the men did not help with the inside work.

Let me give an example of an "admirable" Icelandic farm woman from one of the most celebrated Icelandic autobiographies. Here is how the Icelandic clergyman Jón Steingrímsson (1728-1791) described (1956, pp. 14-15) his maternal grandfather's sister:

> She was tall and thick-set, big-faced, strong and high-minded, upright and outspoken. Still she was gentle and compassionate to those in need and to poor people. She could write and read which was regarded as a notable accomplishment in those days. She could mow hay and was outstanding as a

scythe smithy. . . . She was so good at genealogy that she knew nearly everyone's lineage. . . . She knew the old finger calendar and the ancient way of reckoning time, and so much about the sagas, poetry, and the psalms as to appear truly incredible.

He noted (p. 18) matter-of-factly that she had a child who died immediately after it was born, but he made no mention of whether or not she ever had a husband. This woman was born in the 1650s or 1660s, but she could have been born as late as the 1850s or 1860s.

When the witchcraft craze of the sixteenth and seventeenth centuries reached every country in Europe and colonial America (Trevor-Roper, 1969), only Iceland did not direct its fear toward women. This single exception to Iceland's nonviolent history since the Reformation resulted in approximately 25 witches being burned at the stake between 1625 and 1685, and only two of them were women (Ólason, 1942, p. 253). At the very least, this fact indicates that the perverse fear of, and belief in, magic spells that characterized the Icelanders during this miserable period of Danish exploitation and bad climatic conditions was not directed against women as it was everywhere else.

When we turn to modern Icelandic society and look at it from the point of view of modern equality between the sexes, or more precisely the degree of sexual differentiation, the situation is mixed. Iceland appears quite "backward" in a number of spheres when compared with the other Nordic countries. Let us survey several basic areas:

1. *Labor force.* A smaller proportion of Icelandic women were in the active labor force in 1970 than in any Nordic country, except Norway (Nordic Council, 1977, p. 43). In 1976, only 29 percent of the Icelandic labor force consisted of women (Statistical Bureau of Iceland, *Hagtíðindi*, 1977, p. 184); 27 of the 50 women in my interview sample were "only housewives" (appendix B). The average income of women in 1976 was 38 percent of that of men, partly because a higher proportion of women work part-time and partly because they disproportionately work at lower-paying jobs. (See table 8-1). Particularly significant is the very low proportion of women in the professions and other upper-level positions. In 1976, just over 2 percent (14 of 596) of the active physicians and dentists were women. The percentage of lawyers who are women is even lower; in the years 1911-1963, only 5 of 451 law degrees awarded by the University of Iceland went to women (Agnar Jónsson, 1964); and there are no women clergy in the country. Even in the category teachers and principals, women comprised only 22 percent of the total in 1976; the proportion of women faculty at

Church and turf-farm from southern Iceland, about 1900.
Courtesy of Nationalmuseet, Copenhagen.

Turf-houses in Arbær Folk Museum in Reykjavík. Courtesy
of the Ministry for Foreign Affairs, Reykjavík.

Hveragerði, a village in southern Iceland famous for its greenhouses. Courtesy of the Ministry for Foreign Affairs, Reykjavík. Photo: Kristinn Benediktsson.

A fishing village in one of the western fjörds. Courtesy of the Ministry for Foreign Affairs, Reykjavík. Photo: Kristinn Benediktsson.

Fishing boats. Photo: Guðmundur Ingólfsson.

A fish factory. Courtesy of the Ministry
for Foreign Affairs, Reykjavík.
Photo: Kristinn Benediktsson.

Cod-fishing. Courtesy of the Ministry
for Foreign Affairs, Reykjavík.
Photo: Kristinn Benediktsson.

View from the lake in Reykjavík. Courtesy of the Ministry
for Foreign Affairs, Reykjavík.

A swimming pool in the center of Reykjavík. Courtesy of
the Ministry for Foreign Affairs, Reykjavík.

Reykjavík, city center. Courtesy of the Ministry for Foreign Affairs, Reykjavík.

Reykjavík. Courtesy of the Ministry for Foreign Affairs, Reykjavík.

The National Theater in Reykjavík. Courtesy of the Ministry for Foreign Affairs, Reykjavík.

The Althing (Parliament) Building. Courtesy of the Ministry
for Foreign Affairs, Reykjavík. Photo: Pétur Thomsen.

Bessastaðir, the residence of the president of Iceland. Courtesy of the Ministry for Foreign Affairs, Reykjavík. Photo: Pétur Thomsen.

The Prime Minister's Office, Reykjavík. Courtesy of the Ministry for Foreign Affairs, Reykjavík. Photo: Pétur Thomsen.

The University Building, University of Iceland. Courtesy of
the Ministry for Foreign Affairs, Reykjavík.

The National Museum in Reykjavík. Courtesy of the Ministry
for Foreign Affairs, Reykjavík.

the University of Iceland is miniscule. One area, and a particularly important one in Iceland, where women have come to make a numerical impression is as published poets and writers. Among those poets and writers born after 1935, around 1 of 6 or 7 is a woman (see chapter 5).

2. *Education.* The admission of women into secondary and advanced educational institutions is a phenomenon of the twentieth century in Iceland. The first woman did not graduate from an academic secondary school until 1899, the second not until 1910 (Gils Guð-mundsson, 1950, p. 101); by the mid-1970s, over 40 percent of the graduates of the seven gymnasia (*menntaskólor*) were women, a lower proportion than in the other Nordic countries, where it is now about 50 percent. In the 1975-1976 academic year, 34 percent of the 3,000 university-level students were women, the same level as in Denmark and Norway but below that of Finland (48 percent) and Sweden (40 percent) (Nordic Council, 1977, p. 283). No Icelandic woman received a doctorate before 1926, when Björg Karítus Thorláksson received one in physiology from the University of Paris. The first doctorate to a woman from the University of Iceland went to Selma Jónsdóttir in art history in 1960 (Benedikz and Hjartar, 1964).

3. *Sexual Behavior and Norms.* Enough has been said in this chapter to support the contention of a low level of sexual differentiation in this area, less than has existed elsewhere in Scandinavia.

4. *Child Rearing.* There is as little sexual differentiation in the bringing up of children in Iceland as there is in any modern society. I base this assertion on my own observations and the fact that 83 of my 100 respondents answered same to the question "do you believe girls should be brought up about the same as boys in most ways, or do you believe girls should be brought up differently in most ways?" Most of those who answered differently qualified their answers (appendix A, question 12).

5. *Political Participation.* Almost as high a proportion of Icelandic females as males vote in national elections—89.1 and 91.4 percent, respectively, in 1978, a level of voter participation for both sexes equaled only by Sweden in northern Europe (Statistical Bureau of Iceland, 1978, p. 5). Yet, women today are almost as strikingly absent from leadership roles in politics as they have been all through Icelandic history. The first woman—Ingibjörg H. Bjarnason—was elected to the Althing in 1923 (Sigurðsson and Hjörvar, 1930, p. 38), but she has had few successors. The Althing is like the United States Senate in its paucity of elected female members and unlike the parliaments of the other Nordic countries, which have sizable

numbers of female representatives. In the 1978 general elections to the Althing, three of the sixty elected members were women—all were from Reykjavík; this is the largest female representation ever.

In spite of an egalitarian sexual ethic and a low degree of sexual differentiation in child-rearing practices and socialization, Icelandic women, and men too, are more constricted in their social and occupational roles than are men and women in the other Nordic countries. Relatively few women work full-time outside of the home in Iceland, sex role differentiation in employment is great, and women are barely represented in all the professions, politics, and positions of authority. One factor, above all, appears to be related to this low degree of representation of women in the traditionally male occupational roles; the high fertility of the Icelanders, particularly among women in their teens and early twenties, combined with the fact that a majority of their children are illegitimate (see tables 4-1 and 4-2). Not only does this inhibit the roles open to young women and channel them into the domestic role, but it is also a limiting factor among *their* mothers, who frequently are mother surrogates for their grandchildren. Iceland and Ireland, as I noted in chapter 3, are the only countries in northwestern Europe where the birthrate exceeded 20 per 1,000 population until after the mid-1970s.

KINSHIP

The intergenerational extended family household remains strong in modern-day Iceland and shows no sign of passing from the scene. That such a large proportion of young people, whether engaged or not, continue to establish their own families within the context of their parental families is an uncommon, perhaps unique, pattern in a modern urban society. Yet, there is clear continuity here with older Icelandic patterns of intergenerational extended families that existed in the millennium of the rural society. The continuation, or rather the adaptation of this old pattern, as I noted earlier, has inhibited the role aspirations and possibilities of young women and of their mothers in Iceland. Yet, the pattern also may be viewed, as it is by Rich (1978, p. 182), as a "by-product of a traditional and highly functional form of domestic adaptation that throws the weight of its benefits onto the young people, helping to insure [their] success in an expensive and arduous world."

The first student of kinship to investigate the Icelandic system was the anthropologist Lewis Henry Morgan (1871) in his *Systems of Consanguinity and Affinity of the Human Family*. He obtained his information on Icelandic kinship from the Icelandic patriot-scholar Jón Sigurðsson (p. 509). Morgan (p. 37) wrote:

> The insulation of the Icelandic Teutons would tend to preserve their form of consanguinity free from foreign influence. . . . It follows strictly the natural streams of descent, and makes each relationship specific. This realizes what we mean by a descriptive system. It is evidently nearer the primitive form of the Aryan family than that of any other nation of the Teutonic branch.

Morgan's observations on the antiquity of the Icelandic kinship system are apparently acceptable to current students of kinship, such as George Murdock (Rich, 1976, p. 1).

Robert T. Merrill (1964), one of the few anthropologists to have investigated Icelandic kinship, is impressed with the evidence of the continuity of Icelandic kinship terminology. He wrote (p. 871) that it "consists of two parallel systems; the first for everyday, informal use, constructed basically of pairs of terms, distinguished by sex, for the three most important types of relations: blood, in-laws, and foster; the second carefully distinguishing and grouping relatives in terms of their reciprocal and mutual responsibilities." He went on to state "categorically" that "no term basic to the two original systems has been lost" since the thirteenth century and later suggested (p. 872) that this "may reasonably be projected another three centuries into the past." Merrill, however, sees both systems as "breaking down . . . and amalgamating . . . to form a single new system" (p. 876) under the conditions of modern life.

The most substantive description of Icelandic kinship terminology and its changing directions has been put forth by Rich (1976), who is as impressed as Merrill with its historical continuity. There are descriptive terms for over 99 specific relationships and collectivities of kin, probably more than can be found in any other modern society. Rich analyzes Icelandic kinship terminology as "a coterminous set of self-contained subsystems" (p. 1). He delineates four subsystems, each of which is undergoing change reflecting the radical technological changes of this century. Rich (p. 15) objects to Merrill's depiction of these changes as "breakdowns" and his assertion that there is an "amalgamation" between the systems. Instead, Rich sees that "the amalgamation is occurring within each subsystem, while the subsystems themselves remain intact."

Rich (1976, p. 2) described the subsystems of Icelandic kinship, into which I have inserted examples, as follows:

> There are two major systems of terminology: (1) an Ego-centered system of terms used for designating individuals, and (2) an alliance oriented system of collective terms used for designating groups of kin. Each system is com-

prised of two subsystems which, relative to each other, are more or less class-ifacatory or descriptive. Hence, the Descriptive terms [*faðir, móðir, bróðir*, et cetera, *föður-faðir* (father's father), *móðurfaðir* (mother's father), et cetera] and the Merging terms [*afi* (grandfather, either father's father or mother's father), *barnabarn* (child's child or grandchild for which there are descriptive terms meaning son's son, son's daughter, daughter's son, and daughter's daughter)] are the two subsystems used to refer to specific individuals, the former by purely descriptive means and the latter by relatively classificatory means. The Focal Group terms [for example, *feðgar* (a father and son), *feðgin* (a father and daughter)] and the Indeterminate terms [for example, *frændfólk* (relatives), *tengdamenn* (in-laws)] are the two subsystems used by Ego to designate in the first case, well-circumscribed and delimited groups of kin, and in the second case to designate larger, relatively indeterminate groups of kin.

The Anglo-American societies make do with a bare minimum of kinship terms compared with modern Icelandic society.

Among the notable observations about kinship and kinship terminology in contemporary Iceland are the following:

1. The use of unadorned descriptive terms is always regarded as cold and impersonal. Rather than *móðir*, one uses *mamma* or sometimes *móðir min* (mother mine); instead of *faðir*, *pabbi*; rather than the four descriptive terms for grandfather and grandmother, *afi* and *amma*.

2. Only for parents, grandparents, and great-grandparents are terms of address used; to all other kin given names or nicknames are used; this is an egalitarian pattern.

3. Focal terms that deal with well-defined groups of kin are disappearing from everyday use because of their decreased significance in the modern society (Rich, 1976, p. 8). So too are the specific names for the different kinds and degrees of cousins. Yet, Icelanders continue to have a keen awareness of who their collateral relatives are; they continually point out that so-and-so is their second cousin on their father's side or that he or she is married to his or her spouse's cousin. From the response to the question in my interview schedule (question 11, appendix A) about being related "to any of the great Icelanders," it is clear that nearly all know they are so related but their knowledge is vague and it is not a subject they cultivate. The concern of present-day Icelanders with genealogy is commonly exaggerated.

4. The quality of personal relations between individuals is frequently more important than the formal relationship in determining the degree that kin feel obligations to one another. This "modern" characteristic of Icelandic kinship permeated the sagas, in which the nature of a personal relationship often takes precedence over the ob-

ligations of kinship. This seems always to have been a characteristic of the Icelandic kinship system. As Thompson (1969, p. 134) put it: "The indigenous kindred structure of northern Europe was an open system. . . . It afforded the individual maximum mobility and flexibility to respond to environmental pressures. . . . [It is] based on . . . achievements rather than on formal ascription."

CHAPTER 5

Literacy
and Cultural Life

*Iceland has been uniquely a country of books since the
twelfth century.*

Sigurður A. Magnússon (1977)

*Despite all talk about the literary spirit in Iceland, . . . [the
people are] far from being intellectual.*

Pétur Guðjónsson (1967)

"We publish more books than other people, we buy more books than
others, and, in all likelihood, we read more books than other people
do." So wrote Baldvin Tryggvason (1970), the president of the largest
publishing house in Iceland. Many Icelanders, and perhaps most Icelandic intellectuals, believe assertions like this one. Indeed, the alleged
addiction of Icelanders to reading books and the proportionately large
number of bookstores are among the few items of information about
Iceland that have reached the outside world.

The amount and kind of reading done by Icelanders, the number
of books in their homes, and their general knowledge about literature
were among the kinds of information I was particularly interested in
when I made up my interview schedule. But, before discussing literacy
and cultural life in present-day Iceland, I will deal with two pertinent
background topics: (1) the achievement of nearly universal literacy in
eighteenth-century Iceland, the first country in the world to have accomplished this, and (2) the reports on the literacy of the Icelanders
by the eighteenth- and nineteenth-century travelers.

THE DEVELOPMENT OF UNIVERSAL LITERACY

Of the eleven centuries of settlement in Iceland, no century was more
filled with misery than the eighteenth. Yet, it was during this century

116

that universal literacy was achieved. (*Universal literacy* is defined here as the ability to read, which does not necessarily imply the ability to write.)

Since the twelfth century, writers and poets have been writing the history of Iceland, and they have given the Icelanders a national and historical consciousness that is unique. Indeed, the very survival of the isolated Icelanders during the misery of the five centuries from 1300 to 1800 has sometimes been attributed to the sustenance provided by their history, poetry, and literature. At the beginning of the eighteenth century, a large minority of the Icelandic population could read, and that had probably been more or less the case since the end of the twelfth century. Even in those early times, according to Einar Ól. Sveinsson (1944, p. 197), nearly all the chieftains and the more prosperous farmers could both read and write. The extraordinary amount of manuscript copying and the common practice of reading aloud the sagas, the Bible, and other religious books attest to a high level of literacy. What proportion of the population was literate, however, can only be a guess. Hallgrímur Hallgrímsson (1925, pp. 1-2), an Icelandic librarian who studied the achievement of universal literacy in eighteenth-century Iceland, suggested that around the middle of the eighteenth century less than half of the population could read. At that time, the Swedes and the Danes may have been the most literate of European peoples.

Several sixteenth-century churchmen commented on the literacy of the Icelanders. In a letter written to two Icelandic officials (1546), Pétur Palladíus, a Danish bishop, noted that most Icelanders could read and write their native tongue (Ólason, 1942, p. 212). Absalon Pedersen Beyer, a Norwegian writing in the 1560s, observed (Ólason, 1942, p. 212; Finnbogason, 1933, pp. 292-93):

> This is a land of valiant people, well-bred and independent, adept at all sorts of arts. With these people it is commonly the habit that children are taught to read and write, both girls and boys, and young boys are made to learn the country's lawbook by heart and hold both hands behind their backs and recite the whole lawbook by sections, then every section by chapter, and then each chapter by paragraph.

A Danish priest, Péter Clausen Friis, wrote in 1580 that the Icelanders knew a great deal about chess and law (Ólason, 1942, p. 212). Implicit in these observations was the assumption that the Icelanders were different from the other Scandinavians.

As early as 1634, King Christian IV wrote a letter commanding all bishops, pastors, and church people to make sure that all children were instructed and examined in the teachings of Martin Luther; he further ordered pastors to make home calls to insure the implementation of this directive. In 1736, confirmation and training in religion were made mandatory throughout the Danish realm, but the training did not presuppose the ability to read. During the years 1741-1745, Ludvig Harboe, a remarkably energetic clergyman who had been sent to Iceland by the Danish king, traveled to all parishes in Iceland to question youths aged 12 to 17 on their knowledge of Christian teachings and their ability to read. Many were found wanting, and some of the pastors who should have been teaching them were found to be wastrels and drunkards.

Harboe's visit resulted in legislation based on his proposals that greatly enhanced the role of the clergy and the family in teaching young people to read. In 1744, religious training was ordered for all young people. In 1746, the pastors were ordered to make regular visits to all the homes in their parishes to insure that this training was being carried out. The legislation also contained a provision stating that illiterate parents, whenever they had the necessary means, must engage someone in their place to teach their children to read. Although similar legislation had been promulgated by the king more than a century earlier, it had not been seriously carried out.

The first primary school in Iceland was not set up until 1745, on the Westman Islands, just off the south coast of Iceland. Other schools were generally slow in being established (Fraser and Jósepsson, 1968). As late as 1903, only 5,416 of the 12,030 children aged 7-14 were enrolled in school (Magnúss, 1939, pp. 115-16). The great distances between isolated Icelandic farms made the establishment of schools for rural children difficult, and the tradition of learning to read at home with supervision from the clergy continued into the twentieth century. Of the 100 respondents in my study, 29 had no formal schooling and apparently had been taught at home. In recent times, however, boarding schools accommodating large numbers of pupils from the countryside have solved the problem.

In 1925, Hallgrímur Hallgrímsson was able to verify the achievement of nearly universal literacy during the period 1780-1790 through study of parish registers. These give information, derived from home visits by the clergy, on the personal characteristics and accomplishments of all the people in a parish. From studying the registers of 27 parishes in the northern diocese of Hólar, Hallgrímsson concluded that "saying that all who are over 12 can read is the same as to say that nearly all can read. Those who cannot read are, for the most part, old people who were adults at the time Harboe's proposals were made" (p. 64). Hallgrímsson reached the same conclusions about the 57 parishes of the southern diocese of Skálholt, which he also studied. In the 50 years between 1740 and 1790, the proportion of the population 12 years old and older who could read increased from "nearly half" to "probably all of 90 percent." No wonder Hallgrímsson called Harboe "the best thing Denmark ever sent us."

Hallgrímsson also studied the parish records of some 1,000 homes in the period 1780-1800 and found only seven—all the homes of illiterate farmers—to be without books. He also was able to determine from these records what religious books the Icelanders owned, but, unfortunately, there is no information in the registers on secular literature. More than 900 families owned Jón Vídalín's *Postilla*, a book of sermons of high literary quality; and Hallgrímur Pétursson's *Passíusálmar* (*Passion Hymns*), a prayer book, had an even wider circulation.

The ordinary people's possession of secular books during the second half of the eighteenth century recently was investigated by Sólrún Jensdóttir (1975-1976), who used inventories of estates in the National Archives of Iceland. She found 1,285 inventories for the period 1750-1800; of these, 1,149 dealt with the estates of ordinary people. These inventories were not representative of the country and much overrepresent the north, perhaps because paper rots more readily in the more humid south. The 1,149 estates of farmers, farm workers, and servants listed 9,298 religious books and 627 secular ones (6.3 percent of the total); the average library contained 8.6 books. (The professional class who had many more books, particularly secular ones, are here excluded.) The subjects of the 627 books (pp. 289-90) were these:

Books of law	194
Instructive books in other subjects	156
Sagas, ancient poetry, short stories	118
Rímur (rhyming poetry)	35
Biographies	25
Translated books for pastime	25
Poetry	23
Periodicals	21
Annals	10
Books on other subjects	20

Jensdóttir also looked into book ownership in one county (*sýsla*) for the period 1800-1830 and found libraries to be somewhat larger, with more secular books (pp. 268-71).

By the end of the eighteenth century, then, the Icelanders were the only people in the world to have achieved nearly universal literacy, at least in terms of the ability to read, and—judging from data on popular literacy in Ian Watt's *The Rise of the Novel* (1957, pp. 37-40) —they were far ahead of the English, who are generally recognized as the most "developed" people of the time. The nearly universal ability to read was not achieved elsewhere in Scandinavia and northwestern Europe until the nineteenth century. Indeed, as late as 1850, Carlo M. Cipolla (1969, p. 71) estimated that only about half of all Europeans (excluding the Russians) were able to read.

WHAT THE TRAVELERS REPORTED

Popular literacy of a uniquely high order, along with equality in material conditions and social relationships, are topics on which there is agreement among all of the travelers. Observations range from that of Burton (1875, volume 2, p. 155), one of the more critical nineteenth-century scholar-travelers, who noted that all Icelanders could read and write "more or less," to that of the American Pliny Miles (1854, p. 34) who wrote: "I never saw a child above the age of nine years that could not read in a masterly style." Baring-Gould (1863, p. xxxiv) observed that "every native reads and writes well." A young Swedish geologist, C. W. Paijkull (1866, p. 17), perhaps echoing Baring-Gould, wrote that "not only do all Icelanders read, they read well." In 1872, James Bryce (1923, pp. 30-31) observed:

> Three things no Icelandic farm wants—books, a coffee-pot, and a portrait of Jón Sigurðsson, the illustrious leader of the the patriotic party. . . . Few are the houses in Iceland which do not contain a library; and twice, in spots of rather exceptional wretchedness, I found exceptionally good ones —one chiefly of legal and historical treatises, the other an excellent collection of Sagas and poetry.

Even four decades before Bryce, Arthur Dillon (1840, pp. 106-07), who went to Iceland in 1834, could write that "it is rare to enter a house that is not provided with a very considerable number of books," and von Troil (1780, p. 171) noted in 1772 that he "found better libraries in many parts of Iceland than could have been expected."

Perhaps the first eighteenth-century traveler to Iceland to comment on the Icelanders' literacy was Niels Horrebow, a Danish mathematician and astronomer, who went to Iceland four years after Harboe departed. He (1758, p. 121) commented on the eagerness of the Icelanders for learning in all areas and noted that among "the people in general, more write well than in Denmark." Sir Joseph Banks claimed that "in Iceland education is more general than in other countries; and the lower ranks are clearly much better informed than in other parts; in fact, the lowest ranks of European soceity scarcely exist in Iceland" (quoted by Hermannsson, 1928, p. 40). His companion von Troil (1780, p. 27) later wrote:

We should form . . . a very wrong judgment of Iceland to imagine it absorbed in total ignorance and obscurity: on the contrary, I can affirm, that I have found more knowledge among the lower classes, than is to be met with in most other places. You will seldom find a peasant who besides being well-instructed in the principles of religion, is not also acquainted with the history of his country, which proceeds from the frequent reading of the traditional histories (sagas) wherein consists their principal amusement.

The English geologist George Steuart MacKenzie (1811, p. 286) observed that "education is systematically carried on among all ranks of the inhabitants; and the degree of information existing, even among the lower classes is probably greater than in almost any part of continental Europe." He was impressed that this was accomplished in spite of the absence of schools. Ebenezer Henderson (1818, p. 370) wrote that he was "frequently" astonished by "self-taught peasants" who "discoursed on subjects, which in other countries, we should expect to hear stated by those only who fill the professor's chair, or who have otherwise devoted their lives to the study of science." Samuel Kneeland (1876, pp. 241-45) was impressed with the "high cultivation" of the people. Even Burton (1875, volume 1, p. 142), who was so suspicious of his predecessors and who regarded the Icelanders as "slow and stolid," grudgingly admitted they were "capable of high culture, and of wide learning and deep research." Guðmundur Finnbogason (1933, pp. 361-68; 1943, p. 19), an Icelandic psychologist, described the attributes accorded Icelanders by 24 "prominent" writers on Iceland (20 foreign, 4 native). Of the 21 qualities that he found, the most frequently noted was intelligent (*gáfuður*), mentioned 12 times.

Two twentieth-century scholars who gave currency to the belief in the intellectuality and bookishness of the Icelanders were the great British medievalist W. P. Ker and the prolific American geographer and geographical determinist Ellsworth Huntington. Ker (1908, p. 12) believed that while there were "many towns about the world that could easily take in the whole population of Iceland; there can be few that produce so many men of ability, and so high an average of intellectual power. It is a subject that might be recommended to students of heredity and professors of Eugenics." Huntington (1924, p. 281) wrote scores of pages in a number of books on the magnificent qualities of the Icelanders, explaining these alleged attributes as the result of selective migration from Norway and a thousand years of severe natural selection. He was quite swept away by the bookishness of the Icelanders and reported a number of charming but rather silly anecdotes, such as the one about a boy of twelve who was discovered by a traveler "studying botany from a Latin textbook while he was tending his flock of a thousand sheep." Equally quaint is the story of a girl of 14 who was leading horses laden with milk to the creamery, "reading as she went."

In addition to the popular literary tradition that dates from the twelfth century, the location and climate of Iceland are probably important background factors in the high level of literacy that has prevailed there; people were forced to be indoors for long periods during much of the winter. Lindroth (1937, pp. 179-80) described the family assembly on winter nights (*kvöldvaka* or evening wake), an Icelandic institution dating from the middle ages, which survived as a common practice into the 1920s and in some places until the 1930s:

> When the twilight of the short winter day begins, the people lie down to sleep for about an hour on the beds in the *baðstofa* [combined bed and sitting room] . . . to "take a twilight nap." Then a maid [a young girl] gets up, and after fanning the embers left in the hearth from cooking the dinner, lights the lamp. When all members of the household have gradually awakened, each one takes his assigned seat for some form of work. Now the *kvöldvaka* or "evening wake" begins. The men make ropes out of horsehair, or tethering straps and saddle-girths from waste wool; they weave or repair nets, make tools, pails, and boxes, or carve on wood or horn; and sometimes just continue to lounge about lazily, while the women spin, sew or knit. But one of the men, generally the father of the household or the one who can recite best and most clearly, sits near the lamp and begins to read, often deciding first by common agreement what saga to choose. If there are several good readers in the house they take turns in the entertainment, following each other in regular order, or successive evenings, for their is no change of reader in the same evening. After the reading the different characters of the saga may be discussed, sides taken for or against, etc.

Magnús Gíslason (1977) recently wrote what is probably the definitive work on all aspects of the *kvöldvaka*, using a variety of sources including the abundant Icelandic autobiographies. He observed that, while the institution was universal throughout the island, the activities of the *kvöldvaka* differed "from evening to evening and from farm to farm depending on the resources in the different homes" (p. 88). Books and manuscripts were exchanged. The isolated farms treasured visitors, particularly if they brought books with them and if they had any special talents in reading or reciting or whatever they were compelled to perform. Even many of the vagrants who traveled about the country were welcomed; often they were "not so uneducated and useless as they were poor" (p. 45). Some were celebrated for their ability to tell stories, recite poetry and *rímur*, or pose riddles. A few were poets known throughout the land. The most usual activities of the *kvöldvaka* were (pp. 88-121) these:

1. Most often central to the intellectual activities of the *kvöldvaka* was reading. What was read was both secular and sacred: the old sagas, histories of the country, published folktales (after the middle of the nineteenth century), novels (after 1870, and mostly Icelandic), poetry, newspapers and magazines, the Bible, and Icelandic religious writings.

2. All manner of legends, folk tales, and ghost stories were told. Many were based on the old literature (see chapter 7). Sometimes they were related to the teller's own experiences.

3. Rhymes (*rímur*) were recited during the *kvöldvaka*. The reciting of long and complex poetry has been common in Iceland since at least medieval times. Up until the twentieth century, many Icelanders were able to recite for lengths of time that appear incredible to even modern Icelanders.

4. To compete in composing verses was a common entertainment and one that developed a feel for language and good memory.

5. Riddles and games of all sorts were popular in the households.

6. Occasionally, there were songs and musical instruments were played, but this was never a common practice. Up to the middle of the nineteenth century, music played an almost negligible role in Icelandic culture (as did painting). Sometimes a song or a hymn was sung before the prayers that ended the *kvöldvaka*.

7. House prayers usually concluded the *kvöldvaka*.

The disappearance of the traditional *kvöldvaka* began in the early part of this century with the disintegration of the traditional farm community, but the establishment of schools and, finally, the coming of radio in 1930 were important factors. Still, there is much in Icelandic radio and television that is reminiscent of the activities of the old *kvöldvaka*. Since radio first came to Iceland, there has been a program called "Kvöldvaka" (p. 139). The word is now commonly used as a term for a social evening, particularly one with intellectual or cultural content.

There were at least three major effects on Icelandic culture of the centuries-old institution of the *kvöldvaka*. First, the practice of reading and reciting, particularly of poetry, has been a central factor in maintaining the unique stability of the language (see chapter 6). Second, it enhanced the literary and historical sensibilities that have always characterized the Icelanders. And, third, it strengthened family relationships, particularly between generations, by providing a common fund of interests and knowledge (Magnús Gíslason, 1977, pp. 139-43).

An important point to stress in any account of the justly celebrated literacy of the Icelanders is that the ability to write was not nearly so cultivated as the ability to read until the latter part of the nineteenth century. In a history of the Borgarfjörður district in western Iceland, Kristleifur Thorsteinsson (quoted by Magnúss, 1939, p. 78) wrote:

> Around 1850 there were only two schools in the country, the College of Theology, then just founded, and the Latin School. The common people thought little then about education. . . . Most of the people studied little other than catechism exercises, and only the gifted learned all of the catechism. . . . To learn to write and do arithmetic was certainly thought to be good, but only for gifted boys. For girls and average boys such was thought unnecessary and only as a delay from work. "You shouldn't do that, dear boy," was often the refrain if youths wanted to acquire knowledge or were in the habit of reading books, but it was all the worse if girls took up such bad habits.

Up until around 1870, few children were able to write when they were confirmed, but most, particularly most of the boys, were later "pulled to the letters." These conditions lasted in Borgarfjörður, neither a particularly advanced nor backward area of the country, until the last 15 or 20 years of the nineteenth century. Even then, few women could write and it was considered satisfactory if they could read and knew the catechism and the Bible or Bible stories (Magnúss, 1939, p. 79). Writing in 1930, Lindroth (1937, p. 126) noted that it was "not uncommon" 40 years earlier to find old people who could write only their names.

THE MODERN SITUATION

A 1969 survey of business enterprises in Iceland (Statistical Bureau of Iceland, 1970) listed 89 bookstores in the country, 38 of which were in Reykajavík. This works out to be one bookstore for every 2,300 inhabitants. For comparative purposes, it is sometimes interesting to compare Iceland with the United States because the population of the latter was exactly 1,000 times that of Iceland in 1970. Thus, if a new work by Halldór Laxness sells 6 or 7 thousand copies in hardback in Iceland, this would be equivalent to 6 or 7 million copies in the United States! More remarkable is the sale of *Life's* science series; an average of 9,000 copies of each of the ten volumes of the Icelandic translation had been sold by mid-1971; this would be equivalent to 9 million copies of each title in the United States or a total of 90 million for the series. For a number of years, about 500,000 copies of books published in the Icelandic language have been sold each year. This number includes 400,000 copies of new books, comprising some 300 to 350 titles that are handled through the bookstores. In a typical year 1,000 to 1,500 copies of each new book are sold during the first twelve months after publication. To this is added the sale of 100,000 copies of older titles. These books are mostly hardbacks, although the proportion of paperbacks is increasing. Excluded from these figures are all directories, yearbooks, and textbooks. In addition, unknown but relatively large quantities of foreign books, mostly paperbacks— mainly in English, Danish, Norwegian, and German, in that order— are sold each year. Baldvin Tryggvason (1970) has claimed that young married couples are the best buyers of books, partly because at least one shelfful of handsomely bound books is a necessity in any Icelandic living room, just as it is in the other Scandinavian countries.

Novels, books of poetry, biographies, and genealogies are the most important categories of published works. Despite an uncertain market, a total of almost 800 volumes of poetry, or 20 to 30 volumes per year, were published during the three decades 1940-1970. However, it is unusual for a volume of modern poetry to sell more than 600 or 800 copies, and frequently sales are only 200 or 300 copies. These figures do not include books by the most important Icelandic poets or poets who became popular before 1940; their poetry and poetry collections sell steadily, sometimes in thousands each year. With few exceptions, the younger poets—who have given up rhyme and conventional meters—are not popular with book buyers. Of playwrights there are comparatively few in Iceland, and published plays have a limited market. Short stories, on the other hand, sell well. Icelanders are particularly fond of all sorts of books about their history, especially biographies and travel books (above all, old ones such as those by Uno von Troil and Ebenezer Henderson). In recent years, there has been a marked increase in the sale of books in the natural and social sciences.

Typically, 5 or 6 new children's books are published annually during the two months before Christmas in lots of 1,500 to 2,000 copies and sometimes up to 3,000 copies. Some 40 to 50 works of "light fiction," many in translation, come out each fall in lots of 1,300 to 3,000 copies. Several books on mysticism and psychic experience are published each year; they have a good and secure market, an interest in these phenomena being one of the peculiarities of the Icelanders. Religious books, on the other hand, are published and sold in relatively small numbers. Picture books of Iceland make up another category of books that sells well, probably mostly as presents.

Table 5-1 shows the subject matter of all books published in Iceland during the decade 1965-1974. Besides the publication of such a large number of books for such a small population, several additional observations can be made. First, less than a quarter of the 6,289 books (one-third are really pamphlets with fewer than 49 pages) were transla-

**Table 5-1. Books and Pamphlets Published in Iceland, by Subject, 1965-1974
(In Absolute Numbers)**

Subject of Publication	Total Number of Publications*	Number of Translations in Total
	6,289	1,510
General interest	87	3
Philosophy, psychology	121	46
Religion, theology	191	63
Sociology, statistics	60	7
Politics, government	556	23
Law, public administration, welfare, insurance	484	4
Military affairs	1	0
Education	504†	186†
Trade, communications, transportation	155	1
Ethnography, folklore	46	4
Language, dictionaries, linguistics	174	6
Mathematics	73	10
Natural science	172	26
Medical sciences, public health	131	25
Technology, industries, trades, and crafts	212	18
Agriculture, fishing	218	4
Domestic science	41	6
Business administration, commercial techniques	60	0
Visual art, music, movies, theater, radio, and television	124	7
Entertainment, games, sports	88	8
Literary history and criticism	59	3
Literature	1,977	946
Poetry	356	12
Plays	42	18
Novels	1,454	911
Essays	45	0
Letters	9	0
Miscellaneous	71	5
Geography, travel	180	32
History	575	88
Biography, memoirs, genealogy	338	47
History, other	237	41

Source: Calculated from data in Statistical Bureau of Iceland, 1976, pp. 222-24.

*Includes pamphlets 5-48 pages long and books longer than 48 pages. About a third of the total are pamphlets. This classification is made by the National Library of Iceland.

†These figures include children's books published between 1971-1973. In other years, children's fiction was included in the same category as novels.

tions from other languages. Most of the translations were from English, and a quarter were from the other Scandinavian languages. More than half of the volumes translated are novels, and this is the only category in which a majority of the books published are translations, 911 of 1,454; still, Icelanders published 543 novels during this decade. Second, note that substantial numbers of books are published in *all* categories, except military affairs in which only 1 book was published during the entire decade. Third, note that 356 volumes of poetry were published and that only 12 were translations from other languages. One belief about the literacy of the Icelanders that has substance, as I will show later, is that they have substantial knowledge of their poetry and poets. P. M. Mitchell (1965, p. 333) was not engaging in hyperbole when he wrote that insofar as poetry is concerned "Iceland puts to shame the rest of Scandinavia as well as the United States and every other country on earth." Fourth, note that a relatively large number of books are published in history but that a good majority of these, 338 of 575, fall into the subcategory of biography, memoirs, and genealogy.

The rate of book borrowing from libraries in Iceland was 9.2 volumes per capita in 1974 (table 5-2), compared with 9.0 in Sweden and around 14.0 in Denmark, which has the most developed system of libraries in the Nordic countries (Nordic Council, 1977, p. 295).[1] The high figure for Denmark—probably the highest in the world—is partly because the country is densely populated and a large majority of the population has ready access to the public libraries. In the Nordic countries, library use seems to be related to population concentration.

In 1970, the Icelandic Broadcasting Service commissioned *Sveriges Radio* (Swedish Radio) to do a sample survey of radio listening and television viewing in Iceland (Berg, 1971). The results were revealing, and they provide one key to the high level of general knowledge among the Icelanders. The amount of time devoted to poetry reading, lectures,

Table 5-2. Number of Books Borrowed from Libraries in Iceland, 1970 and 1975

Library	1970	1975
Reykjavík Public Library	775,332	1,140,344
Other town and district libraries	369,668	685,656
Rural libraries	156,000*	160,000*
Home, mobile libraries, et cetera	53,000*	25,000*
Total	1,354,000	2,011,000
Per capita	6.6	9.2

Source: Statistical Bureau of Iceland, *Hagtíðindi*, 1974, p. 134; 1977, p. 202.

*Estimates.

and other cultural programs on the Icelandic radio is high, in constrast to television, on which the cultural fare is lighter. In spite of the fact that 85 percent of Icelanders had direct access to television in 1970 (98 percent by 1976), 86 percent of the population between the ages of 14 and 79 listened to the radio on an average day during the week of 8-14 Novermber 1970. Still more striking is the observation that the average listening time per day was 3 hours and 10 minutes. The old Icelandic tradition of people listening to someone read while they worked has a modern counterpart in radio listening. Bus drivers frequently listen to the radio while they are driving, and so do people in fish factories and in stores. My impression is that radio listening on

Table 5-3. Programming Content of Icelandic Radio (1971-1974) and Television (1974)

Type of Programming	Percentage of Programming
*Radio**	
News	10.4
Weather reports and forecasts	4.1
Announcements and advertisements	7.2
Talks	5.6
Recitals	6.9
Conversations	3.8
Plays	1.6
Children's programs	3.5
Educational programs	0.4
Religious services	1.2
Other spoken matter	6.3
Classical music	16.8
Other music	32.2
Television†	
News	24.0
Advertisements	4.3
Sports	11.7
Educational programs	12.8
Classroom programs	2.9
Plays	7.8
Entertainment	7.3
Serials	9.6
Films	11.2
Children's programs	6.4
Religious programs	1.0
Music	1.0

Source: Statistical Bureau of Iceland, 1976, p. 226.

*Average programming day is 16.54 hours long.

†Average programming week is 24.60 hours long.

the job is more common in Iceland than in the United States, but what is clearly different is the more substantial cultural content of Icelandic radio. Table 5-3 gives the programming content of Icelandic radio and television (each media has one station that broadcasts to the entire country).

The sale of daily newspapers in Iceland was 555 copies per 1,000 population per day in 1977 (Nordic Council, 1979, p. 296), probably the highest in the world and almost double that of the United States (United Nations, 1973, pp. 933-38). There are six dailies in Iceland, all published in Reykjavík; five are affiliated with political parties. They are smaller in size and circulation than the major dailies in the other Scandinavian countries, their general quality is lower, and they are given to acrimonious and often petty criticism of their political opponents, which is why Icelandic intellectuals are so intensely critical of their press. M. Michel Sallé (1968, p. 91), a French observer of the economic and political life of Iceland, referred to the country's press as "in a perpetual Dreyfus affair." It should be noted, however, that the cultural articles in the newspapers are frequently of high quality. In addition to these six dailies, there is a paper published three times a week in Akureyri and there are a number of weeklies published in other parts of the country. I know of no study reporting on newspaper reading in the general population, but Broddason (1970, pp 82-83) found that 85 percent of a sample of 598 Icelandic children aged 10-14 claimed that they read a newspaper "daily or almost daily."

Many of the specialized journals published in the other Scandinavian countries have their counterparts in Iceland. In 1976, there were 257 different magazines, journals, and annuals published in the country, fewer than in previous years (Statistical Bureau of Iceland, Hagtíðindi, 1977, p. 201). Four highbrow periodicals deal with literary and cultural topics, two are quarterlies and two are annuals; the annual Skírnir, published since 1827, is the oldest periodical published in Scandinavia. Two monthly chess journals are published. The weekly Vikan, a relatively lowbrow magazine similar to its weekly counterparts in Scandinavia, has a circulation of about 14,000.

Table 5-4 lists the paid theater attendance in Iceland for the years 1974 through 1976. The average for the country is around 1.3-1.5 paid attendances per capita for the population over age 15; this seems to be very high. In Reykjavík, which has both the National Theater and the Reykjavík Theater, per capita attendance is much higher than elsewhere in the country. Particularly remarkable (Table 5-5) is the observation that nearly half (123 of 271) of the plays produced during this three-year period were Icelandic.

Movie attendance is extraordinarily high in Iceland. Per capita attendance in 1976 was 11.2, compared with 3.7 in Denmark, 1.9 in Finland, 4.2 in Norway, and 2.9 in Sweden (Nordic Council, 1978, p. 298).

Table 5-4. Paid Theater Attendance in Iceland, 1974-1976

Theater	1974	1975	1976
National Theater of Iceland	115,192	98,665	126,280
Reykjavík Theater*	48,000	44,242	48,741
Akureyri Theater	9,788	9,073	13,162
Other theater groups*	22,000†	45,000†	42,000†
Total attendance	194,980	196,980	230,183
Per capita attendance‡	1.3	1.3	1.5

Source: Adapted from data in Statistical Bureau of Iceland, Hagtíðindi, 1977, p. 204.

Note: About 25 percent of the total attendance is accounted for by students who are allowed a discount on the price of their tickets.

*Figures are for the seasons of 1973-1974, 1974-1975, and 1975-1976, and not for calendar years.

†Estimates.

‡Based on 1974, 1975, and 1976 population over the age of 15.

Table 5-5. Number of Plays Produced in Iceland, 1974-1976

Theater and plays produced	1974	1975	1976
National Theater of Iceland			
Number of Icelandic plays	13	9	7
Number of foreign plays	5	11	16
Reykjavík Theater*			
Number of Icelandic plays	9	3	3
Number of foreign plays	4	5	4
Akureyri Theater			
Number of Icelandic Plays	0	2	2
Number of foreign plays	5	3	4
Other theater groups*			
Number of Icelandic plays	18	29	28
Number of foreign plays	21	33	37

Source: Adapted from data in Statistical Bureau of Iceland, Hagtíðindi, 1977, p. 204.

*Numbers are for seasons 1973-1974, 1974-1975, and 1975-1976, and not for calendar years.

The Statistical Bureau of Iceland collects and publishes data on concert attendance and the numbers of museum visitors, as well as on theater attendance. Table 5-6 lists data for 1971 and 1976 for attendance at concerts of the Iceland Symphony Orchestra and the Philharmonic Society, together with the numbers of visitors to the National Archives, the National Gallery of Iceland, the National Museum, the Reykjavík Local History Museum—all of which are located in the capital city—and the district museums located outside of Reykjavík. Included in these figures are all the institutions of their kind in the country, except for a few small museums devoted to the works of individuals in Reykjavík and a still smaller number in places outside of Reykjavík. The data on museum attendance are of limited value because some unknown but large proportion of the visitors were tourists. There was particularly low attendance at concerts in 1976; 1971 is more typical.

Table 5-6. Attendance at Concerts and Visits to Museums in Iceland, 1971 and 1976

	1971	1976
Iceland Symphony Orchestra	23,450	13,766
Philharmonic Society	8,930	6,000*
National Archives	4,166	3,942
National Gallery of Iceland	27,842	31,051
National Museum	47,835	33,929
Reykjavík Local History Museum	15,352	10,634
District museums	22,000*	40,000*
Total visits	149,575	139,322
Per capita attendance†	1.1	0.9

Sources: Statistical Bureau of Iceland, Hagtíðindi, 1974, pp. 135-36; 1977, pp. 203-6.

*Estimates.

†Of population age 15 and over.

AN EMPIRICAL STUDY

During April through July of 1971, I interviewed a representative sample of Icelandic adults born during the first half of this century on a wide range of topics. (See Appendixes A and B.) One of my central concerns was their cultural life: the books they read and owned and their familiarity with literature. About 90 of the interviews were conducted in Icelandic; English was used when a respondent was fluent in the language. Of the sample, which was roughly representative of the total adult population aged 21-70 in 1971, half were men and half were women; only 15 of the 100 had an academic secondary education (*menntaskóli*), and 29 had no formal schooling at all. The names and addresses of potential respondents were taken randomly from the National Register. Of the 100 respondents who agreed to be interviewed, 50 were from Reykjavík; 17, from Hvolsvöllur, a small farm village in the south; 17, from Stafholtstungnahreppur, a typical farm parish in Borgarfjörður; and 16, from Ísafjörður, a fishing town on the northwestern peninsula. These three smaller communities were chosen in order to represent the residential and occupational characteristics of the half of the Icelandic population that lives outside of the Reykjavík metropolitan area. All of those selected to be in the sample received a letter of explanation before I telephoned or visited their homes. Only 3 males and 6 females with whom I made contact refused to be interviewed, and a few others could never be found at home or were incapacitated for some reason; two foreign-born individuals were eliminated from the list.[2]

Although this sample of Icelanders born during the years 1903-1950 is small, it has, to my knowledge, no major sources of bias; it might even have a certain statistical validity (Siegel, 1956, pp. 8-11). Still, the small sample size discourages detailed internal comparisons of differences by sex, age, place of residence, education, and so forth. In the concluding section of this chapter however, I give the results of simple breakdowns based on the number of correct responses to the questions about literary knowledge (numbers 29 through 35, appendix A). The respondents were cooperative beyond any reasonable expectations. Since there was no tradition of interviewing for either social science or commercial purposes in Iceland in 1971, being interviewed was a new experience for almost everyone. Most of the respondents treated me as a guest. Of the 100 respondents, 62 offered me food or drink—from dinner to coffe and cake; 4 of them offered me strong drink. In many cases, a spouse was present during the interview; in a few cases, a whole family. I was careful, however, to prevent anyone from helping the respondents answer the knowledge questions; I was less particular with the other questions.

Among the most basic questions I asked was whether the respondent had read any books in the past month, other than texts and work-related books (question 16). Almost half (48 of the 100 respondents) answered that they had not, but, when I asked whether they had read any books in the past year, all but 4 answered yes. The following is a list of the numbers of books that the 100 respondents had read in the month preceding their interviews (the interviews took place in April, May, June, and July of 1971):

No books 48
One book 20
Two books 19
Three or more books 13

The numbers of books the respondents had read during the year before their interviews were these:

No books 4
One book 4
Two books 3
Three books 8
Four books 10
Five to nine books 27
Ten to nineteen books 25
More than twenty books 19

The great difference in the number of books read during the preceding month and during the preceding year—so my respondents informed me—was a consequence of the fact that the interviews were taking place during the lightest months of the year, when most people were less likely to read than during the winter months, when there are only five or six hours of daylight per day. Surprisingly, 89 of the 100 respondents in my sample claimed to have read three or more books during the previous year. This is an extraordinarily high figure compared with the amount of book reading reported in other countries. Sample surveys of book reading in France (Rudorff, 1970, p. 173), West Germany (Dahrendorf, 1967, p. 345), and the United States (Gallup, 1964, p. 42) all indicated that less than half the adult populations had any contact with books at all at the times the surveys were conducted.

Even though the respondents may have somewhat overstated their case, I have no reason to believe their replies were not generally realistic. After the questions on book reading, I asked them to name the titles of the last *two* books they had read (question 17). (See table 5-7.) Of 200 titles that could have been named, I obtained 171 titles and 29 "I don't remember" responses. (I always allowed people to go and get the book or to ask members of the family whether they could remember the title or the author.) Most significant about these responses is the consistent preference for Icelandic over foreign fiction and poetry and for Icelandic over foreign nonfiction. It is indeed remarkable that this tiny nation can sustain so much native writing, considering that most of the world's greatest literature, and much of that not so great, has been translated into Icelandic.

Table 5-7. Kinds of Books Read by 100 Representative Icelanders, 1971

Kinds of Books	Frequency Mentioned	Percentage
Icelandic fiction and poetry	72	36.0
Icelandic nonfiction	33	16.5
Foreign fiction and poetry	48	24.0
Foreign nonfiction	18	9.0
No response*	29	14.5
	200	100.0

*Responses of "I don't remember" are included in this category.

Each of my respondents were asked to estimate the number of books in his or her house or apartment (question 19). (See table 5-8.) In many cases, however, I counted or estimated the number of books myself and found that the respondents had a tendency toward underestimation. They often failed to include paperback mysteries in English (such as those by Alistair McLean and Agatha Christie) or the lowbrow Danish novels that many Icelanders read. These were, some people thought, unworthy of the designation *book*. The median number of books in the 100 dwellings of my respondents was about 200, the modal number was in the 200-300 range, and the mean number was about 338. I regard these estimates as having a high degree of validity, although they may be a bit low because of books—frequently in bed-

Table 5-8. Number of Books in 100 Representative
Icelandic Homes, 1971

Number of Books	Frequency
None	1
Few than 50	13
About 50	2
50-100	11
About 100	5
100-200	8
About 200	13
200-300	13
About 300	2
300-400	6
About 400	4
400-500	2
About 500	3
500-1,000	9
More than 1,000	8

Note: The median number of books was about 200.

The modal number of books was 200-300.

And the mean number of books was about 338.

rooms—that were missed by the respondents or myself. Generally, individuals who lived alone and young couples had fewer books than others. The only respondent in the sample who had no books was the driver of a school bus who lived in a rented room.

I asked my respondents whether they themselves had ever had anything published (question10); 27 of the 100 answered in the affirmative, 15 of the males and 12 of the females. The only comparable data I have come by is for Denmark; P. M. Mitchell (1965) cited data showing that 8 percent of Danes have published something, 5 percent among the males and 10 percent among the females; for the upper, or professional, classes the figure was 28 percent.

In relation to the size of the population, the number of published Icelandic authors, both living and dead, is probably unparalleled in the world. To tap the knowledge the Icelanders have of their native writers, I asked my respondents to name, if they could, five living Icelandic writers (of novels, poems, plays, essays, and/or short stories) and then five dead ones (questions 30 and 31). Similar questions were asked regarding five living foreign writers and five deceased ones (questions 32 and 33). The Icelanders' knowledge of their native writers vastly exceeded their knowledge of foreign ones. Indeed, 89 of the respondents could name at least five living Icelandic authors, and 87 could name at least five that were dead. Most were able to list a greater number. All told, at least 64 living and 55 deceased writers were named by the 100 respondents; on the other hand, 46 could not name a single living foreign writer and 31 could not name a single dead one. Some were embarrassed by their ignorance.[3] The 100 respondents' scores on question 30 (naming five living Icelandic writers and poets) were these:

Five names	89
Four names	4
Three names	2
Two names	3
One name	0
No names	2

Their scores on question 31 (naming five dead Icelandic writers and poets) were these:

Five names	87
Four names	3
Three names	3
Two names	3
One name	0
No names	4

Their scores on question 32 (naming five living foreign writers and poets) were these:

Five names 18
Four names 9
Three names 10
Two names 9
One name 8
No names 46

Their scores on question 33 (naming five dead foreign writers and poets) were these:

Five names 36
Four names 11
Three names 5
Two names 6
One name 11
No names 31

Table 5-9 lists in descending order the living Icelandic writers who were named in the sample; 473 responses out of a possible 500 were elicited. Nobel laureate Halldór Laxness was named by 91 of the respondents. Most of his many novels deal with Icelandic farm life. Gunnar Gunnarsson, also internationally known, was named by 56 respondents in the sample; he too has taken Icelandic history and farm culture as the subject of his novels. Sigurður A. Magnússon (1970, p. 135) observed that "more than 90 percent of all Icelandic novels up to about 1960 dealt with rural themes." Indeed, most of the novelists and poets on this list have written on Icelandic themes. This is less true of the younger writers, those who have made their literary debut since the late 1950s; they are less parochial in their subject matter and more international in their orientation. Most of the younger poets have broken away from the traditional and stringent rules of poetic form and do not write in rhyme, and all of them have less popular appeal than their predecessors. Note that only seven of the 34 living literary figures listed in Table 5-9 were under age 40 at the time of the interviewing in 1971.

When the Icelanders were asked to name five deceased Icelandic writers (see table 5-10), they did about as well as with the living. Most notable, however, is their overwhelming tendency to choose poets rather than other kinds of writers. The eight most frequently mentioned names were all poets, and all but two of them lived during this century. The exceptions were Jónas Hallgrímsson (1807-1845), a leading romantic poet of the 1830s and 1840s, and Hallgrímur Pétursson

(1614-1674), the most recited and influential poet and hymn writer in Icelandic history. The only poet and writer from Iceland's golden age to be mentioned two or more times was Snorri Sturluson (1179-1241).

The living and deceased foreign authors named by the Icelanders are a potpourri of diverse types from diverse countries. (See tables 5-11 and 5-12.) First and second among the leading living foreign

Table 5-9. Living Icelandic Writers and Poets Named by 100
Representative Icelanders, 1971

Rank	Name or Pen Name	Born	Principal Medium	Frequency
1.0	Halldór Laxness	1902	Novel	91
2.0	Gunnar Gunnarsson	1889	Novel	56
3.0	Tómas Guðmundsson	1901	Poetry	45
4.0	Guðmundur G. Hagalín	1898	Novel	29
5.0	Kristmann Guðmundsson	1901	Novel	24
6.0	Jóhannes úr Kötlum	1899	Poetry	21
7.0	Guðrún frá Lundi	1887	Novel	20
8.0	Hannes Pétursson	1931	Poetry	17
9.0	Svava Jakobsdóttir	1930	Short story	16
10.0	Thórbergur Thórðarson	1889	Novel, essay	14
11.0	Matthías Johannessen	1930	Poetry	11
12.0	Guðmundur Böðvarsson	1904	Poetry	10
13.0	Jökull Jakobsson	1933	Novel, play	9
14.0	Guðmundur Daníelsson	1910	Novel	8
15.0	Guðbergur Bergsson	1932	Novel	7
16.5	Jón úr Vör	1917	Poetry	6
16.5	Thor Vilhjálmsson	1925	Novel	6
18.5	Jakobína Sigurðardóttir	1918	Novel, short story	5
18.5	Thorsteinn frá Hamri	1938	Poetry	5
20.0	Indriði G. Thorsteinsson	1926	Short story, novel	4
21.5	Jón Helgason	1899	Poetry	3
21.5	Thorsteinn Valdimarsson	1918	Poetry	3
	Ármann Kr. Einarsson	1915	Children's story	2
	Dagur Sigurðsson	1937	Poetry	2
	Gunnar Dal	1924	Poetry	2
	Hannes Sigfússon	1922	Poetry	2
	Ingibjörg Jónsdóttir	1933	Novel, children's story	2
	Ingibjörg Sigurðardóttir	1925	Novel	2
	Jóhann Hjálmarsson	1939	Poetry	2
	Jóhannes Helgi	1926	Novel, biography	2
	Kristján frá Djúpalæk	1916	Poetry	2
	Nína Björk Árnadóttir	1941	Poetry	2
	Rósberg G. Snædal	1913	Poetry	2
	Sigurður Nordal	1886	Scholarship, poetry, essay	2

Note: At least thirty other names were mentioned one time each; several names could not be identified.

Table 5-10. Deceased Icelandic Writers and Poets Named by 100
Representative Icelanders, 1971

Rank	Name or Pen Name	Life Span	Principal Medium	Frequency
1.0	Davíð Stefánsson	1895-1964	Poetry	56
2.0	Jónas Hallgrímsson	1807-1845	Poetry	54
3.0	Matthías Jochumsson	1835-1920	Poetry	45
4.0	Einar Benediktsson	1864-1940	Poetry	36
5.0	Steinn Steinarr	1908-1958	Poetry	28
6.0	Thorsteinn Erlingsson	1858-1914	Poetry	27
7.0	Hallgrímur Pétursson	1614-1674	Poetry	26
8.0	Hannes Hafstein	1861-1922	Poetry	16
9.0	Jón Trausti	1873-1918	Novel	15
10.0	Grímur Thomsen	1820-1896	Poetry	13
11.5	Guðmundur Kamban	1888-1945	Novel	12
11.5	Jón Thoroddsen	1818-1868	Novel	12
13.0	Bólu-Hjálmar	1796-1875	Poetry	11
14.0	Steingrímur Thorsteinsson	1831-1913	Poetry	10
15.0	Stephan G. Stephansson	1853-1927	Poetry	9
16.0	Jón Svensson (Nonni)	1857-1944	Novel	8
18.5	Einar H. Kvaran	1859-1938	Novel	7
18.5	Snorri Sturluson	1179-1241	Poetry, saga, history	7
18.5	Stefán frá Hvítadal	1887-1933	Poetry	7
20.5	Bjarni Thorarensen	1786-1841	Poetry	6
20.5	Guðmundur Guðmundsson	1874-1919	Poetry	6
22.5	Jóhann Sigurjónsson	1880-1919	Play	4
22.5	Thorgils Gjallandi	1851-1915	Short story	4
24.5	Benedikt Gröndal	1826-1907	Poetry	3
24.5	Kristján Jónsson	1842-1869	Poetry	3
	Eggert Ólafsson	1726-1768	Poetry	2
	Guðmundur Friðjónsson	1869-1944	Poetry, short story	2
	Jón Arason	1484-1550	Poetry	2
	Jónas Jónsson frá Hriflu	1885-1968	Journalism, poetry	2
	Jón Thorláksson	1744-1819	Poetry, translation	2
	Örn Arnarson	1884-1942	Poetry	2

Note: Twenty-four other names were mentioned one time each.

writers are Alistair McLean and Agatha Christie, both English mystery writers. William Heineson (the leading Faroese novelist) and Arthur Miller (the American playwright) are tied for third place. Next on the list are Françoise Sagan (the French novelist) and Aleksandr I. Solzhenitsyn, tied for fifth place. These are followed by three more novelists: Klaus Rifbjerg (Danish), Jean-Paul Sartre (French), and Pearl Buck (American). The deceased writers make a more consistently distinguished collection. The leading eight in rank order are Ernest Hemingway (American), Hans Christian Andersen (Danish), William Shakespeare (English), Henrik Ibsen (Norwegian), John Steinbeck (American), Björnstjerne Björnson (Norwegian), Selma Lagerlöf (Swedish), and Leo Tolstoy (Russian). Two observations about these lists can be made; first, in spite of the extraordinary concern with poetry on the part of Icelanders, only two of the then living foreign writers listed were primarily poets (W. H. Auden and Ezra Pound), and none of the deceased, were primarily poets; second, some of the living writers are known for activities other than their writing. W. H. Auden and Peter Ustinov had earlier come to Iceland and received much publicity as visiting celebrities; Arthur Miller's play *Death of a Salesman* was performed in the National Theater and received much publicity; Frank Slaughter's books have been widely advertised. Aside from a relatively small number of translated bestsellers, Icelanders read relatively little modern foreign literature.

An easier exercise than recalling literary names without any cues is recognizing names. The 100 respondents were asked to identify by country 15 world-famous playwrights and novelists whose works had been translated into Icelandic (questions 34 and 35). Table 5-13 lists the results of these questions. Henrik Ibsen was correctly identified as a

Table 5-11. Living Foreign Writers and Poets Named by 100 Representative Icelanders, 1971

Rank	Name	Nationality	Frequency
1.0	Alistair McLean	English	17
2.0	Agatha Christie	English	16
3.5	William Heineson	Faroese	11
3.5	Arthur Miller	American	11
5.5	Françiose Sagan	French	10
5.5	Aleksandr I. Solzhenitsyn	Russian	10
7.0	Klaus Rifbjerg	Danish	9
8.0	Jean-Paul Sartre	French	7
9.0	Pearl Buck	American	6
11.0	W. H. Auden	English/American	5
11.0	Desmond Bagley	English	5
11.0	Frank Slaughter	American	5
14.5	E. B. H. Cavling	Danish	4
14.5	Tove Ditlevsen	Danish	4
14.5	Torkild Hansen	Danish	4
14.5	Ezra Pound	American	4
19.5	Enid Blyton	English	3
19.5	Theresa Charles	English	3
19.5	A. J. Cronin	Scot	3
19.5	Per Olof Sundman	Swedish	3
19.5	Valeriy Tarsis	Russian	3
19.5	Peter Ustinov	American	3
	Per Hansen	Danish	2
	Hammond Innes	English	2
	Agnar Mykle	Norwegian	2
	Tennessee Williams	American	2

Note: Thirty-five other names were mentioned one time each.

Table 5-12. Deceased Foreign Writers and Poets Named
by 100 Representative Icelanders, 1971

Rank	Name	Nationality	Frequency
1.0	Ernest Hemingway	American	21
2.0	Hans Christian Andersen	Danish	20
3.0	William Shakespeare	English	19
4.0	Henrik Ibsen	Norwegian	18
5.0	John Steinbeck	American	15
6.0	Björnstjerne Björnson	Norwegian	14
7.0	Selma Lagerlöf	Swedish	13
8.0	Leo Tolstoy	Russian	8
11.5	Johann Wolfgang von Goethe	German	6
11.5	Knut Hamsun	Norwegian	6
11.5	W. Somerset Maugham	English	6
11.5	Kaj Munk	Danish	6
11.5	Boris Pasternak	Russian	6
14.5	Edgar Allan Poe	American	5
14.5	Mark Twain	American	5
16.5	T. S. Eliot	English	4
16.5	John Galsworthy	English	4
20.5	Olav Duun	Norwegian	3
20.5	Ian Fleming	English	3
20.5	Jack London	American	3
20.5	Friedrich Schiller	German	3
20.5	Sigrid Undset	Norwegian	3
20.5	Stefan Zweig	Austrian	3
	Isak Dinesen (Karen Blixen)	Danish	2
	Bertolt Brecht	German	2
	Robert Browning	English	2
	Peter Freuchen	Danish	2
	Maxim Gorky	Russian	2
	Johannes V. Jensen	Danish	2
	Nikos Kazantzakis	Greek	2
	John Keats	English	2
	Martin Anderson Nexø	Danish	2
	George Bernard Shaw	English	2
	August Strindberg	Swedish	2
	Françoise-Marie Voltaire	French	2

Note: Forty-three other names were mentioned one time each.

Norwegian by 72 of the respondents; the same number correctly identified Shakespeare's nationality. At the other extreme, only 21 identified Balzac as French. Not infrequently, respondents familiar with a
playwright or an author incorrectly identified his nationality. A few
identified Ibsen as Swedish, Eugene O'Neill was sometimes identified
as Irish, and Jack London was frequently thought to be English.

About themselves Icelanders have the belief—also held by many
foreign observers—that virtually all of them have read the major sagas

and are in close contact with the old literature. While it is true that many (most?) Icelanders have sets of the sagas in their living rooms (a practice corresponding to having encyclopedias in the other Scandinavian countries), my observation is that the great majority of present-day Icelanders, including the active readers among them, have only a distant schoolbook knowledge of the sagas. Of the 171 responses to my question about the last two books read (question 17), only one title was that of a saga, just as there was only one mention of the Bible. To test the respondents' basic knowledge of the sagas, I asked them to name the sagas in which five famous characters are most prominent (question 29.). The first was Njal, the major character in *Njal's Saga*, the longest saga and the one universally regarded as the greatest of the sagas of the Icelanders. Analogous questions for Americans, one might suppose, would be asking in which novels Huckleberry Finn and Moby Dick are most prominent. But this would really not be comparable because in America familiarity with the national literature is of a different order than it is in Iceland. A better comparison would be to ask who the first president of the United States was, where failure to give the correct answer might raise serious doubts about the intelligence or the mental state of the individual. Still, 9 of the 100 respondents could not identify Njal with *Njal's Saga*. Fourteen could not identify Grettir of *Grettir's Saga*, the best-known outlaw in Icelandic

Table 5-13. Deceased Foreign Playwrights and Authors Correctly Identified by 100 Representative Icelanders, 1971

	Nationality	Number of Times Correctly Identified
Playwrights		
Henrik Ibsen	Norwegian	72
William Shakespeare	English	72
George Bernard Shaw	Irish or English	65
August Strindberg	Swedish	58
Eugene O'Neill	American	43
Ludvig Holberg	Norwegian/Danish	35
Authors		
Boris Pasternak	Russian	69
Leo Tolstoy	Russian	64
Charles Dickens	English	63
Ernest Hemingway	American	61
Johann Wolfgang von Goethe	German	57
William Faulkner	American	50
Jack London	American	38
Jane Austin	English	27
Honoré de Balzac	French	21

literature, and 25 could not identify Gunnar of Hlíðarendi, the most magnificent hero in all of the sagas, with *Njal's Saga*. Even more astounding was the finding that 53 of the respondents did not identify Guðrún with *Laxdaela Saga*, which deals with the four loves of Guðrún and which is one of the three or four most famous of the sagas. Guðrún's only female rival for a leading place in the popular repertoire of saga characters is the passionately evil Hallgerd in *Njal's Saga*. Admittedly, some of the respondents knew vaguely about Guðrún, but they could not identify the saga in which she is a central character. The least known of these five saga characters, but by no means an obscure character, is Helga the Fair, the central female character in the short romantic saga *Gunnlaug Serpent-Tongue*. Eighty-two of the respondents were unable to identify Helga with this saga.

Table 5-14. Saga Characters Correctly Identified
by 100 Representative Icelanders, 1971

Character	Saga	Frequency
Njal	Major figure in *Njal's Saga* (the greatest of the family sagas)	91
Grettir	Main character in *Grettir's Saga*	86
Gunnar of Hlíðarendi	Major heroic figure in *Njal's Saga*	75
Guðrún	Main female character in *Laxdaela Saga*	36
Helga the Fair	Main female character in the short romantic saga *Gunnlaug Serpent-Tongue*	18

Several Icelandic writers reacted to these results with surprise, their view being that, with the possible exception of Helga the Fair, *all* Icelanders "should" be able to identify these famous characters. Today, Icelanders are apparently further removed from and more ignorant about their classical literature than was the case with earlier generations. There is no basis in fact, if there ever was, for the many assertions like that of Sigurður A. Magnússon (1977, p. 83): "A large number of these [saga] characters have through the centuries been familiar figures in the homes of Icelanders of all classes, and they have been more real to the people in every epoch than the contemporary leaders of the nation." Magnússon's claim, however, is modest compared to that of older Icelanders, for example Jón Stefansson's (1902, p. 13) statement to an English audience: the "Icelander of today knows them [the sagas] by heart. It is as if every Englishman from pauper to king, knew Shakespeare's historical plays and could retell them more or less in his or her own words."

To illustrate how little knowledge there is about saga reading in Iceland even among those who should be most informed, let me quote two opinions from a round-table discussion on culture in Iceland ("Perspectives," 1973). One extreme is represented by Baldvin Tryggvason, the director of the largest publishing firm in Iceland who was quoted at the beginning of this chapter, who said "The Sagas are being read today, both by young and old. This is indicated both by their sales and their usage in the public libraries. . . . I think they satisfy a real need." Of a strikingly different opinion is Haraldur Ólafsson, a lecturer in sociology at the University of Iceland, who said:

> In my work at the University I have quite another experience. I had a group of 50 students in sociology and tried to use examples from Icelandic history, the Sagas, the *Book of Settlements*, etc., when discussing certain cultural phenomena, but it was of no use. These young people simply didn't know this literature, not even what we were supposed to have learned in the abbreviated textbooks in Icelandic history in school.

Two of my questions asked the respondents to name their two most admired living Icelanders and the two most admired deceased Icelanders (questions 4 and 5). My purpose was to discover how frequently literary and cultural figures would be mentioned. It is important to stress that these two questions were asked *before* any of the literary questions, so these answers were not influenced by the talk of literary figures. Because many of the respondents refused to single out certain individuals as most admirable, I obtained a total of only 113 responses out of 200 potential responses to the inquiry about living Icelanders most admired. The respondents were less reluctant to answer the question about the two deceased Icelanders most admired; on that question 161 responses were given out of a possible 200. Of the many and varied questions asked in the interviews, these two were the only two that the respondents were reluctant to answer. My explanation of this reticence is the strong egalitarianism of the Icelanders; many expressed clear disdain and discomfort when asked to single out certain individuals as more admirable than others!

The importance of literary and cultural personages among the most admired Icelanders is, I propose, high in comparison to what one would find elsewhere. Of the 113 living Icelanders mentioned at least twice, Nobel laureate novelist Halldór Laxness was most frequently mentioned, followed by Kristján Eldjárn, the president of Iceland and an internationally known archaeologist. Tied for third place were Jóhannes S. Kjarval, a dramatic painter of Icelandic seascapes and landscapes, and Sigurbjörn Einarsson, bishop of Iceland and well known for his strong cultural nationalism. All told, six of the 13 names listed in table 5-15 are wholly literary or artistic figures.

Table 5-15. Living Icelanders Most Admired by
100 Representative Icelanders, 1971

Rank	Name	Born	Career	Frequency
1.0	Halldór Laxness	1902	Novelist	34
2.0	Kristján Eldjárn	1916	President of Iceland, archaeologist	28
3.5	Jóhannes S. Kjarval	1885	Painter	10
3.5	Sigurbjörn Einarsson	1911	Bishop of Iceland	10
5.0	Hannibal Valdimarsson	1903	Union leader, member of parliment	6
6.5	Geir Hallgrímsson	1925	Mayor of Reykjavík	5
6.5	Gunnar Gunnarsson	1889	Novelist	5
8.0	Jóhann Hafstein	1915	Prime minister, 1970-1971	4
9.0	Ásmundur Sveinsson	1893	Sculptor	3
	Ásgeir Ásgeirsson	1894	Second president of Iceland	2
	Gunnar Thoroddsen	1910	Leading Independence Party politician	2
	Ríkarður Jónsson	1888	Sculptor	2
	Sigurður Nordal	1886	Literary scholar	2

Note: Only 113 out of a possible 200 responses were obtained in the interviews. Some respondents gave only one name (rather than the two requested), some said something like "but there are so many," and some refused to answer at all. Note also that ten other individuals were mentioned one time each.

Among the most admired deceased Icelanders, literary and artistic figures loomed larger than among the living. Of the 17 persons listed in table 5-16, 8 are wholly literary and artistic figures and three more have a substantial literary reputation in addition to another source of recognition. In other words, only 5 of the 17 most admired deceased Icelanders are without literary or artistic reputation. It is also of interest that only two medieval Icelanders were mentioned two or more times, Snorri Sturluson (1179-1241) and Leifur Eiríksson (970-1020), discoverer of America, and that saga characters were so infrequently mentioned. Gunnar of Hlíðarendi, that most splendid of saga heroes was mentioned only once, and Egill Skalla-Grímsson, the greatest and most complex of medieval Icelandic poets, was mentioned not at all, which is further confirmation that modern Icelanders are not as deeply involved with their ancient literature as earlier generations are alleged to have been.

CONCLUSION

This chapter presents data on a topic about which there is much discussion but little empirical data: the literacy of the Icelanders. The

Table 5-16. Deceased Icelanders Most Admired by
100 Representative Icelanders, 1971

Rank	Name	Life Span	Career	Frequency
1	Jón Sigurðsson	1811-1879	Statesman, scholar	51
2	Bjarni Benediktsson	1908-1970	Prime minister, 1963-1970	26
3	Ólafur Thors	1892-1964	Prime minister five times, 1942-1963	15
4	Hallgrímur Pétursson	1614-1674	Hymn writer	8
6	Davíð Stefánsson	1895-1964	Poet	6
6	Jónas Hallgrímsson	1807-1845	Poet	6
6	Sveinn Björnsson	1884-1958	First president of Iceland	6
9	Jónas Jónsson frá Hriflu	1885-1963	Founder of Farmers' Party, journalist	5
9	Matthías Jochumsson	1835-1920	Poet	5
9	Snorri Sturluson	1179-1241	Poet, historian, saga writer	5
11	Skúli Magnússon	1711-1794	Public official, reformer	4
12	Hannes Hafstein	1861-1922	Poet and statesman	3
	Einar Benediktsson	1864-1940	Poet	2
	Einar Jónsson	1874-1954	Sculptor	2
	Friðrik Friðriksson	1868-1960	Founder of Icelandic YMCA	2
	Leifur Eiríksson	970-1020	Discoverer of America	2
	Steinn Steinarr	1908-1958	Poet	2

Note: Only 161 of a possible 200 responses were obtained in the interviews. Some respondents gave only one name; some gave answers like "but there are so many," and others refused to answer. Note also that eleven other individuals were mentioned one time each.

contention that virtually all Icelandic homes at whatever class level contain books is substantiated. So is the belief that the overwhelming majority of Icelanders read books, at least occasionally. Such statements probably cannot be made of any other society. The bookishness of the Icelanders can be partially explained by the unique tradition of popular literacy that developed in the rural culture. The Icelanders also have an extraordinary knowledge of their native writers, both living and dead; yet, discussion of these authors permeates the mass media and does not necessarily imply any reading knowledge of their works on the part of the general population or the 100 respondents in my survey. Literary and cultural figures loom large among those Icelanders most admired by the respondents. The Icelanders' knowledge of foreign writers, on the other hand, appears scanty when compared to their knowledge of native writers. My guess is that the other Scandinavians have less knowledge of their native writers, but probably know more about foreign writers because of the much larger number of works translated into their languages. There is little in the data I collected to support those who contend that many Icelanders continue to read the sagas or are involved with their classical literature. There is, I am afraid, little reading of those bound volumes of the sagas that adorn so many Icelandic living rooms. My data on what Icelanders read also supports the finding of a subsequent study (see Haraldsson, 1978, p. 147) that the overwhelming majority of Icelanders (92 percent) seldom or never read the Bible.

No attempt has been made so far to investigate differences within the sample based on sex, age, place of residence, and education because of the relatively small size of the sample. However, I have made some simple divisions of average literary scores of the sample by these variables, and the results are reasonable and should enhance confidence in the reliability of the general findings.

1. Men are more knowledgeable about literature than women. Of the forty knowledge questions on this topic, the men had an average score of 25.9 correct answers (65 percent), while the women received an average score of 23.4 (59 percent). This sex difference is maintained in the Reykjavík and the non-Reykjavík halves of the sample taken separately.

2. There is no difference in literary scores between people living in Reykjavík and those living outside of Iceland's only metroplitian area; the respondents living in the urban area had an average score of 24.3 (61 percent); those from rural areas, 24.9 (62 percent). However, there is a difference in knowledge of saga characters between those living in Reykjavík and those living elsewhere in the country; those from Reykjavík identified an average of 2.8 (56 percent) of the five saga characters; the others, 3.2 (64 percent).

3. Formal education is positively related to literary knowledge as it might be expected to be, but the difference between the 15 respondents with an academic secondary education and the 85 without such education (and 29 of these had no formal schooling at all) is not great; those with secondary education had an average literary score of 31.5 correct answers (79 percent); and those without, 23.4 (59 percent). The mean number of books in the households of the 15 respondents with an academic education was 444, compared with 320 among the 85 respondents without such education. This is certainly not a large difference.

4. The younger half of the sample, those born after January 1937, had a greater overall literary knowledge than the older half of the sample, the respective scores being 25.6 (64 percent) and 23.6 (59

percent). Not surprisingly, and in accord with what Haraldur Ólafsson and others might suspect, the better educated younger half of the sample knew less about the sagas than the less formally educated older half of the sample. The average numbers of saga characters correctly identified by the two groups were 2.9 (58 percent) and 3.2 (64 percent) out of a possible five.

CHAPTER 6

The Language

Icelandic is the "classical" language of Scandinavia [and has] preserved for posterity a wealth of traditional prose and poetry from the past of all Germanic peoples. . . . Grammatical and lexical conservatism is a source of pride to Icelanders. . . . Among the factors that account for the conservatism through the centuries of obscurity may be mentioned the inner coherence and contact within the Icelandic community, the isolation from outside influence, and the force of the living literary tradition.

Einar Haugen (1976)

Whatever we may think of the poetical value of the rímur *and other verse in the old tradition, there is no question of the important consequences of the general devotion to this kind of poetry—the most obvious of these, perhaps, being the preservation of the classical language of the thirteenth century as the living Icelandic of today.*

Sigurður Nordal (1954b)

Icelandic is related to the other modern Scandinavian languages as Latin is related to the modern Romance languages (Wessén, 1965, p. 30). The major difference is that Icelandic has remained a living language. It is as though there were some isolated island in the Mediterranean where Latin was still the native tongue. Icelandic is unique among Indo-European languages in that its written form took shape during the twelfth and thirteenth centuries and has changed *relatively* little since that time.

But what do I mean when I say that the language has changed *relatively* little? How much the language has been transformed in the more than eight centuries it has had a written form using the Latin alphabet depends on what frame of reference is used. Linguists who have studied the history of the language generally focus on the *changes* in it (for example, Hreinn Benediktsson, 1959, 1961-62, 1962a, 1962b, 1964a, 1964b; Jakob Benediktsson, 1964; Böðvarsson, 1964; Chapman, 1962; Helgi Guðmundsson, 1972, Halldórsson, 1964, Haugen, 1975, 1976; Haugen and Markey, 1972, pp. 171-79). Phonemic shift, particularly in the vowels, in Icelandic has been radical and greater than in the dialects of the Norwegian west coast. Syntactical and grammatical changes, mostly minor, also have been numerous; the Icelandic linguist Hreinn Benediktsson (1962a, columns 486-93) took several paragraphs just to list them. Orthographic changes, however, have been relatively few, and the inflectional system has shown a stability remarkable by any standard. Although the degree of change in Icelandic is greater than many scholars who are not linguists seem to realize, "it is clear that, compared with its related neighbors in the same period, Icelandic has undergone only small and insignificant changes" (Hreinn Benediktsson, 1961-1962, p. 102).

THE DEVELOPMENT OF MODERN ICELANDIC

Many Icelanders, including some of the older students of the language, disdain or ignore the now conventional distinction between Old Icelandic (Old Norse) and Modern Icelandic. Alexander Jóhannesson (1953, p. 6), professor of Icelandic at the University of Iceland 1930-1958, for example, has written that "Icelanders . . . speak only of one Icelandic language through the whole thousand-year period and therefore do not need to distinguish an Old Icelandic, a Middle Icelandic, and a Modern Icelandic as some scholars commonly do with regard to the development of the other Germanic languages."

Occasionally, some people have even assumed that the language spoken today is the same as the language spoken a millennium ago. Sigurður Nordal (1924, p. xxvi) once wrote that there "is a certain priceless value to be soulmates with Egill Skalla-Grímsson and Völu-Steinn [ninth- and tenth-century poets], to hear from their lips the same language our mothers taught us." This is romantic hyperbole. If through H. G. Wells's time machine, present-day Icelanders could go back ten or eleven centuries to hear these poets, they would probably understand little of what they heard. Because of the shortening of vowel sounds that occurred in the Middle Ages, Jón Helgason (1931, p. 36) even suggests that an Icelander of 1600 would have difficulty understanding one from 1200. A more recent and more typical example of romantic overstatement is that of Craigie (1957, p. 3) who wrote in the preface to the Cleasby-Vigfusson-Craigie *Icelandic-English Dictionary* that after Iceland was settled

> new dialects formed themselves throughout Scandinavia, in Iceland the old tongue rose to the dignity of a literary language, and thereby retained its original form. It has thus been preserved to our days. . . . Only in Iceland did a living literature spring up and flourish; there alone the language has been handed down to us with unbroken tradition and monuments, from the first settlement of the island to the present day.

On the other hand, when the history of the Icelandic language is compared with the histories of the other Scandinavian languages, its extremely conservative nature is readily apparent. An Icelandic child can read with little difficulty the sagas of the Icelanders, written mainly in the thirteenth century, in normalized Old Icelandic orthography. When I first attempted to read the sagas in Old Icelandic after I had learned some Modern Icelandic, it was a thrill to find it so much easier than the modern language. This is because of the limited vocabulary and the large number of stereotyped phrases in the ancient writing. In a study cited by Hreinn Benediktsson (1975, p. 64), about 500 of the 520 most frequent Icelandic words (reduced from 1,000 by regarding all inflectional forms as the same word) were found to be of Old Icelandic provenance. And only half of the remaining 20 were clearly younger than the Reformation.

Let me give an example (Hallberg, 1952, pp. 153-54) of how little the written language has changed with a brief passage from *Njal's Saga*, written around 1280. Translated into English it reads as follows: "Gunnar had his wares and those of his brother brought to the ship. And when this had been done and the ship was about ready to sail, Gunnar rode to Bergthorsknoll and to other farms to say farewell and to thank those who had given him support." The first Icelandic rendering below shows how these sentences were written around 1300 in the oldest and one of the best preserved of the manuscripts of *Njal's Saga*. At that time, there was no standard orthography and the scribes differed greatly in their spelling and in the abbreviations they used. The second rendering uses the normalized Old Icelandic spelling used in the standard editions of the sagas and in the school anthologies. The third version is in Modern Icelandic.

(1) G. letr flytia voro þeira brøðra til skips ok þa er oll favng. G. voro komin ok skip var miok bvit. þa riðr .G. til bergþorshvals ok aðra bei at fina menn ok þackaði liðveizlv ollvm þeim er honvm hofðv lið veitt.

(2) Gunnarr lætr flytja voru þeira brœðra til skips. Ok þá er oll fong Gunnars váru komin ok skip var mjok búit, þá rídr Gunnarr til Bergþórshváls ok [á] aðra bœi at finna menn ok þakkaði liðveizlu ollum þeim, er honum hofðu lið veitt.

(3) Gunnar lætur flytja vöru þeirra bræðra til skips. Og þá er öll föng Gunnars voru komin og skip var mjög búið, þá ríður Gunnar til Berg-
þórshvóls og á aðra bæi að finna menn og þakkaði li veizlu öllum þeim,
er honum höfðu lið veitt.

Relatively few changes in spelling occurred between the twelfth
and twentieth centuries. The most important are that final -r has become -ur (for example, lætr to lætur), œ has become æ (for example,
brœðra to bræðra), unstressed final -t and -k have become -ð and -g
(for example, þat and mik to það and mig), initial kn- has become
hn- (for example, knífr [knife] to hnífur), and second rs at the ends
of words have been dropped (for example, Gunnarr to Gunnar). Such
long-term continuity of the written language is characteristic of no
other Indo-European language.

Icelandic is an archaic language. For this reason, few foreigners,
including students of Icelandic literature, have been able to master
the language in detail. Icelandic has retained the four cases (nominative, accusative, dative, genitive), singular and plural forms, the three
genders (masculine, feminine, neuter), strong and weak models for the
declension of nouns and adjectives, which have 48 potential forms.
Personal names as well as numbers are inflected. Verbs have different
declensions, strong and weak, plus tense and aspect, voice and mood,
person and number. The other Scandinavian languages, English, and
the Romance languages have shed much of this traditional grammatical baggage in their transition to their modern forms. They have moved
from what linguists call synthetic languages to analytical languages
and use prepositions to do the work of the case endings. German, like
Icelandic, has remained an inflected language, and it has a grammatical structure analogous to Icelandic. Because of this characteristic,
German provides a better background for learning Icelandic than do
the Modern Scandinavian languages, even though they share more
cognates with Icelandic than German does.

While Icelandic has undergone numerous minor changes in its
written form in its eight-century history, it remains the only Indo-
European language whose speakers can read their medieval literature
without special training and even with ease. This is a much celebrated
virtue of Icelandic (Finnbogason, 1933, pp. 76-78); once the ancient
form of a language is lost by a people, it is lost forever. W. P. Ker
(1908, p. 4), that most Icelandophilic of medievalists, claimed that
the cultural superiority the Icelanders assumed (an assumption now
much attenuated) was something they had "mainly through pride in
their language."

The settlers, at least the dominant majority among them, were
Norwegians speaking the dialects of western and southwestern Norway.

Some came directly from Norway, and others came by way of Britain, Ireland, the Hebrides, and Orkney. Persons from the same area in the old country did not settle together in the new country; the mixture of dialects resulted in an extremely uniform language. As I stressed in chapter 1, one consequence of long-distance overseas migration and the resultant breakdown of traditional kinship and communal ties and the mixture of people is the homogenization of culture; this is particularly notable in language and the attenuation of dialects.

In the beginning, then, the language of the Icelanders was a blend of the dialects of the Norwegian west—those of Sogn, Rogaland, and Telemark. The Icelanders' language was the same one (Old Norse) spoken in the west of Norway, except that the dialectical differences had been smoothed away. The Celtic influence of the Old Norse spoken in Iceland was slight and consisted of only a few proper names (for example, Njáll and Kjartan) and some place names (for example, Patreksfjörður and Papey). A few nouns for everyday objects may also be of Irish origin. Whether these loanwords came from the Irish monks who lived in Iceland before the settlers arrived or from the Celts who accompanied the settlers is not known. Some new words were introduced into the early language for phenomena not experienced before settling in Iceland, such as *hraun*, a common word meaning a burnt-out lava field, and *hver*, a word meaning hot spring (of which there are many in Iceland). Other terms were invented for new institutions, for example, *goði* (chieftain) and *alþingi* (national assembly). Also, the Norse immigrants certainly did not bring the whole of the Old Norse vocabulary with them, and some words that had no use in Iceland, we can assume, were lost.

Around the year 1000, the *Dönsk tunga*, the earliest recorded name of the common Scandinavian language, was spoken not only in Iceland, Greenland, and Scandinavia but in the east in Russia; around the Baltic and as far south as Constantinople; in the west in Britain, Ireland, the North Atlantic islands; and as far as the coast of North America. This *Dönsk tunga* was to some degree intelligible to those speaking the Germanic languages from what later became Prussia west to Frisia. To what degree there was mutual intelligibility we can only speculate; Jespersen (1938, pp. 66-67) posed the question but came to no conclusive answer. The assertion in the fourteenth-century Icelandic saga *Gunnlaug Serpent-Tongue* (1938, chapter 7) that in the latter part of the tenth century the "language in England was one and the same as that in Norway and Denmark" is certainly an overstatement. So, too, is the observation of Wulfstan, who wrote of the Viking invaders as "people who do not know your language" (Napier, p. 295; quoted by Jespersen, 1938, p. 67).

In the centuries before the year 1000, the common Scandinavian language began to branch into East Scandinavian (spoken in Denmark, the southern two-thirds of Sweden, and southeastern Norway) and the more conservative West Scandinavian (spoken in most of Norway and the Norwegian settlements in the North Atlantic) (Haugen, 1976, p. 92). A comparison of the languistic developments of the three existing varieties of West Scandinavian—West Norwegian, Icelandic, and Faroese—is a linguistically interesting topic (Haugen, 1976; Haugen and Markey, 1972; Chapman, 1962). There are numerous independent but similar historical changes in these languages (Hreinn Benediktsson, 1961-1962, pp. 104-5; Dahlstedt, 1958).

The first great foreign addition to the Icelandic language after the almost negligible Irish contribution came with the introduction of Christianity into Iceland around the year 1000. Words like *prestr* (priest), *munkr* (monk), *kirkja* (church), *kristinn* (Christian), *biskup* (bishop) and *djöfull* (devil) came into the language at that time (Jakob Benediktsson, 1964). These words have Greek or Latin roots but came into Icelandic mediated through other Germanic languages, especially Anglo-Saxon and Old Saxon, either directly from England or Germany or via Norway. Most of these words could easily have been given an Old Norse form such as *guðsmaður* (God's man) rather than *prestr* and *guðshús* (God's house) rather than *kirkja*. However, at this time the Icelanders were doubtlessly quite oblivious to the purity of their language. It was not until about 1600 that there seems to have been any consciousness of the subject, and it was not until the second half of the eighteenth century with the beginning of the romantic folk movement that there was any concerted effort to rid Icelandic of words of foreign roots and to invent neologisms from Old Norse roots.

During the Middle Ages, a few hundred loanwords from Low German came into Icelandic. These words entered the language via Norwegian and, after 1380 when control of Iceland passed to Denmark, increasingly from Danish. Yet, the overall effect of Low German on Icelandic was slight compared with the lexical and grammatical transformation it caused in the other Scandinavian languages. This influence was a result of the growth of the German-controlled Hanseatic League in thirteenth-century Scandinavia and the movement of many Germans into the towns of the North.

From the time of the Reformation, the involvement of the

Danes in the religious and economic affairs of Iceland accelerated. The influence of Danish vocabulary, orthography, and syntax increasingly affected spoken and especially written Icelandic in the southern part of the country. During the latter part of the sixteenth century, the Danes began harassing the German and English merchants; this culminated in the Danish trade monopoly ordered in 1602. The monopoly lasted until 1787; during that time, only merchants licensed by the Danish crown (that is, Danes) could trade in Iceland. The seventeenth and the eighteenth centuries, and particularly the eighteenth, were the times when there was the most intense Danish influence on Icelandic. However, this influence did not permeate very deeply into the interior of the island. What was happening to Icelandic was similar to what was happening at the same time to Norwegian and Faroese; the Norwegians and the Faroese people were also under Danish suzerainty. But only the Icelanders were later successful in purging their language of most of the Danish influences. Much of the official written Icelandic from the seventeenth- and eighteenth-centuries was Dano-Icelandic, probably comparable to the Dano-Norwegian and Dano-Faroese of the same period.

The New Testament was translated into Icelandic by Oddur Gottskálksson in 1540; Gottskálksson used Luther's German translation as his main source. In addition to a Germanic syntax, above all with verbs placed at the ends of dependent clauses, its style is based on the older Icelandic religious literature that deviated from the classical Icelandic saga style in its attempt to imitate Latin speech. Because of similar influences, "from a purely syntactical point-of-view the New Testament is in many ways closer to the Danish and Swedish prose from the same period than to genuine Icelandic speech" (Jón Helgason, 1931, p. 39). In Iceland, as everywhere in Protestant Europe, the vernacular translation of the Bible shaped the form of the written language.

The first Icelander to discuss seriously the Icelandic language was Arngrímur Jónsson (1568-1648), who was called "the learned," an appellation the Icelanders used to bestow only on their most scholarly and knowledgeable compatriots. At the beginning of the seventeenth century, he warned against allowing Icelandic to be corrupted by Danish and German words. He believed (mistakenly) that the language of the Icelanders, unlike the languages of their neighbors elsewhere in the North, had remained relatively "pure" since antiquity. Knowledge of languages had not progressed far enough to allow Arngrímur to distinguish native Icelandic words from those of Low German and other origins (Helgason, 1931, p. 41). His explanation for the purity of Icelandic was the scarcity of intercourse with other countries and the continual reading of the old literature by the people. Other Icelanders in the seventeenth century also began to show concern over the purity of the language, but there was no popular movement until the first half of the nineteenth century.

Most important during these centuries were the efforts of two Icelanders, Eggert Ólafsson (1726-1768) and Bjarni Pálsson (1719-1779), who were commissioned by the Danish government in the 1750s to undertake a thorough study (originally published in Danish in 1772 and published in Icelandic in 1943) of the conditions of Icelandic society, the geography of the country, and its animal and plant life. Among the topics that most concerned them in the middle of that miserable century in Icelandic history was the condition of the language. They noted that "in the rural areas the language is spoken relatively purely and without bad grammar, but along the seacoast, particularly near harbors where many foreigners come the language is blended with foreign words, particularly from German and Danish" (volume 1, pp. 31-32). Near the end of their two-volume study, they dealt with the sparsely settled and isolated east and noted that here "the accent and timbre of the language . . . are something like the Norwegian," that the language was particularly pure, and that the old ways of speaking [were] maintained more than elsewhere (volume 2, p. 150). But they concluded that the writing of the language was best in the north and in all ways, written and spoken, "worst" in the south. Ólafsson and Pálsson accounted for the corruption of the language in the south by four reasons (volume 2, pp. 253-54): (1) the influence of German merchants during the sixteenth century was strongest there; (2) contact with Danish officials and merchants was closer and shared by more people; (3) the Althing, which met in the south and was most attended by people living nearby, used the corrupted Dano-Icelandic of the administration and of judicial procedures; and (4) the presence of the Latin School at Skálholt brought many foreign words and phrases to the people.

The clearest and purest Icelandic is still generally believed to be spoken in the rural north, particularly in the vicinity of Lake Mývatn. There the old "hard speech" (tense and aspirated) has been maintained more than in other parts of the country, where it has become more "lax." The universal advice of Icelanders to any foreigner seriously interested in learning Icelandic is to go live on a farm, preferably in the north. As the Icelandic linguist Halldór Halldórsson (1962, p. 8) has noted: "In Iceland it is the folk speech, above all the farmers' language, which is the standard language."

The beginning of organized activity aimed at purifying Icelandic and returning it to its ancient form was the founding of the Icelandic Society of Learned Arts (*Hið íslenzka Lærdómlistafélag*) by twelve Icelandic students in Copenhagen in 1779 (Thorkell Jóhannesson, 1950, pp. 421-24). Like Eggert Ólafsson, they had been influenced by early German romanticism, which culminated about this time in the romantic history of Herder. Every people should have its own language, particularly a people with such a magnificant historical language and history as the Icelanders—such was the ideology of these students. And their language was still spoken in relatively pure form in the interior of the country, even if it had been Danified by Icelandic officials and thoroughly corrupted in the south. The society published a journal, which came out for 15 years 1781-1796, devoted to diverse scientific and literary topics. From its beginning, the society was dedicated to preserving and purifying what the students believed was the Old Norse language. In the journal, they refrained from using words of foreign origin except those that had come into Icelandic in the distant past. For concepts not in the Icelandic language, they gave old words new meanings or made up neologisms from Old Norse roots. The society planned to publish a book on the correct writing of Icelandic, but it never did.

Of importance in the movement to purify Icelandic was the great Danish linguist Rasmus Rask (1787-1832), who spent the years 1813-1815 in Iceland. There he accomplished what few foreigners have, he became fluent in Icelandic. When Rask first came to Iceland, he asserted that, in 100 years, no one in Reykjavík would understand Icelandic and, in 200 years, no one in the entire country would (Thorkell Jóhannesson, 1950, pp. 430-431). But later, when he traveled about the country, he heard an Icelandic that was "pure and powerful." Long before 1913, a century after the arrival of Rask, however, the people of Reykajvík had assimilated the language of the country and not the country, the language of the city (Jón Helgason, 1931, pp. 45-46). Under the initiative of Rask, the Icelandic Literary Society (*Hið íslenzka Bókmenntafélag*) was founded in 1816, with branches in both Copenhagen and Reykjavík. It was dedicated to preserving the Old Icelandic language and publishing Icelandic literature, both old and new.

Of greatest direct importance in the effort to purify Icelandic, however, was the romantic movement. The leaders were "partly educators, partly politicians, and partly poets" (Stefán Einarsson, 1957, p. 221). The preeminent theme of the romanticism that came as a flood upon Iceland in the 1830s was patriotism. It had three elements: the glorification of the Icelandic past, particularly the heroic

Saga Age; the love of country and simple country life; and the admiration for the "pure" native tongue. The campaign for the purification of the language and the restoration of the Old Icelandic began
a movement that quickly cleansed the language of "two centuries of
Danish-German dross and its baroque style" (Stefán Einarsson, 1957,
p. 222). A number of young poets who made their debut during the
1830s were committed to purifying the language; they set in motion
a popular movement that has continued to the present day. The early
success of the Icelandic movement led to its becoming the model for
similar archaic language movements in Norway and the Faroe Islands
in the middle of the nineteenth century.

During the nineteenth century, Iceland had only one academic
school (*menntaskóli*), the Latin School at Bessastaðir, just outside of
Reykjavík, to which it moved in 1846. From the 1820s, the teachers
at the school were strongly committed to "kindling in" their pupils
"love and admiration for their mother tongue" (Stefán Einarsson
1957, p. 222). Most notable of the teachers was Sveinbjörn Egilsson
(1791-1852), who insisted that his pupils give pure Icelandic translations of the Greek and Latin classics. He also translated Homer's
Odyssey and *Iliad* into impeccable Icelandic. Another early major
influence on the purification of Icelandic was Jón Espólin (1769-
1836), who wrote a popular history of Iceland in twelve volumes in
the saga style, the first of which appeared in 1821. The style was
strikingly different from the eighteenth-century Dano-Icelandic best
exemplified by his near-contemporary and fellow historian Magnús
Stephensen (1762-1833). Jón's history subsequently shaped the
writing of popular history in Iceland, but it also served as a model
of good Icelandic prose.

The movement to purify Icelandic began the tradition of con-
structing words (*orðsmiði*, literally word smithing) to replace
Danish and German words that had entered Icelandic, many originally of Greek and Latin provenance, with Old Norse roots. This is a
vigorous tradition that has continued to the present. Table 6-1 lists
several such neologisms from different periods.[1]

By the middle of the nineteenth century, the Icelanders had
made great strides toward purifying their language. But, it is important to note, the language had always been relatively pure in the interior and less accessible parts of the country. Also, the purification
of the language has never been complete. There are still numerous
Danicisms in the spoken language, though fewer in the written language. A modern Icelander eats a *kartafla* (potato) and not a *jördepli*
(earth-apple) and goes to the *bíó* (movies) and not the *kvikmyndahús*
(quick-picture-house).

Table 6-1. Some English and Swedish Variants of International Words
Compared with Icelandic Neologisms

English	Swedish	Icelandic
radio	radio	útvarp (out-casting)
television	television	sjónvarp (view-casting)
telephone	telefon	sími (thread)
microscope	mikroskop	smásjá (small see)
philosophy	filosofi	heimspeki (world-wisdom)
chemistry	kemi	efnafræði (substance-study)
sociology	sociologi	þjóðfélagsfræði (people-association study)
geology	geologi	jarðfræði (land-study)
democracy	demokrati	lýðstjórn (people-control)
liberalism	liberalism	framsókn (forward-pursuing)
conservative	konservativ	íhaldsmaður (in-holding-man)
atom	atom	eind (unit)
captain	kapten	skipstjóri (ship-leader)
electricity	electricitet	rafmagn (amber-power)
film	film	kvikmynd (quick-picture)
taxi	taxi	leigubíll (rent-car)
motor	motor	hreyfill (from verb *hreyfa*, meaning move or stir)
dessert	dessert	ábætir (an-addition)
fantastic	fantastisk	ímyndunarfullur (in-composition-full)
cigarette	cigarrett	vindlingur (from *vindling*, meaning twisting)
margarine	margarin	smjörlíki (butter-likeness)

The reasons for the success of the Icelandic movement are more obvious when the Icelandic movement is compared with analogous movements in Norway (Haugen, 1966) and the Faroe Islands (Haugen and Markey, 1972, pp. 93-100; Margolin, 1975). In Norway, the brilliant linguist Ivar Aasen (1813-1896), reacting to the strong linguistic nationalism that came in the wake of Norway's independence from Denmark in 1814, proposed a radical solution to the problem of forging a new Norwegian, which he called *landsmål*, by basing it on the Norwegian dialects, particularly those of the west and midlands. These were the most archaic of the dialects and the closest to Old Norse and Icelandic. Aasen was the leader of a movement to accomplish for the rural Norwegian dialects what the Icelanders had already largely accomplished for Icelandic: the establishment of a standardized version of the old language. But in Norway there was no body of literature written in Norwegian. The literature of Norway was written in Danish, and the spoken language of the upper classes and the urban population was Danish spoken with Norwegian pronunciation (which is close to Swedish). In addition, only a small minority of the Norwegian population spoke the dialects upon which *landsmål* was based, and no one really spoke that particular language because it was made up of a mixture of dialects. Today, Norway continues to use two closely related languages, *nynorsk* (New Norwegian, the preferred name for *landsmål*) and *riksmål* (official language, or *bokmål*, book language, sometimes called in English Dano-Norwegian [Haugen, 1976]). *Nynorsk* is now the language of less than a fifth of the whole population. It has been unable to retain its purity and readily incorporates foreign loan words, and it has been deliberately altered by official language commissions to bring it closer to *riksmål*. *Riksmål* is the language of the great majority and is growing in strength at the expense of *nynorsk*. However, the two languages are slowly coming together.

Faroese also was affected by the movement for a national language during the middle of the nineteenth century, and the Icelandic movement also served as a model for the Faroese movement. However, Faroese became a written language only in the latter part of the eighteenth century, when some ballads were written down phonetically, with Danish orthography. Like Norway, but unlike Iceland, the country is sharply divided dialectically. Danish had been the language of religious and political life since medieval times and, consequently, had a more pervasive effect on the spoken language than it did in rural Iceland and Norway. The attempt to purify the language had limited success. Modern Faroese, the closest language to Icelandic, has kept three genders, but the declensional system has been retained to a lesser extent. The Faroese alphabet is the same as the Icelandic, with the exception that the old runic thorn *þ* (the unvoiced English *th* as in *thin*) has been replaced by *t,* as it has been in the other Scandinavian languages.[2] The percentage of Danish words used in Faroese remains high, even though many Faroese (Old Norse) words have been substituted for Danish words. Many Danish conventions also are found in the language, such as with numbers (for example, one-and-twenty rather than twenty-one). Standard Faroese also has been affected by Danish syntax.

In summary, then, we can say that the Icelandic purification movement was successful to a degree that the Norwegian and Faroese movements were not for several quite obvious reasons. First, in spite of all the Danish influence on official Icelandic, the isolated rural areas where the majority of the population lived were never much affected. Second, the influence of Danish on Icelandic was strongest among officials and in the coastal trading stations, and even there the influence of Danish was less pervasive than in the towns of Norway or anywhere in the Faroes. Third, there was a uniquely high degree of literacy among the Icelanders from the latter part of the twelfth century and the literary tradition was wholly Icelandic. The factors that explain the historical stability of rural Icelandic will be dealt with later in this chapter.

Still, the dialects of west Norway and Modern Faroese are to some degree intelligible to modern Icelanders even though they have been separated from their Norwegian and Faroese cousins for over a millennium. This may be the only case of such mutual intelligibility among historical peoples separated by great distances for such a long period. The migration from northern Germany to Britain, for example, occurred only a few centuries earlier than the migration to Iceland, but there has been no mutual intelligibility between German- and English-speaking peoples for many centuries. This is because neither of these peoples has been isolated from foreign linguistic influences.[3]

Several Icelanders have informed me that Icelanders can understand some of the inner west coast Norwegian dialects; the student of Icelandic-Norwegian linguistic relationships Kenneth G. Chapman (1962, p. 25) also agrees that this is the case. The relationship between the two languages was confirmed for me by two first-hand encounters. Óttar Thorgilsson (born 1925), an Icelander living in Massachusetts, attended a music festival in Bergen in 1954, where he heard a 79-year-old woman from an isolated inland valley in the eastern part of Gudbrandsdal sing three songs she had learned from her grandmother. According to Óttar's account to me in the summer of 1973, the songs were in "perfect Icelandic," which he understood while Norwegians in the audience did not. A second example is that of a Norwegian pilot from outside of Trondheim who is employed in Iceland. He was a classmate of mine in Modern Icelandic at the University of Iceland in 1970-71. He told me that, when he was a boy, he had a great-uncle then in his 90s who used numerous words and expressions that he never understood until he studied Icelandic. Several Icelanders have assured me that Faroese spoken slowly is intelligible to them. I could vouchsafe that this is the case after a short visit to Torshavn in 1971; even with my poor Icelandic, I could understand some Faroese. Written Faroese looks like Icelandic with a number of words misspelled, but it is pronounced very differently.

I have shown that Icelandic has changed *relatively* little, particularly orthographically, through the centuries, at least that version of it spoken in the rural areas of the country. It is also noteworthy that Icelandic has never delveloped any true dialects. There are some systematic differences in vocabulary, pronunciation, and morphology, but they are not great. Hreinn Benediktsson (1961-1962, p. 109) has suggested the term *variety* for these minor, noninvidious differences.

They are fewer than, say, those between the English or eastern Massachusetts and downstate Illinois. It is particularly difficult to render dialect into Icelandic. For example, in Hardy's *Tess of the D'Ubervilles*, the Icelandic translation (1954, for example, chapter 3) in no way suggests the west country speech of some of the characters. (How, I wonder, was the Icelandic production of *My Fair Lady* handled?) The absence of dialects is perhaps surprising in this island nation larger than Ireland and with so many natural barriers to communication—glaciers, mountains, deserts, and impassable rivers. But, as I will show later, the barriers were not insurmountable because there has always been a great deal of internal migration in Iceland.

In spoken Icelandic, particularly among the young and in the southwest (the Reykjavík-Keflavík area), there is a well-developed slang (Oscar Jones 1964b; Groenke, 1966; Dóra Bjarnason, 1974). The slang is used in conversation but usually is avoided in the written language. Much of it consists of borrowings from English (for example *okeh, beibí, sjoppa*) and Danish (for example, *reddara*, a clumsy and troublesome helper, from Danish verb *redda*, meaning to help), although some of it is from conventional Icelandic (for example, *tryllitæki*, meaning a big fine car, literally a crazy apparatus). There is disagreement between Hreinn Benediktsson (1961-1962) and Groenke (1966) over the extent that substandard Icelandic is used; Benediktsson minimizes its development and Groenke claims that it is well developed in the towns. Dóra Bjarnason (1974, p. 160), however, in her study of Reykjavík teenagers, claimed that their argot "at times is quite incomprehensible to older people."

A number of factors can be suggested that help explain the historical stability of the Icelandic language:

1. In the ten and a half centuries since the close of the Age of Settlement, there has been virtually no immigration to Iceland. And, from the middle of the fourteenth century—the time of the Black Death in Norway—through the eighteenth century, there was relatively little intercourse with the rest of the world, except for the interaction with German and Danish merchants and Danish officials. The Icelanders, except those in the south, were free of the simplifying and disinflecting effects of immigrants speaking a *closely related language*. Jespersen, (1938, p. 84) pointed out that the "wearing away and levelling of grammatical forms" in English occurred in those parts of Britain where the Danes settled and that the disinflecting "was a couple of centuries in advance of the same process in the more southern parts of the country." Jespersen went on to say that "the conclusion does not seem unwarrantable that this acceleration of the tempo of linguistic simplification is due to the settlers, who

did not care to learn English correctly in every minute particular and who certainly needed no such accuracy in order to make themselves understood." The same explanation is given by Bergman (1947, pp. 44-61) for the breakdown of the Old Swedish case system in the latter part of the Middle Ages, which he attributes to "the mangling of Swedish by German immigrants." German- and Russian-speaking areas, by contrast, never experienced large-scale immigration of people speaking a closely related language, and German and Russian have remained, like Icelandic, highly inflected languages.

2. From as early as the latter part of the twelfth century, a large proportion of Icelanders have been literate (Sveinsson, 1944, 1956). The popular reading of the old literature, as Arngrímur Jónsson pointed out almost four centuries ago, together with the copying of manuscripts by a large proporation of the population into the eighteenth century are major factors making for the historical stability — if not necessarily the temporal stability — of the language. The conservatism of a language is related to the extent that it is used as a literary medium. No language has ever been used more as a literary medium than Icelandic.

3. The Icelanders have a pervasive and deep poetic tradition (P. M. Mitchell, 1965). The other Scandinavian countries also have popular poetic traditions, but theirs are minor by comparison. Consider the development of *rímur* (rhymes), a very artificial, very difficult, and wholly indigenous form. This genre consists of verses of four (or, rarely, three) lines (Beinteinsson, 1966). In the most difficult form of *rímur*, every word in the first line must rhyme with the corresponding word in the third line, the same with each word in the second and fourth lines. In addition, the verse must make sense read backward word by word as well as forward! Here is an example cited by Stefán Einarsson (1957, p. 185).

> Mettur rómur, meyrnar mér
> máttur glettu-góma,
> dettur ómur heyrnar hér,
> háttur sléttu óma.

The composing of *rímur* began in the fourteenth century and was well established among the whole Icelandic population by the first half of the fifteenth century, although its practice has declined greatly in this century. The result of the development of this verse form (Craigie, 1937, p. 21) has been to preserve "throughout all classes of the population, a feeling for language and rhythm, a knowledge of the past, an interest in myth and legend, which helped as much as anything to maintain the continuity of Icelandic literature."

I would add "and language" to Craigie's observation. The maintenance of the complex Icelandic grammar has been functionally necessary for the composition of *rímur* and other complex poetic forms.
The alternatives possible with the ancient grammar give Icelandic its
enormous flexibility for a formal rhyming and alliterative poetry, a
plasticity that the languages that have shed their old grammar have
lost. Variation in syntax and word form are infinitely greater in inflected languages than in, for example, English and the Modern Scandinavian languages, which necessarily have a rigid word order, few
forms for nouns and adjectives, and a heavier reliance on prepositions.

4. A complex system of case endings further acts as a buffer
against the adoption of foreign loan words. When foreign words are
adopted into Icelandic, their forms are usually changed (for example,
tubercle became *berkill, jeep* became *jeepi*) in order to be compatible
with the necessary declensions. As noted earlier, the dominant pattern for Icelandic, however, is to translate foreign words, particularly
those of Greek and Latin provenance, into words using analogous
Old Norse roots. (See table 6-1 for examples.) A consequence of this
pattern, incidentally, is to make Icelandic an extraordinarily egalitarian language in that virtually the entire vocabulary is accessible to
the whole population; jargon and words for complex ideas are constructed from roots universally understood. The Germans did this,
particularly during the Nazi years, but not to the extent that this is
practiced in Iceland. In languages with large proportions of loanwords, particularly from Greek and Latin—above all English—only
the sophisticated even passively understand a large proportion of the
vocabulary.[4]

5. Two old institutions, the Church and the Althing, played a
central role for centuries in maintaining the historical and temporal
stability of the language. From the late eleventh to the nineteenth
century, the Church educated the clergy at two schools, Hólar in the
north and Skálholt in the south. The clergy, then, supervised the education of the young in their parishes. The Althing met for two
weeks in the second half of June almost every year from 930 to
1800. Large numbers of people came from all over Iceland to attend
this annual national reunion, which was at once political assembly,
fair, and marriage mart. It was attended by a sizeable portion of the
population.

6. A peculiarity of Iceland from the beginning (compared with
the other Nordic countries and Europe in general) that both contributed to the historical stability of the language and inhibited the
development of dialects has been the high degree of internal migration. Icelanders have never had much of that attachment to place

that characterizes traditional agricultural peoples; "love of the soil" is not a common theme in their poetry (Stefán Einarsson, 1957, p. 279). This is because grain growing never contributed much to the material well-being of the Icelanders; and, after the fifteenth century, it ceased completely. This was the result of a slight but significant decline in the temperature that made the cultivation of grain unworthwhile because the growing season was neither warm enough nor long enough to produce a good crop. From the beginning, Icelandic agriculture has consisted, above all, of producing fodder for livestock. The Icelandic geologist and geographer Sigurður Thorarinsson (1958, pp. 8-9) wrote about this.

> There was thus from the beginning a basic difference between Icelandic farming and farming in the Scandinavian countries and on the British Isles, where grain-growing was a basic industry, a difference which exerted a profound influence on Icelandic civilization. The farmer's attachment to his farmstead depends first and foremost on agriculture and the cultivation of the soil. With cultivation goes stability and immobility, but Icelandic farming has always had a touch of nomadism. . . . The Icelandic farmer has never been so closely attached to his farmstead as his Scandinavian counterparts. The movement of homes between districts and different parts of the country has been much commoner over here.

A high level of internal movement within a country maintains and enhances the uniformity of its culture, and this is particularly true of language.

7. Urban culture had no effect on the language because of the almost total absence of towns until the latter part of the nineteenth century. As recently as 1901, there were only three towns in the country with as many as a thousand people; Reykjavík, the largest, had a population of 6,682 in that year. The changes that sophisticated urban life can exert in shaping a national language were totally absent from the development of Icelandic. Because of the migration to the towns during the twentieth century—the Reykjavík area now has a population of well over 100,000—and the absence of any prestigious urban form of speech, the language of the country has shaped the urban speech rather than the other way around. There was no "high culture" and no crystallized class system until the time Iceland embarked on the path to being a modern society since 1900. High culture encourages a self-consciousness about language. Typically, the presence of an upper class or a distinct educated class encourages this process and some distinction between upper-class and common speech develops. Such processes have not affected Icelandic linguistic development. There remains no difference between literary Icelandic

and popular Icelandic. Modern Icelandic remains a language that was developed and refined by farmers.

NAMES AND NAMING PATTERNS

Only in Iceland has the centuries-old Scandinavian pattern of naming continued down to the present. One's given name is one's primary name. Individuals are listed in the telephone book, in library card catalogs,[5] and in directories and files as Jón or Guðrún. Recently, the United States Library of Congress even made the decision to catalog modern Icelandic authors by their given names rather than last names (P. M. Mitchell, 1978, p. 30). One's last name is a patronymic formed by adding *son* or *dóttir* to the possessive of one's father's name. Women do not change their names after marriage. Everywhere else in Scandinavia family names became legally necessary in the nineteenth or early twentieth century.

In 1913, legislation was passed in Iceland that required one to petition the government in order to adopt a family name; the legislation also required that the name be of a suitable type (Hjörleifsson et al., 1915). This legislation further required that official lists of acceptable Icelandic family names and given names be drawn up. This legislation was enacted in order to curtail the popular practice of adopting family names and using given names of foreign origin. Such practices had begun in the seventeenth and eighteenth centuries and had rapidly increased during the nineteenth century among Danophilic Icelanders (Thorstein Thorsteinsson, 1915, p. 14). In 1855, there were 108 different family names in Iceland; by 1910 the number had increased to 297. In 1925, additional legislation was passed to prohibit the adoption of family names altogether, although it allowed those who already had them to keep them; it also made the adoption of an Icelandic name and patronymic a prerequisite for obtaining Icelandic citizenship. A cursory check of the Icelandic telephone directory indicates about 15 percent of Icelanders continue to have family names; only 9 of the 100 individuals in my interview sample bore family names (see appendix B). This percentage probably will decline in the future as Icelanders with family names drop them and revert to the traditional naming system.

The continuity of names throughout Icelandic history has been striking, as a look at tables 6-2 and 6-3 will demonstrate. These tables list the rank order frequency of male and female names for six periods in the 1,100 years of Icelandic history; all names are spelled

Table 6-2. Rank Order of Frequency of Icelandic Male Names
from Saga Times to the Present

Rank	Saga Times	1100-1299	1703	1855	1910	Circa. 1970
1	Thorsteinn	Þórður	Jón	Jón	Jón	Jón
2	Þórður	Jón	Guðmundur	Guðmundur	Guðmundur	Guðmundur
3	Thorkell	Thorsteinn	Bjarni	Sigurður	Sigurður	Sigurður
4	Þórir	Einar	Sigurður	Magnús	Ólafur	Gunnar
5	Bjõrn	Guðmundur	Ólafur	Ólafur	Magnús	Ólafur
6	Grímur	Eyjólfur	Magnús	Einar	Kristján	Magnús
7	Thorbjõrn	Snorri	Einar	Bjarni	Einar	Kristján
8	Helgi	Bjõrn	Thorsteinn	Árni	Bjarni	Einar
9	Thorgeir	Ólafur	Þórður	Gísli	Jóhann	Jóhann
10	Þórarinn	Brandur	Árni	Björn	Björn	Kristinn
11	Thorgrímur	Thorkell	Gísli	Kristján	Gísli	Helgi
12	Sigurður	Halldór	Björn	Thorsteinn	Árni	Björn
13	Thorvaldur	Sigurður	Halldór	Stefán	Stefán	Halldór
14	Ketill	Magnús	Eiríkur	Jóhannes	Thorsteinn	Stefán
15	Einar	Hallur	Páll	Jóhann	Helgi	Bjarni
16	Thorgils	Árni	Sveinn	Jónas	Guðjón	Þór
17	Bárður	Þórarinn	Oddur	Þórður	Halldór	Ragnar
18	Eyjólfur	Thorgeir	Pétur	Sveinn	Kristinn	Árni
19	Thormóður	Páll	Eyjólfur	Halldór	Páll	Pétur
20	Eyvindur	Thorgils	Helgi	Páll	Jóhannes	Gísli
21	Thorleifur	Oddur	Tómas	Pétur	Pétur	Páll
22	Þórólfur	Grímur	Thorleifur	Eiríkur	Þórður	Guðjón
23	Oddur	Ketill	Thorkell	Helgi	Sveinn	Thorsteinn
24	Ormur	Helgi	Snorri	Eyjólfur	Gunnar	Sveinn
25	Hrafn	Bárður	Sigmundur	Benedikt	Jónas	Karl
26	Ólafur	Thorbjõrn			Ágúst	Örn
27	Thorfinnur	Þórir			Sigurjón	Jóhannes
28		Thorvaldur				Haukur
29						Óskar
30						Ágúst
31						Ingi
32						Birgir
33						Sigurjón

Sources: Rank order of frequency of names in saga times was calculated from Guðni Jónsson, 1968, and was based on about 6,800 names. Twelfth- and thirteenth-century data are from about 4,000 names in index to Jóhannesson, Finnbogason, and Eldjárn, 1946, volume 2, pp. 363-473. Data for 1703 are based on frequency counts from census of that year (Ólafur Lárusson, 1960). Data for 1855 are based on frequency counts from the census of that year (Hansen, 1858). Data for 1910 are also based on census frequency counts (Thorstein Thorsteinsson, 1915). The rank order of names for circa 1970 is based on a frequency count of the names of all children born in Iceland between 1921 and 1950 (Thorstein Thorsteinsson, 1961, p. 13).

Note: The names from 1703 until 1970 include all names accounting for at least 1 percent of the names used.

Table 6-3. Rank Order of Frequency of Icelandic Female Names
from Saga Times to the Present

Rank	Saga Times	1100-1299	1703	1855	1910	Circa. 1970
1	Thorgerður	Guðrún	Guðrún	Guðrún	Guðrún	Guðrún
2	Thórdís	Helga	Sigríður	Sigríður	Sigríður	Sigríður
3	Thuríður	Thórdis	Ingibjörg	Margrét	Kristín	Kristín
4	Helga	Valgerður	Margrét	Kristín	Margrét	Margrét
5	Guðrún	Thuríður	Helga	Ingibjörg	Ingibjörg	Ingibjörg
6	Thóra	Halldóra	Thuríður	Helga	Anna	Anna
7	Thórunn	Sigríður	Kristín	Anna	Helga	Helga
8	Sigríður	Steinunn	Valgerður	Guðbjörg	Jóhanna	Jóhanna
9	Thorbjörg	Hallbera	Halldóra	Guðný	Guðbjörg	Sigrún
10	Valgerður	Herdís	Ólöf	Jóhanna	Jónína	María
11	Rannveig	Thorgerður	Guðný	Guðríður	María	Jóna
12	Vigdís	Ingibjörg	Guðríður	Halldóra	Guðný	Guðbjörg
13	Thorkatla	Thóra	Steinunn	Steinunn	Halldóra	Erla
14	Ingibjörg	Kolfinna	Thóra	Thuríður	Guðríður	Hulda
15	Gróa	Oddný	Thórunn	Thórunn	Steinunn	Guðný
16	Jórunn	Álöf	Thorbjörg	Ólöf	Elín	Elín
17	Halldóra	Guðný	Ragnhildur	Valgerður	Thórunn	Ragnheiður
18	Hildur	Hallfríður	Ingveldur	Elín	Guðlaug	Steinunn
19	Hallbera	Vigdís	Thórdís	Thorbjörg	Ólöf	Ólöf
20	Álöf	Thorbjörg	Sesselja	Guðlaug	Sigurbjörg	Björg
21	Thórhildur	Halla	Katrín	Sólveig	Valgerður	Jónína
22	Ragnhildur	Margrét	Guðlaug	María	Thuríður	Ásta
23	Ástríður	Álfheiður	Sólvieg	Hólmfríður	Hólmfríður	Haldóra
24	Auður	Birna	Gróa	Björg	Ragnheiður	Thóra
25	Guðríður	Jórunn	Thorgerður	Ragnheiður	Thorbjörg	Sigurbjörg
26	Gunnhildur		Vigdís	Ragnhildur	Kristjana	Lilja
27	Ólöf		Oddný	Sesselja	Elísabet	Thórunn
28			Vilborg		Thóra	Guðlaug
29			Anna		Björg	Unnur
30					Sólveig	Sólveig
31						Elísabet
32						Valgerður
33						Erna

Sources: Same as for table 6-2.

Note: The names from 1703 until 1970 include all names accounting for at least 1 percent
of the names used.

with modern orthography, except for substituting th for the Icelandic þ. They are based on name counts of about 6,800 persons
from the Saga Times (A.D. 870-1030); about 4,000 persons from the
twelfth and thirteenth centuries (the Age of the Sturlungs); complete
counts of names enumerated in the censuses of 1703, 1855, and
1910; together with a frequency count of the names of all children

born in Iceland during the years 1921 through 1950, which I take as an approximation of the rank order frequency of names for the years around 1970. These name frequencies indicate that a large majority of Icelanders have the same names as their ancestors of seven and eight centuries ago. More remarkable, however, is the observation that most of the names of the men and women who settled Iceland in the years 870-930 are still used in Iceland today. Of the twenty-seven most common male names from saga times (almost 5,000 of the 6,800 known persons were males) *all* are at least fairly common in Iceland today and most are among the most common. The same is true, with one exception (Álöf) of the 27 most common female names (about 2,000 of the known persons from saga times were females). There are no Álöf's born in 1921-1950 (Thorsteinn Thorsteinsson, 1961); nor are there any listed in recent Icelandic telephone directories. However, the very similar name Ólöf is now a common name in Iceland, as it was in saga times. No such continuity characterizes the Anglo-Saxon names in use a millennium ago; most of the Anglo-Saxon names sound ancient and distant to our ears.[6]

In spite of the continuity in names over the eleven centuries of Icelandic history, a number of trends can be noted:

1. There has been a marked decline in the number of persons named after Thor. In pre-Christian times, about 25 percent of all names commemorated this most vigorous and vital of the Viking gods. During the twelfth and thirteenth centuries, after Christianity had been established for several generations, the number of Thor names had declined to about 14 percent of all names. In the census enumerations of 1703, 1855, and 1910, 8 or 9 percent of all names were Thor names; there was no decline over these two centuries. Around 1970, however, only about 4 percent of all names were Thor names. In an overwhelming majority of cases, Thor is the first part of a compound name, but, in a minority of cases, it is the end part as in Bergthór or Bergthóra, Steinthór or Steinthóra. Sometimes, the *th* (*þ*) becomes *d* as in Halldór and Halldóra. In one case, there is a vowel change, the leading female name Thuríður (from the male Thorríður) must be reckoned a Thor name (Janzén, 1947, p. 95).

2. From the beginning, there has been a continual increase in the use of biblical and Christian names. A very small number of the 3,500 original settlers listed in the *Book of Settlements* had biblical names such as Jón, Pétur, Páll, and Margrét (Janzén, 1947, p. 29; Jakob Benediktsson, 1969: *Landnámabók*, 1968, pp. 441-525). Still, however, the great majority of Icelanders down to the present have borne Old Norse names.

3. Until the eighteenth century, virtually no Icelanders had more than one name; among those born in the years 1941-1950, 52 percent had two or more given names (Thorstein Thorsteinsson, 1961, p. 11). In the 1703 census, only two individuals in the whole country, a brother and a sister, were enumerated as having two given names (Ólafur Lárusson, 1960, p. 3).

4. From the beginning, Icelanders have continually made up new names by compounding names, but the process greatly accelerated during the nineteenth century, when many new combinations came into existence, such as Friðjón and Bergjón.

5. Since the nineteenth century, there has been an increasing tendency toward using foreign names, a few of which have become common (for example, Kristinn and Hulda), a trend distressing to some Icelanders. Most of the leading foreign names have come to Iceland via Denmark.

6. The use of nonintimate nicknames has nearly disappeared. During heathen times (Steffensen, 1967-1968, pp. 179-81) 24.9 percent of the males listed in the *Book of Settlements* had nicknames, not counting those names compounded with an occupation or a place name or those referring to age (the older, the younger); during the Christian twelfth and thirteenth centuries (based on names in *Sturlunga Saga*), the percentage of males with nicknames dropped to 19.3 percent; it has been much lower in all subsequent periods. The same trend is characteristic of women's names, but in all periods women have been much less likely than men to have nicknames. The old nicknames were graphically descriptive and frequently derogatory; Auðun the Stutterer, Eystein Foul-Fart, Ulf the Squint-eyed, Stubby-Lína, Thorberg Ship-Breast, Thorkell Prick, Ófeig Thin-Beard, Auðun the Rotten, and Ljótur the Unwashed are not atypical examples. Affixing place names to one's name is sometimes done now as it was in antiquity; some modern writers in Iceland are named, for example, Jóhannes úr Kötlum, Guðrún frá Lundi, Jón úr Vör, and Thorsteinn frá Hamri. The Scandinavian pattern of identifying oneself by the name of a farm has always been rare; a case in point is Halldór Laxness, born Halldór Guðjónsson, who grew up on a farm called Laxnes.

Throughout Icelandic history, relatively few names have been used by the majority of the population. In the 1703 census, 387 male and 338 female names were counted (Ólafur Lárusson, 1960, p. 3). However, 23.5 percent of the males were named Jón, probably the most common male name during all times since the thirteenth century. The ten most frequent male names in this early census were held by over half of the males. Among the females, the most common name in 1703, as it has been since at least the twelfth century, was Guðrún; this was the given name of 19.7 percent of all the females. As with males, the ten most common names accounted for a majority of the females enumerated.

Among Icelanders born in the years 1921-1950, the number of recorded names more than tripled to 1,234 for males and 1,463 for females (Thorstein Thorsteinsson, 1961, p. 12). Yet, between a third and a half of both males and females had the ten most frequent names. Sixty-four percent of the male names were held by fewer than fifty individuals and 31 percent were held by only one person. Among female names, 73 percent were counted fewer than 50 times and 30 percent, only once. The use of Jón had declined to 6.5 percent of all males; Guðrún, to 7.8 percent of all females.

The most common male names have close to the same rank order of frequency at present as they had in 1703, and perhaps for several centuries before that. The most notable exception is Gunnar, which moved from 35th place in 1703, to 33rd place in 1855, to 24th place in 1910, and to fourth place in the present era. Significantly, this is the name of the greatest of all heroes in the sagas of the Icelanders, Gunnar of Hlíðarendi in *Njal's Saga*. The name Bjarni, on the other hand, declined from third place in 1703, to seventh place in 1855, to eighth place in 1910, and to 15th place among males born in 1921-1950. Of the 33 most common male names listed in table 6-2, for the most recent period *at least* 24 go back to the Age of Settlement (870-930) (Hermann Pálsson, 1960). Kristján and Kristinn are Danish imports and were rarely used in Iceland before the eighteenth century. Jóhann and Jóhannes, variations of the biblical name Jón, came into Iceland in the seventeenth century or earlier; there were only eleven Jóhann's and one Jóhannes enumerated in 1703. Stefán dates from the thirteenth century. Guðjón is a name that was unknown in 1703, but it became common in the nineteenth century; it is a typical Icelandic compound and is simply Icelandic for God's Jón. Óskar and Ágúst date from the late eighteenth or early nineteenth century. Sigurjón, in thirty-third place, is another nineteenth-century compound but, unlike Guðjón, it has no meaning.

There is clearly less continuity with female names than with male names. Of the 33 most common female names for the present period listed in table 6-3, not fewer than 18 go back to the Age of Settlement. Kristín, the third most common name among females born in the period 1921-1950, is a Christian name that was introduced into Iceland in the thirteenth century, since which time it has always been one of the most common names. Anna came to Iceland in the fifteenth century and is the sixth most common female name among those born in the years 1921-1950; it was 29th in frequency among those enumerated in 1703, but it jumped to eighth place in 1855 and to sixth place in 1910, where it has remained. Jóhanna, a feminine form of Jóhann, is of Danish origin and goes back to the seventeenth century. Sigrún was not used in Iceland before the fifteenth century, although the name is found in the *Saga of the Volsungs*, written in the thirteenth century. María, another Christian name, did not come into use until the eighteenth century; there was not one María enumerated in 1703. There were, however, four women enumerated in this first census with the male-sounding name Marío (Ólafur Lárusson, 1960, p. 38). Jóna, the feminine of Jón, became popular in the late nineteenth century; only one Jóna was enumerated in 1703. Erla is of very recent vintage in Iceland; none was enumerated as recently as 1910. Hulda is a late-nineteenth-century import from Denmark. Elín is not of Norse origin (it is from the Greek Helena) and was not used in Iceland before the fifteenth century. Jónina, a feminine diminutive of Jón, is probably a nineteenth-century invention. Ásta is a shortening of the ancient Norwegian name Ástríði and was not used in Iceland before the thirteenth century. Six Sigurbjörg's were counted in 1703, a compound name of old Norse roots probably invented in the seventeenth century. Lilja was not used in Iceland before the eighteenth century. Elísabet dates from the seventeenth century; however, a Nordic version of this name was Ellisif and it was used in Iceland from the thirteenth through the eighteenth centuries (Hermann Pálsson, 1960, p. 38). The name Erna is from the mythological literature of ancient Iceland (*Rigsþula*); only three were enumerated in 1910.

Some of the wives and slaves who accompanied the original Norse settlers were Irish. They are responsible for the small number of Irish words in the Icelandic language, including a few proper names. The most common have been the male names Kjartan (Certán), Kormákur (Cormac), and Njáll (Níall), together with the female name Melkorka (Mael Curcaig). All of these are the names of well-known saga characters, yet not since the earliest generations have more than a fraction of 1 percent of Icelanders borne Irish names. By far the most common has been Kjartan, also the name of an enormously illustrious and handsome figure in *Laxdaela Saga*; but, of the males born in 1921-1950, only 261 had this as a single, first, or auxiliary name; only 15 were enumerated in 1703.

Several patterns in the naming of children have persisted since saga times and earlier (Janzén, 1947; "Namngjeving," 1968). Sometimes sons have been named after their fathers, but this has never been a common pattern either among the old Norse nor among modern Icelanders. Of about 1,100 Jón's listed in the Reykjavík section of a recent Icelandic telephone directory, only 21 had the patronymic Jónsson; two of the 50 men in my interview sample had the same given names as their fathers (appendix B). Rarely, at any time, have daughters been named after their mothers. Three naming patterns have been common from the beginning: alliteration, variation, and commemoration. A stunning example of the alliterative pattern is the successive list of kings of the Uppsala dynasty who were named Agni, Alrek, Yngvi, Iǫrund, Aun, Egil, Óttar, Adils, Eystein, Yngvar, Ǫnund, Ingiald, and Olaf (Foote and Wilson, 1970, p. 115). That this was a pervasive old Germanic pattern is suggested by the names of Alfred the Great's children: Ethelflaed, Edward, Edmund, Ethelgifu, Aelfthryth, and Ethelweard (Duckett, 1956, p. xviii). Today, some Icelandic parents continue to name their children with alliterative combinations, such as Gunnar, Gunnilla, and Guðbjörg.

Probably always more commonly used, however, has been the variation principle, and it is probably older than alliteration, having arisen before the Germanic languages were separated from the main stock; it appears in Greek (Withycombe, 1950, pp. xxiii-xxiv). Here names with similar beginnings or endings are used to show family relationships. In Iceland and ancient Scandinavia, variations of the first element rather than the last element have been much more common. In the *Book of Settlements*, there is an account of a settler from Sogn in Norway named Végeir (which means Temple-Geir or Holy-Geir); he had six sons named Vébjǫrn, Vésteinn, Véthormur, Vémundur, Végestur, and Véthorn, plus a daughter named Védís. The helpful brothers in *Hrafnkel's Saga* were named Thorgeir and Thorbjǫrn, and they had a third brother named Thormóður. Such a combination would not be unusual in Iceland today. Once again it is appropriate to use Alfred the Great as an example; his father was named Ethelwulf and his brothers were Ethelbald, Ethelbert, Ethelred, and Ethelswith.

Far more common, however, than either of these patterns has been commemoration, particularly the naming of a son after an ancestor, above all a paternal grandfather. Ari Thorgilsson (1067-1148), the father of Icelandic history, had a son named Thorgils Arason, who in turn, had a son named Ari Thorgilsson. It has always been common in Iceland, and it is as common now as in the past, to have name reversals such as this. A sizable proportion of living Icelandic males have the same names as their paternal grandfathers.

CHAPTER 7

Religion, Literature, and Alcohol

However great the spiritual importance of the conversion [to Christianity], it was not, as in some lands, a social and cultural revolution. This may help to explain why the traditions of pre-Christian Scandinavia survived the conversion in Iceland, as they could not survive in Norway or in any other northern land.

G. Turville-Petre (1953)

Iceland, and Iceland alone, was the true home of the family saga in the narrower and more technical sense of the term. That the Icelanders had special aptitudes and tastes in this direction is clearly indicated by the circumstance that they still have an exceptional flair *for genealogies and memoirs.*

Knut Liestøl (1930)

Drunkenness is [the Icelanders'] only vice; but they cannot easily afford it, or have the opportunity of often indulging. . . . Inebriety is not, as with us, attended with violence and brutality, but generosity and stupidity.

Charles S. Forbes (1860)

The grouping of religion, literature, and alcohol in the same chapter may appear incongruous; it is at least unusual. But there is some justification for such an arrangement. First, all three are fundamentally leisure-time pursuits; all involve activities that individuals and societies choose to devote their time and resources to after they have satisfied their requirements for sustenance and survival. Second, they are all modes of altering consciousness. Religion directs attention toward spiritual and supernatural concerns with various individual and social consequences. Literature (and all art) transports individu-

173

als to a different reality and enhances aesthetic sensibilities. Alcohol contributes to losing self-consciousness and shyness and to throwing off inhibitions; it dulls the pains and discomforts of existence. And, finally, religion, literature, and alcohol are three aspects of culture in which the Icelanders have manifested remarkable patterns of cultural continuity from the beginning.

RELIGION

In their whole history, Icelanders have shown a striking tolerance in matters of religious belief and practice. Few Icelanders have ever been intense pagans, intense Catholics, or intense Lutherans. As far as is known, no one has ever died for his or her religious beliefs in Iceland (Finnbogason, 1943, p. 21). In the latter decades of the tenth century, a few pagan poets were killed by proselytizing Christians for writing scurrilous verse about them, but this was an affront to their honor and so by the standards of the time was justifiable cause for homicide. The last Catholic bishop of Iceland, Jón Arason, was beheaded, along with his two sons, in 1550 (the most famous killings in Icelandic history); but these were political killings that occurred after the bishop, leading a force of 400 men, attempted to reestablish Catholicism in Iceland. During the seventeenth century, some 25 people accused of being witches were burned at the stake, but this unusual Icelandic behavior was a result of Danish and German influences at a time of acute misery in Iceland. The witches' crime was casting malevolent magic spells, not their religious belief.

In 1829 Jón Espólín, a popular historian, wrote (quoted by Finnbogason, 1933, p. 305) that the Icelanders are "a cool-tempered people" who "usually show no serious devotion, neither to their priests nor other authorities" and they "are generally not pious, as some [foreign observers] have maintained." In 1902 Valtýr Guðmundsson (p. 20), a professor of Icelandic at the University of Copenhagen, wrote a book on Icelandic culture and national character for a Danish audience in which he observed that in religion the Icelander "is certainly a full-blooded rationalist. Pietism and intolerance are foreign to him. He wishes complete freedom for every sort of personal conviction. He is above all a man with a desire to understand, who prefers the absolute rule of reason over sentiment, feeling, and mysticism." Guðmundur Finnbogason (1943, p. 21), the foremost writer on the character of the Icelanders, noted that in religion "Icelanders have always been very liberal, and all extremist tendencies have been coldly received and soon died out. . . . Such theological works as have acquired great popularity have combined religious sincerity with great worldly wisdom and exceptional genius." Sigurður A. Magnússon (1977, pp. 164-65), an Icelandic editor and writer, observed that while Icelanders "are naively intolerant in political matters, they are exceedingly tolerant in moral and religious affairs." But, he went on to note, even though they "care little about Christianity and organized religion, they are still an essentially religious people in a more general sense." He supported this last contention with the results of Haraldsson's (1978) study that found that 92 percent of Icelanders "never" or "seldom" read the Bible but that 97 percent considered themselves "quite, somewhat, or slightly" religious. (My guess is that the great majority of people in *all* modern Western countries are religious in this sense; religion is pervasively and vaguely regarded as a good thing.)

These observations of native observers on religion stand in contrast to the observations of some foreign observers. In 1772, von Troil (1780, p. 89) described the Icelanders as "very zealous in their religion." MacKenzie (1811, p. 269), four decades later, observed that they "deserve a high place on the scale of morality and religion." Henderson (1818, p. 88) wrote that the "exercise of domestic worship is attended to, in almost every family in Iceland, from Michaelmas to Easter." He saw the Icelanders as religious, devout, and wanting Bibles. Dillon (1840, p. 107) comments on the "universal attention paid to religion." The naive American Pliny Miles (1854, p. 223) claimed Icelanders had "a devotional spirit, and ardent love of the precepts and practices of Christianity." Lord Dufferin (1910, p. 28) once called them "the most devout . . . people in the world."

What are we to make of these differences in perception between the native observers and the travelers? I suggest that the observations of these visitors may be suspect for several reasons. First, those who claimed the Icelanders to be such devout Christians held strong, positive opinions of them, were themselves religiously oriented, and—except for Henderson—did not know the language. Second, many other observers, particularly the best ones (for example, Morris, Bryce, Burton, Lindroth), never observed the Icelanders to be such devout Christians. And, third, the travelers did not comment on any particular piety among the clergy about whom they wrote so much and who were their chief sources of information and their interpreters.

But there was some change in religious belief and practice during the nineteenth century. Thórir Kr. Thórðarson (Nordal and Kristinsson, 1975, pp. 303-10), a professor in the theology faculty of the University of Iceland, views the cataclysmic seventeenth and eighteenth centuries as a time when "the religious tradition achieved a unity and strength never since equalled" (p. 305). Personal and communal piety were universal, he claims, but were "lost" by the beginning of this century, a discontinuity "symptomatic of the breach of tradition characterizing the present situation in Iceland, both in culture and religion" (p. 305). The pervasiveness of religious books in the homes of ordinary people during the eighteenth century (chapter 5) seems to support Thórðarson's argument. Even Bryce (1872, p. 42) and his companions, interestingly enough, were confused on the general question of the religiosity of the Icelanders: "one . . . maintaining the Icelanders to be an exceptionally religious people; a second, exceptionally unreligious; while a third thought them neither more nor less religious than the rest of the world." No observer, native or foreign, however, has ever questioned the Icelanders' general tolerance in religious and moral affairs.[1]

In 1977, 97.2 percent of the Icelandic population was formally Lutheran (93.0 percent being affiliated with the National Evangelical Church and 4.2 percent with three Free Lutheran churches); 1.6 percent had a non-Lutheran affiliation (Catholic, Pentacostal, Seventh-Day Adventist, and Bahai); and 1.2 percent claimed no affiliation (Statistical Bureau of Iceland, *Hagtíðindi*, 1978, p. 17). There is full freedom of religion. For example, one does not need to be a member of the Lutheran Church or any religious congregation in order to teach religion in the schools. This is similar to Sweden and Finland but unlike Denmark and Norway, where religious training continues to be officially confessional (Jósepsson, 1970). There are around 110 clergymen in Iceland; this works out to about 1 per 2,000 population.

Church attendance on an average Sunday, I would estimate, is not more than 1 or 2 percent of the population; there are no national statistics on the subject. Björn Björnsson's (1971, p. 128) observation as a temporary minister in the only State Lutheran Church in Akranes, a town of over 4,000, is probably not atypical. He noted "the number of empty seats in the small church, Sunday morning after Sunday morning. In at least one instance only five seats were taken and the attendance never rose to more than some thirty persons." He was "reassured by members of the church choir and the Church Warden that this standard of attendance was just about normal."

My interview schedule contained only one direct question about religious belief: "Which of the following statements best expresses your belief in God?" (appendix A, question 6). After asking the question, I presented the respondents with a card listing four alternatives and asked them to give me only the letter of their preference. The alternatives and the number choosing each were these (one person refused to answer):

I do not believe in any God   4
I believe in God, though not necessarily the Christian God   29
I believe in the Christian God   61
I do not know what I believe   5

No differences that could approach having any significance were found between men and women, nor between the Reykjavík and non-Rekjavík halves of the sample. Not one respondent volunteered a response critical of religion or the clergy, and only one respondent made any spontaneous statement friendly to religion or religious belief. However, when I inquired into what are the two worst things about living in Iceland (question 9), two respondents mentioned the lack of religion in the country. When I asked about the two best things about living in Iceland (question 8), no one mentioned freedom of religion or religion in any way.

Today, the Church of Iceland is highly liberal compared with the Lutheran churches elsewhere in northern Europe. As Sigurbjörn Einarsson (1967, p. 22), the bishop of Iceland, has written, "the liberalism associated with the turn of the century acquired greater and more lasting popularity here in Iceland than in Western European countries." This "liberalism" was manifest in the tendency of many Lutheran Icelanders in North America to move toward Unitarianism (Walters, 1953, pp. 97-99); indeed, the schism caused by the inroads of Unitarianism on the Icelandic pioneers in North America was deep and bitter (p. 100). Icelandic Lutheranism also is distinguished by its having been much influenced by occultism, particularly spiritism and theosophy, in the latter part of the nineteenth century (Sigurbjörn Einarsson, 1965). Christianity in twentieth-century Iceland has been syncretistic and tolerant, just as it was during the period of the Commonwealth.

The original settlers knew about Christianity, and some had been baptized in the British Isles before emigrating to Iceland. But most of them and their children lapsed back into paganism in Iceland, and not until the end of the tenth century did a few Icelanders begin to accept Christianity.

The old Scandinavian heathens were tolerant and did not decry the falseness of their neighbors' gods. The old religion of the North was like the Eastern religions in that it was open and nonfanatical. As H. R. Ellis Davidson (1964, p. 219) has written, this heathen religion had "no real central authority, no recognized body of doctrine to which to appeal, few deep certainties for which men were prepared to die. The worship of the old gods was a very individual affair suiting the independent people who practiced it." Acceptance of one god didn't necessarily mean that one had to reject others. So it is understandable that these Icelanders showed little hostility toward Christianity and many came to believe they could accept Christ along with their old gods. Many of the early Icelanders were probably like Helgi the Lean, one of the original settlers who, the *Book of Settlements* (paragraph S218) tells us, was "very mixed in his beliefs: he believed in Christ, and yet called on Thor for sea-voyages and in difficult situations."

The conversion of Iceland in the year 999 or 1000 is a remarkable instance of pragmatism and compromise in matters of religion. In the two decades prior to the conversion, four missionaries are known to have gone to Iceland. First was an Icelander named Thorvaldur, who had converted to Christianity in Germany and had gone to Iceland with a German bishop named Frederick. They made themselves disliked and had to flee the country. In 995, Olaf Tryggvason took the Norwegian throne. He was an evangelical Christian, and he wanted to convert all of the Norse peoples to Christianity. In 996, he dispatched one Stefnir Thorgilsson to bring Christianity to the Icelanders. He failed and only aroused opposition. The next year King Olaf sent the German priest Thangbrandur to convert the Icelanders. Thangbrandur succeeded in converting a number of powerful Icelanders, but he also aroused hostility among many pagan Icelanders. He left Iceland in 999 and returned to Norway. King Olaf was outraged at the failure of Thangbrandur's mission and decided to have the Icelanders then in Norway "maimed or killed" because of the report that their fellow Icelanders would not adopt Christianity.

Shortly after Thangbrandur's return to Norway, two leading Icelandic chieftains, Hjalti Skeggjason and Gizurr the White, whom Thangbrandur had converted, arrived at King Olaf's court. They tried to persuade the king not to persecute the Icelanders then in Norway but to let the two of them return to Iceland as missionaries and convert the country to Christianity at the Althing in June. King Olaf apparently agreed to their plan.

At the meeting of the Althing, two parties had formed, those who opposed the adoption of Christianity and those who favored it. Each party had elected its own lawspeaker (presiding officer), and each party declared the other outside of the law. However, after negotiations and some bribery, the two parties agreed to put the decision in the hands of the pagan lawspeaker, Thorgeir, a much respected man. Ari the Learned tells us that "later when men had returned to their booths, Thorgeir lay down and spread his cloak over him, and lay quiet all day and the night following, and spoke never a word" (Gwyn Jones, 1964, p. 107). The next morning, he told the men to proceed to the Law Rock, where he informed them of his decision. He told them, again in the words of Ari (p. 107), that the people would be in a

> sorry plight if men were not to have one law, all of them, in this land; and he put this to men in many ways, how they must never let such a state of affairs come about, maintaining that strife would be the result, so it could be taken as certain that such contention would arise among men that the land would be laid waste by reason of it.

Thorgeir then urged that they "not let those prevail who are most anxious to be at each other's throats, but reach such a compromise in these matters that each will win part of his case, and let all have one law and one faith" (p. 108). He then declared it to be law that all Icelanders were to be Christians and that all were to be baptized. This certainly satisfied the Christians, but to satisfy the pagans he allowed the exposure of infants to continue. In that, he said, "the old laws should stand, and for the eating of horse-flesh too" (p. 108). Thorgeir even allowed sacrifices to the old gods, but only in secret. However, should anyone witness such sacrifice and testify to it, the culprit would be liable to a charge of lesser outlawry (with a punishment of three years banishment).

Thus, Christianity came to Iceland. The sagas and old histories contain no, or very few, instances of belief or religious—as opposed to moral—conflict in Iceland after the conversion. The Reformation came just as peacefully, being enforced from the top down by the Danish authorities. There was no need for persecution; the new faith was formally accepted with hardly a murmur. It is true that Jón Arason and his sons were killed by the Danes, but their deaths are best interpreted as political killings. Bishop Jón in his time and since his beheading is a hero of nationalism, not religion, standing for the opposition of the Icelanders to their treatment by the Danes; that he did not accept the new faith was irrelevant. The witch craze of the seventeenth century was not a religious inquisition either; it was a perverse persecution of individuals thought to be dangerous because of their ability to do evil through magic spells.

From the fifteenth century until the end of the eighteenth, the Icelanders, as I have emphasized repeatedly, lived a particularly terror-filled and miserable existence. During that period, there was a growth of superstitious folktales "passionately concerned with the workings of magic in evil arts" (Benedikz, 1964, p. 23). Many of the folktales from the late sixteenth, seventeenth (especially), and eighteenth centuries have been preserved. Everywhere the people wanted protection from the agents of the devil, but they did not much turn to Jesus, Mary, or the saints for help. One of the ways they protected themselves was by creating the "good master wizard," who became a partial solution to the problem of good and evil in their frightening world. "And out of their distorted memories of the Sagas, the scattered lines of verse from the Eddas which still hung in their minds, and from other more romantic sources, the medieval romances and the *rímur* . . . they gradually built up this outstanding phenomenon of the folklore of modern Iceland, the good master wizard" (p. 23). During the dark centuries, the literary activity of the people was so stifled by horror and hysteria that it manifested itself in the "perverted form" (p. 33) of clumsy folktales of magic, evil, and superstition. This, as much as Christianity, is the heritage that has shaped the supernatural and religious beliefs of modern Icelanders.

Central to the belief system of modern Icelanders are all manner of psychic phenomena: prescience, foretelling of the future; second sight, as the Scots call it, the ability to know what is happening at a distant place or to a distant person; the meaningfulness of dreams; a belief in "hidden people"; a belief that people can communicate with the dead or those absent; and so forth. An example of the kind of tales that have abounded (Jón Árnason, 1866, p. lxxxiv) is about a man who was thought to be very clever and to be virtually infallible in foretelling the deaths of people. Concerning his own death, he would always say, "I am not clear about my death; it is forever veiled in smoke." He died in 1832, suffocated by smoke! Many analogous tales are told about fishing accidents. There is a belief that many of those with psychic abilities have eyebrows that grow together or hairy crosses on their chests—presumably only the men (p. lxxxiv). There remains something uncommon about those with prescience or second sight, and it has always been regarded as a special gift. For example, Snorri the Priest is described in *Njal's Saga* (chapter 114) as being "reckoned the wisest man in Iceland, not counting those who were prescient." One of the reasons why Njal himself had such great authority and why so many people sought his advice was his gift of prescience.

The old literature is filled with psychic phenomena. The average saga contains three or four dreams (Hallberg, 1962, p. 81), most of which prophesy the future. Turville-Petre (1972, p. 30) claims there is a total of some 250 dreams in the extant saga literature. Speaking generally, he observed (p. 30): "Among no people in Europe is the cult of dreams so deeply rooted. In no literature are dream-symbols more sophisticated, nor their interpretation more subtle and intricate." Psychic phenomena have transcended the more formal religious beliefs of Icelanders during pagan, Catholic, and Lutheran times.

The classical literature and the popular folklore partially descended from it have predisposed the Icelanders to a belief in psychic phenomena unique among a universally literate and technologically sophisticated people. The Norwegian psychologist Harald Schjelderup has claimed that spiritualism is more prevalent in Iceland, along with Puerto Rico and Brazil, than anywhere else in the world (Sigurður A. Magnússon, 1977, p. 166). The Lutheran Church of Iceland, as I have pointed out, has been much influenced by spiritualism in the twentieth century, to the dismay of purists (Sigurbjörn Einarsson, 1965, 1967). Books on psychic phenomena outsell purely religious books. The books of Jean Dixon, the American psychic, have been translated into Icelandic and her column appears in the largest daily newspaper, *Morgunblaðið*.

My 1971 interview study was, I believe, the first systematic inquiry into the beliefs of the Icelanders regarding psychic phenomena. Unfortunately, I asked only two questions on the topic. Question 13 was: "Do you believe that it may be possible for some people to communicate with people who are not present? Would you say yes, no, or maybe?" Of the 100 respondents, 50 answered affirmatively, 17 answered negatively, and 33 considered the possibility by suggesting that this might be the case. Question 14 was: "How about with people who have died? Would you say yes, no, or maybe?" To this question 51 answered affirmatively, 10 answered negatively, and 39 gave answers such as maybe, perhaps, and could be. It is striking, I think, that only 10 percent of these adult Icelanders denied that communication with the dead might be possible. Men were more likely than women to answer both questions in the negative.

A later mail survey of a random sample of 1,132 Icelanders between the ages of 30 and 69 carried out by Erlendur Haraldsson (1978) at the University of Iceland in 1974-1975 revealed a great deal about the religious and psychic beliefs and practices of present-day Icelanders. Almost 80 percent of the original sample (902 of the 1,132 persons surveyed) eventually answered the questionnaire, a most impressive rate of return. The topics of the 54 questions on the questionnaire fell into six categories: dreams, psychic experiences (clairvoyance, telepathy, communication with the dead, out-of-body experiences, memories of previous lifetimes, poltergeists, apparitions of "hidden people" and fairies, and so forth), religion (beliefs and practices), visits to psychics, attitudes toward all manner of psychic phenomena, and demographic information. Some of the findings of this enormously interesting study are:

- 64 percent of the sample reported experience with psychic phenomena, 59 percent of the males and 70 percent of the females
- 91 percent believed it possible (37 percent), likely (29 percent), or certain (25 percent) that dreams can reveal the future
- 88 percent believed it is possible (31 percent), likely (26 percent), or certain (31 percent) that some people can foretell the future
- 44 percent believed reincarnation is possible (30 percent), likely (10 percent), or certain (4 percent)
- 55 percent believed the existence of elves or hidden people (*huldúfolk*) is possible (33 percent), likely (15 percent), or certain (7 percent); about the same percentages believed in ghosts (34, 12, and 9 percent, respectively)
- 72 percent believed the existence of accompanying spirits called *fylgjur* (singular *fylgja*) is possible (35 percent), likely (21 percent), or certain (16 percent)
- 52 percent have visited a fortune-teller at some time, but only 28 percent of these claimed to have benefited from the experience
- 41 percent have visited a faith healer, with 91 percent of these believing they benefited from the experience
- 8 percent claimed that they read the Bible often, 59 percent seldom did, and 33 percent never did
- 25 percent often read books dealing with psychic phenomena, 53 percent seldom did, and 22 percent never did
- 88 percent believed that a life after death is possible (20 percent), likely (28 percent), or certain (40 percent)
- 97 percent believed themselves to be very religious (15 percent), somewhat religious (66 percent), or a little religious (19 percent); only 3 percent claimed to be not at all religious.

It is notable that the proportion which is certain about anything is never a majority and usually only a modest minority. The extent of formal education is negatively associated with all manner of supernatural belief, practice, and experience (pp. 146-52).

LITERATURE

The continuity of Icelandic prose and poetry has been attenuated among writers since the Second World War by the internationalization of Icelandic letters and the passing of rhyming and alliterative poetry. But, until the last three decades, there were uniquely well-defined national literary traditions. The emphasis on the graphic portrayal of individual characters (their physical appearance and mental qualities, their abilities and shortcomings) runs through the whole of Icelandic prose for seven centuries. So does a concern with establishing the genealogy of all the characters described.

Even the writing of the national history, most of which has been only serial biography, is characterized by this pattern. Not until 1956, wrote Haraldur Bessason (quoted in Jón Jóhannesson, 1974, p. 360), and the publication of Jóhannesson's *A History of the Old Icelandic Commonwealth* was a major work in Icelandic history published in which "biographical accounts were carefully subordinated to the analysis of . . . social forces and conditions. . . ." Bessason (pp. 360-61) also observed:

> Until the middle of the twentieth century the biographical form may be said to have dominated Icelandic historical writing. Historians were not only inclined to follow their time-honoured Saga traditions but also allowed themselves to be unduly influenced by the fact that in a nation as small as their own every individual receives a wider stage for the personal performance than he would find in a more populous society.

These "Saga traditions" have not only affected the writing of formal history, but they also have affected the writing of memoirs, genealogies, and fiction. Halldór Laxness (quoted by Hallberg, 1962, p. 150) wrote in 1946 that "an Icelandic author cannot live without constantly having the old books in his thoughts."[2] But such is no longer the case—at least not among younger writers.

Let me illustrate one aspect of the continuity of the saga style: the empirical, sparse description of individuals. Indeed, until not very long ago, an Icelandic prose writer could hardly introduce a character without giving a detailed realistic portrait. Let us begin our chronological account with a description of the morose, tenth-century barbarian poet Egill Skalla-Grímsson from *Egil's Saga* (chapter 55), written around 1230:

> Egill had course features: a broad forehead, bushy eyebrows, and a short and extremely thick nose. His long beard covered much of his face, and his chin and jawbone were terribly broad. His neck was so thick and his

shoulders so broad that he stood out from all other men. His expression was harsh and grim when he was angry. He was of great stature, being taller than anyone else. His hair was gray and thick, but he became bald quite young. But as he sat there, as here described, he alternately pulled one of his eyebrows down to his cheek and the other one up to his hair-line. Egill had black eyes and eyebrows.

Another graphic description, one taken almost at random from the sagas of the Icelanders, is that of Snorri the Priest from *Eyrbyggja Saga* (chapter 15):

Snorri was a man of average height and rather slender. He was of hand-some appearance, with regular features, a fair complexion, blond hair, and a red beard. It was not easy to detect whether he liked or disliked a thing. He was a shrewd man and foreseeing in many things. He was unforgiving and revengeful. To his friends he gave good counsel, but his enemies rather thought they felt the cold heartedness of his counsels. . . . He became a great chieftain, but he was rather envied for his prestige since there were many who felt they were not inferior to him as to birth and believed they were better men in regard to strength and proven hardihood.

The thirteenth-century bishop Magnús Gizurarson is described in the historical *Bishops' Sagas* (Leith, 1895, p. 56) as follows:

Magnús was a comely man of face, and rather a tall man in growth, fair-eyed and well-limbed, amiable and pleasant, and noblest of all men in ap-pearance and manners. He was gentle and humble with all, large-minded and steadfast of soul, full of good counsel, attached to his kinsmen, much learned and clear of speech. He was tried and well-experienced in both household affairs and journeys, and he was conciliatory to all men.

Jumping ahead five centuries, one can find *identical* patterns of character description. An Icelandic clergyman (quoted by Hermanns-son, 1925, pp. 53-54) described Eggert Ólafsson (1726-1768), poet, co-author of the most important study of Icelandic society of the eighteenth century, and one of the most admired men of his time, as follows:

He was a tall man, handsome of face, strongly built, excelled in all kinds of sport, and added to his learning an artistic talent. He was resolute, some-what grave, yet in daily intercourse cheerful. He was complete master of his emotions in joy and sorrow. In minor matters he might show excite-ment but in affairs of greater importance he remained calm. He expressed his opinion frankly and generally in slow speech. He was very sensitive as to his dignity and honor, temperate in high degree, most regular in his habits, and generous to those who were in need. He was kind and helpful to his kinsmen when they deserved it. . . . Popular prejudices and errors he tried to eradicate. All his life he kept aloof from quarrels among men, only interfering when he saw the possibility of settling them or bringing about reconciliation.

Jón Thoroddsen published the first modern Icelandic novel in 1850. It is entitled *Piltur og stulka (Lad and Lass)*; it is a country love story. The author was much influenced by the English literature of his time, particularly by Scott and Dickens, but the saga style in his character descriptions and dialogues is unmistakable. Here (1890, pp. 7-8) is how he described a young boy, the major male character:

> Indrid was a handsome, personable boy, and was believed to be stronger than other boys his age. . . . He was sprightly and clever beyond his years in everything except learning the Catechism. . . . Indrid was never so happy as when he had something to whittle; his next greatest pleasure was in tending his father's flock. He was keen of sight and swift of foot, and luckier than most shepherds, often being able to find missing sheep when others had abandoned the search.

Matthías Jochumsson (1835-1920), one of Iceland's greatest poets, once described his father (quoted in Thórðarson, 1946, p. 5) as follows:

> Jochum was of medium height, slender, and red of hair and beard. It grayed a little with age. He was energetic of temperament, so perservering that few were his equals, and so swift and light on his feet that he was an example to others. He had such a healthy chest, that he claimed never to have caught cold. But with all the good health and pluck that he possessed, he had a weak heart and was nervous. . . . He was a hospitable and benevolent man.

A 1945 description of Thórdis Jónsdóttir (1772-1862), the mother of Jón Sigurðsson (the great nineteenth-century scholar and patriot), by the late historian Páll Eggert Ólason (1945-1946, pp. 28-29) is as follows:

> Thórdis was a stately woman, clever and judicious, reknowned for her intelligence and discernment. She was reckoned an excellent teacher, and was knowledgeable about the ancient language. She was of middle height, personable, the face open and intelligent, the eyes small and brownish but full of life. Gentle and good-natured in speech, but authoritative in the house, a woman of few words, but she could be witty as well as sarcastic if she were annoyed. . . . She was a kind woman, helpful and quick to give money to the poor.

Only with difficulty would one find examples of the saga style in current Icelandic fiction, even in the enormous corpus of Halldór Laxness (who was born in 1902).[2] However, Alfgrim's description of his grandmother in Laxness's 1957 novel *The Fish Can Sing* (1966, pp. 30-31) is reminiscent of the old style:

> She was an extremely thin and fragile-looking woman . . . bowed and toothless, with a bit of a cough and red-rimmed eyes. . . . There might sometimes have been a little soot in the wrinkles of her face, and her head would dither slightly when she looked at you with those mild eyes of hers. Her hands were long and bony.

In 1924, Sigurður Nordal published an essay entitled "Continuity in Icelandic Literature," in which he asserted that there is a "continuity in our language and literature from the beginning of Iceland." There is no more striking exemplification of this continuity than the romantic poets of the first half of the nineteenth century, who were nurtured on the national literature and who "were in an unbroken relationship to the poetry of the ninth and tenth centuries" (p. xxv). In a study of Icelandic poets during the years 1800-1940, Richard Beck (1950, p. 1) also observed that the Icelandic poetic tradition "is as old as the nation itself, its roots buried in the ancient German and Scandinavian soil." Sir William A. Craigie (1937, p. 33), a lifelong English student of Icelandic literature, noted that one of the ways in which "Icelandic poetry as a whole" is remarkable is that it has "an unbroken continuity, with little change in the language, from the tenth century to the present day." As an example of the continuity of Icelandic literature, which he contrasted with the English, Craigie noted the "unbroken admiration . . . throughout the centuries" for the 100-stanza poem *Lilja (The Lily)*, composed around 1340 and always regarded as the most perfect poem ever composed in Icelandic. (See also Stefán Einarsson, 1957, pp. 74-76.)

Icelandic poetry from the time of the Vikings until a couple of decades ago has been characterized by an extreme emphasis on form. Alliteration is always central and is used according to precise rules; end rhymes are strictly adhered to, and internal rhyming is important. This is the kind of poetry that Icelanders still buy and read (chapter 5). Henry Wadsworth Longfellow could have been an Icelandic poet if his rhyming and form had been more precise; he deals with many of the sorts of concerns that the pre-1950s Icelandic poets did. This is not surprising; Longfellow was absorbed in ancient Scandinavian literature and even had a dictionary knowledge of Icelandic (Hilen, 1947, p. 105). The Icelandic poetry that flourished during the nineteenth century and, to a lesser extent, during the first half of the twentieth century concerns itself with patriotism, love of the land, admirable people, saga times, independence, and all manner of homely topics. It is empirical, restrained, close to home, nonintellectual, and without literary allusions.

The folklore of Iceland, incredibly abundant for having come from such a small population, is the contribution of the common people to the Icelandic literary tradition. The printed collection of Jón Árnason, only one of three leading collectors of Icelandic folklore in the nineteenth century, fills five huge volumes divided into ten classes: (1) mythic stories, (2) ghost stories, (3) stories of witchcraft, (4) stories of natural phenomena, (5) legends (in the more specific sense), (6) historical legends, (7) stories of outlaws, (8) tales, (9) comic stories, and (10) superstitions.

All of these diverse forms have their roots in pagan Scandinavia. Stories of giants and trolls, for example, are a favorite topic from the earliest Eddic songs to the folklore of the 1970s. Trolls are just giants in the narrow sense, but in the broader sense they are "beings that combine preterhuman strength with demonic malice" (Jón Árnason, 1866, p. lxi)." *Grettir's Saga* and *Erbyggja Saga* from the thirteenth century are the direct ancestors of many of the ghost stories collected during the nineteenth century (p. lxx), and they continue to thrive today. In Craigie's collection of folklore from the five Nordic countries, he observed (1896, p. 440) that "(t)he most impressive ghosts . . . , it will be seen, are those of Iceland, both ancient and modern." A professor of theology told me with enthusiasm about a book of 39 ghost tales, "all about the same ghost." Stories of elves and hidden people, which thrive as much as ghost stories in present-day Iceland, also can be traced back to the beginning. (For modern examples of these phenomena, see Sigurður A. Magnússon, 1977, chapter 7). In Icelandic folklore, the old and the new have always been inseparable. However, as we have already noted, there is remarkably little Christian content in this enormous body of folklore; there is little of the legends of the saints, although the Virgin Mary was popular during the Middle Ages.

ALCOHOL

There is some similarity between the patterns of alcohol use among the Icelanders and the patterns among the American Indians. The Icelanders may drink less than the Indians do and they have not undergone any comparable disruption of their social fabric, but, when Icelanders do drink, they drink relatively large quantities and show marked changes in their behavior. They get very drunk. Few Icelanders drink frequently, partly because of strict governmental regulation of the sale of alcohol and partly because of the cost of alcohol (which is some four or five times what it averages in the United States).

In a mail questionnaire study of the drinking patterns of a sample of 292 young people aged 15, 20, and 25 in Reykjavík (Frímannsson, 1971), inquiry was made into the drinking patterns of the parents of the youth. These patterns can probably be taken as an approximation of those of the Reykjavík population between the ages of 35 and 64. As is shown in table 7-1, only 18 percent of the fathers and 5 percent of the mothers drank as frequently as once a month. Among the fathers, 64 percent drank less frequently than once a month and 17 percent did not drink at all; among the mothers, 37 percent drank less frequently than once a month and a majority of 58 percent did not drink at all. The amount of drinking done outside of Reykjavík is smaller than this, if only because there are no state liquor stores in most communities. (State liquor stores are the only legal source of alcoholic beverages in Iceland.) Alcohol consumption is generally limited to special occasions, holidays, parties, and nights out. A greater proportion of Reykjavík young people drink than do their parents, according to Frímannsson's data.

Dóra Bjarnason (1974, pp. 136-40), from her intimate study of Reykjavík teenagers, observed that " drinking appears to be the rule, rather than the exception among older teenagers." Among the 15-year-olds in Frímannsson's study, a third of the males and a quarter of the females have used alcohol; among those 20 and 25 years old, 90 and 92 percent, respectively, of the males and 83 and 84 percent of the females have. While the young people drink more frequently than their parents do, not more than 15 percent of the male drinkers in any of the three age categories drank as frequently as four times a month and still lower percentages of the females drank that frequently. However, on the occasions when males do drink, they consume great quantities. Table 7-3 shows that more than a third of the large majority of youths who drink averaged more than 15 centiliters of pure alcohol on the three most recent occasions when they drank; this translates into more than 12 ounces of 86-proof whiskey.

Table 7-1. Drinking among Parents of Reykjavík Youth, 1970.
(In Percentages)

	Fathers	Mothers
Drinks once a month or more frequently	18	5
Drinks less frequently than once a month	64	37
Never drinks	17	58
	100	100
	(N = 272)	(N = 273)

Source: Data from Frímannsson, 1971, pp. 26-27.

Table 7-2. Alcohol Use by Reykjavík Youth, 1970.
(In Percentages)

	15-year-olds		20-year-olds		25-year-olds	
	Males	Females	Males	Females	Males	Females
Have used alcohol	38	24	90	83	92	84
Have never used alcohol	62	76	10	17	8	16
	(N = 60)	(N = 62)	(N = 49)	(N = 40)	(N = 39)	(N = 44)

Source: Data from Frímannsson, 1971, p. 28.

Table 7-3. Average Alcohol Consumption on
Three Most Recent Drinking Occasions of Reykjavík Youth, 1970
(In Percentages)

	Males	Females
Less than 4.0 centiliters pure alcohol per occasion	16	47
4.0-7.4 centiliters	20	36
7.5-14.9 centiliters	29	15
More than 15 centiliters	35	1
	100	99
	(N = 102)	(N = 85)

Source: Calculated from Frímannsson, 1971, pp. 43-45.

The rate of traffic offenses involving alcohol is appreciably higher in Iceland (5.4 per 1,000 population in 1974) than in the other Nordic countries—the rates there ranged from a high of 3.6 in Finland to a low of 1.8 per 1,000 population in Norway for the year 1976 (Nordic Council, 1978, p. 281). The relative number of criminal court cases involving alcohol—including drunk driving, smuggling, and other alcohol offenses but excluding violations of "order and peace"—accounted for more than one-third of all criminal cases (15,235 of 43,084) in courts of first instance over the six-year period 1966-1971 (Statistical Bureau of Iceland, 1976, p. 215). My guess is that a large proportion of the conventional crimes in this relatively law-abiding society is alcohol related.

Sporadic excess is an apt description of the predominant drinking patterns of Icelanders. Even though Iceland has long been the *lowest* of the five Nordic countries in per capita consumption of pure alcohol—3.07 liters per capita in 1977 compared with the high of 8.89 liters for Denmark in the same year (Nordic Council, 1979, p. 227)—this is not the impression a superficial observer would have. Unlike elsewhere in the North, over 80 percent of the alcohol consumed is in the form of hard liquor. Few Icelandic men drink more often than occasionally and at special events, but they often drink them-

selves into a state of advanced incapacitation or until they have consumed every ounce available. Icelandic women drink to excess much
less frequently than the men. Nowhere else in the Nordic countries
(with a possible occasional exception in the Faroe Islands) does one
see so much public drunkenness, even of 14, 15, and 16 years old, as
in Iceland on Independence Day (June 17) or on Saturday nights
when the weather is warm. The most lasting impression of a 1975
"Sixty Minutes" television documentary on Iceland was made by
scenes of very drunk Reykjavík youth drinking from their *brennivín*
bottles. Such drunkenness was interpreted as a "social problem" in
an otherwise modern and admirable society. Icelandic parties commonly do not end until all of the liquor on the premises has been
consumed; then the party may move to a place where there are fresh
supplies to be tapped. I was told by an Icelandic editor in 1973 that
the Soviets had stopped serving drinks to visiting Icelandic delega-
tions—part of the courting of this strategically located people—
because of the disastrous effects on their capacity to function. Some
Icelanders even lamented the replacement of propeller aircraft with
jets on the route between Reykjavík and Copenhagen in the mid-
1960s because their speed did not allow sufficient time to get enjoy-
ably drunk on the cheap drinks served on the flight. In Iceland, it is
not at all common to drink modest amounts frequently; there are
few conventional patterns of moderate social drinking. Alcohol is not
integrated into everyday life. It is revealing that, when Frímannsson
(1971) asked his sample of Reykjavík youth about the drinking patterns of their parents, "once a month or more" was the polar category for the *most frequent* drinkers.

As elsewhere in the Nordic countries, except beer-drinking
Denmark, there has been a strong temperance movement since the
last century. In Iceland, the temperance movement culminated in a
1905 decision of the Althing to hold a referendum on total prohibition. In 1908, 60.1 percent of the male voters—women did not get
the franchise until 1915—favored it (Statistical Bureau of Iceland,
1976, p. 235). Prohibition was introduced in 1912, but the sale of
the alcohol still in the country was allowed; total prohibition came in
1915. Iceland was the first country to enact total prohibition, seven
years before the United States. Finland had actually passed prohibition legislation before Iceland, but it had been vetoed by the czar
(Frímannsson, 1971, pp. 20-21).

Prohibition ended in 1922 for a practical reason: the Spanish
threatened to refuse to buy Icelandic fish if the Icelanders did not
buy Spanish wine. However, the importation of alcohol was limited
to wines with an alcohol content not in excess of 21 percent. In

1934, this stipulation was removed, allowing the importation of stronger wines and liquors. However, a prohibition on the importation of beer with an alcoholic content in excess of 2.25 percent alcohol has continued. To this day, one cannot legally buy "normal" beer in Iceland. The rationale for this seeming irrationality is the relationship in the minds of many Nordics of the drinking of beer and *brennivín*. The availability of beer, it is thought, just enhances the appetite for the more potent *brennivín*.

The sagas describe enough incidents of drunkenness to indicate that sporadic excess was not uncommon among the ancient Icelanders. The admonitions against excess in drink found in the *Hávamál* (*Words of the High One*), put to parchment in the thirteenth century, contain numerous apothegms against excessive drinking (Taylor and Auden, 1970, pp. 37-60). Some examples include these.

> A more tedious burden than too much drink
>   A traveler cannot carry. (Number 15)
>
> A man knows less the more he drinks,
>   Becomes a befuddled fool. (Number 16)
>
> Best is the banquet one looks back on after,
>   And remembers all that happened. (Number 18)
>
> Drink your mead, but in moderation,
>   Talk sense or be silent. (Number 23)
>
> A gluttonous man who guzzles away,
>   Brings sorrow on himself. (Number 24)
>
> Be not overwary, but wary enough,
>   First, of the foaming ale. (Number 124)

Niels Horrebow, the Danish astronomer who spent the years 1749-1751 in Iceland, made observations (1758, p. 112) about Icelandic drinking patterns that are similar to those I made more than two centuries later and that are typical of the kind of observations made by numerous travelers in the intervening years. He wrote:

> Generally speaking, there is not a more sober people than the Icelanders. . . . When they come to the factories about business, they indulge themselves with brandy, and other liquors. A merchant or stranger, on first coming to these places, may be induced to deem them a drunken, beastly people; and I myself was almost of that opinion, till I came into the country to be better aquainted with their manner of living. It is certain that at the factories which they resort to but once a year, they drink brandy to excess; for it comes but seldom in their way, and is a great treat to them.

Uno von Troil noted (1780, p. 91) that the Icelanders have "no aversion to a bottle if they can find opportunity." The Scottish biologist W. J. Hooker kindly observed in a footnote (1813, pp. 135-136) to a description of a tipsy clergyman that regular drinking was not really characteristic of the Icelanders and that was why they became so easily drunk. The same observation was made by his fellow Scot Ebenezer Henderson (1818, pp. 94-95), who wrote a few years later:

> Drinking is certainly a vice by no means common among the natives of Iceland. Neither their means nor their opportunities admit of their indulging in it to the same extent with the inhabitants of other countries; yet it cannot be denied, that the factories sometimes present scenes of drunkenness, when the peasants repair thither for the purpose of trade; though even then it is not so much the quanitity of liquor they drink, as their being unaccustomed to the use of it, that occasions this temporary derangement.

Many of the multitude of author-travelers who subsequently went to Iceland commented on the drunkenness of Icelanders, but they also generally made the observation that it was of an occasional nature. Sometimes it was isolated as one of the few vices of the Icelanders; such was the case with Lord Dufferin (1910, p. 82), an intemperate admirer of the Icelanders who traveled to Iceland in 1855, and for Charles S. Forbes (1860, p. 312), who traveled there a few years later and made a typical observation (it heads this chapter). C. W. Paijkull, (1866, pp. 103), the young Swedish geologist from Uppsala, observed that the Icelanders drank less than the Swedes but drank more on the special occasions when they did drink (just as they do today). J. Ross Browne (1867, p. 437) simply noted that Icelanders were "too often drunk."

There is one section of the population that has been particularly prone to drunkenness: the clergy. During the years 1741-1745, Ludvig Harboe, the clergyman sent by the Danish king to investigate the ability of Icelandic youth to read and their knowledge of Christian teachings, found a number of the priests, who should have been teaching the young, to be drunkards (Hallgrímsson, 1925). Jón Steingrímsson in his *Autobiography* (1956) made several gentle observations about the drunkenness of his fellow clergymen during the mid-eighteenth century. A century later, James Nicoll (1841, p. 212), an English traveler, reported that many members of the clergy were still drunkards. In the twentieth century, however, members of the clergy have not been particularly noted for their tippling, just as they are no longer noted for their fathering of illegitimate children.

One hypothesis, and a rather strained one, has been put forth by Hjalmar Lindroth (1937, p. 116), a temperance advocate, to explain "the central position that aquavit [*brennivín*], or drinking in general, occupied in the life of the Northern peoples." According to him:

Brennevín is the heir of mead and, particularly in Iceland, of ale. And ale was a holy beverage, a sanctified drink which did not produce the requisite feeling or state of mind in the festal hall until proper quantities of it had been imbibed. He who could not consume large draughts was simply excluded from the innermost social circle. Even the Christian ministers continued to bless the brew. Such things stick.

Even if we regard Lindroth's hypothesis as farfetched, there are several long-term observations that we can make about Icelandic drinking patterns. The use of alcohol is seldom a part of daily life. It is largely consumed on special occasions, on holidays, and at parties. The emphasis is on hard liquor, not wine or beer, which is not even sold in present-day Iceland. Men, and to a much lesser extent women, have a tendency to drink until they are in a state of total incapacitation. And there is an extraordinary general tolerance for this kind of behavior when it is occasional. This is a manifestation of the pervasive tolerance that characterizes the Icelanders, the same tolerance that accepts illegitimacy, common-law marriages, modest embezzlement, minor nepotism, and smuggling consumer goods from abroad.

CHAPTER 8

Values

If we are to engage in the tracings of cultural genealogies, and to look for the origin of ideas and cultural themes in Hesoid and Plato, then we have an equal duty to look as best we can at the folk underpinnings of European civilization.

Rosalie Wax (1969)

In [ancient] Iceland . . . all the leading families were animated by a high sense of pride and a pervading sentiment of equality. This love of equality remains among the sons of the old Norsemen both in Iceland and in Norway and is indeed stronger there than anywhere else in Europe.

James Bryce (1901)

In no modern Western society has there been as much obvious continuity with a distant past as in Iceland. But this continuity is rapidly being attenuated by the pressures of the modernization of the society and the internationalization of the culture. In conclusion to this book, let me give a brief overview of Icelandic value orientations with concern for their continuity and how they are changing. Values may be vague and abstruse and difficult to get hold of, but this does not make an attempt to articulate them any less significant. A sophisticated definition of *value orientations* is that of Florence Kluckhohn, who defined them as "complex but definitely patterned (rank-ordered) principles, resulting from the transactional interplay of three analytically distinguishable elements of the evaluative process—the cognitive, the affective, and the directive elements—which give order and direction to the ever-flowing stream of human acts and thoughts as these relate to the solution of common human problems" (Kluckhohn and Strodbeck, 1961, p. 4).

EGALITARIANISM

There is perhaps no more pervasive value held throughout Icelandic history than egalitarianism, and this has been true since the founding of the society.[1] Icelandic egalitarianism rose out of the very conditions of life that faced the Icelanders from the beginning. Frontier life produces an independence of spirit because the cake of custom is broken and the old authorities lose their legitimacy; a consequence of this independence is the refusal to turn over to someone else any economic surplus and so there is no capital for establishing a dominant leisure class. Frontier conditions, as the Lenskis (1978, p. 229) pointed out, tend to "break down the sharp inequalities and exploitive patterns characteristic of agrarian societies." These tendencies were intensified by the harshness of the environment and the closeness to sheer survival that characterized the lives of the Icelanders for a millennium. Also, the pioneering Icelanders did not have to face the complexities of interaction with an indigenous people in their new land.

In modern Icelandic society, equality could even be singled out as the most dominant value orientation. It pervades the mass media and literature, and it shapes the mode of social interaction (Dóra Bjarnason, 1974, pp. 36-39). This in no sense means that Icelanders do not make invidious distinctions among themselves, that there are not vaguely defined social classes, that certain occupations (those involving high levels of education) are not more highly evaluated than others (p. 87), or that the schools that prepare the young for high-status occupations are not disproportionately filled by the children of the more educated (Broddason, 1974). This is all true. Yet, there are few things Icelanders believe more about themselves than that theirs is a country where there is equality among interacting individuals and equality of opportunity, even if some people have more money and more education than others. Icelanders with high occupational status continually claim they have a cousin or another relative who is a seaman; nearly all adults had a grandfather who was a farmer. Barbershop owner Páll Sigurðsson told me that on his passport he gives his occupation as "director" because of the low status of barbers in England and Scotland, where haircuts cost only "a third" what they do in Iceland. Truck driver Pétur Pétursson expressed pride in the vehicle he owned—most taxi and truck drivers in Iceland own the vehicles they drive—and, like most of those similarly situated, he has an entrepreneurial, not a worker's, ideology.

This pervasive belief in equality is probably declining as a result of increasing awareness in the society of how much material, educa-

tional, and sexual inequality there in fact is. Table 8-1 lists the declared incomes for 1976 of men and women in fifteen occupational
categories. Income differentials are large, even if they are smaller
than in most other modern societies.

The Icelandic sociologist Thorbjörn Broddason (1974) wrote a
paper entitled "On the Myth of Social Equality in Iceland," in which
he claimed that the pervasive belief in social equality is "largely un-
founded," that the arguments supporting the belief in equality are
"better construed as explanations for the lack of consciousness of inequality," and that Icelandic society is becoming more similar to
other western European nations. All of this is clearly true, yet *relative* to any other modern society Iceland remains radically egalitarian
in ideology. Even Broddason (1974, p. 1) recognized this when he
wrote: "It is not argued that social divisions in Iceland are in any

Table 8-1. Mean Declared Incomes for Selected Occupations in Iceland, 1976
(In United States Dollars)

Occupation	Males' Income (N)	Females' Income (N)
Doctors and dentists	$26,265 (582)	$14,254 (14)
Trawler captains (including coxswains)	18,378 (358)	13,984 (2)
Fishing boat captains (including whale boats)	14,714 (1,364)	7,000 (3)
Employees of Energoproject and Sigöld works	13,097 (553)	7,416 (42)
Teachers and principals	12,951 (1,808)	6,546 (513)
Employees of banks, savings and loan associations, and insurance companies	12,930 (1,158)	5,368 (961)
Employees of Icelandic associations	12,573 (683)	5,454 (44)
Civil servants (except those mentioned in other categories)	12,443 (5,977)	5,103 (1,776)
Municipal employees (except those mentioned in other categories)	11,719 (1,760)	5,011 (767)
Trawlermen (except captains)	11,508 (853)	5,665 (5)
Employees of the cooperatives, political parties, political papers, et cetera	11,449 (627)	4,459 (248)
Truck and taxi drivers	10,665 (2,793)	6,843 (17)
Domestic servants and charwomen (excluding those in health facilities)	10,492 (86)	3,930 (620)
Employees of hospitals, old age homes, childrens' homes, asylums, and related institutions (including midwives, et cetera)	9,832 (941)	4,573 (3,487)
Crews of fishing boats, including repairmen on land	9,438 (3,616)	4,449 (42)
Cleaning men and women, window washers	8,686 (55)	4,292 (293)
Municipal workers, skilled craft workers, et cetera	7,427 (1,649)	2,427 (344)
Food handlers	4,654 (5,766)	3,086 (7,670)

Source: Calculated from data in Statistical Bureau of Iceland, *Hagtíðindi,* 1977, p. 182.
Based on an average of 185 krónur to 1 dollar, the mean exchange rate for 1976.

way as pronounced as in other Western European countries. Nor do we expect them to become so in the near future. But what we are saying is that, while Iceland is not a 'class society' in the full sense of the term, . . . neither may it be equated with a Rousseauan paradise of equality."

ACHIEVEMENT

As is perhaps inherent in egalitarian frontier societies, the Icelanders place great value on achievement and success. Here again the similarity between Icelanders and Americans is striking. For example, in her (1974, pp. 3-4) study of Reykjavík youth, Dóra Bjarnason observed that they were "extremely achievement oriented, viewing educational and occupational goals mainly as instrumental to material advancement." She also noted that "the different socioeconomic background of the teenagers appeared to make hardly any difference to their expectations and ambitions." Sigurður A. Magnússon (1977, pp. 161-62), with his more literary-humanist orientation, called this same value "excellence," and used it as a synonym for "fame and fortune." He observed that, in "the Icelandic hierarchy of values," fame and fortune "precede honor when the need arises." This emphasis on achievement (excellence) Magnússon called "the supreme ideal of Icelandic culture" (p. 161). In my interview study, I asked: "Which of the qualities on this card [intelligent, good-natured, ambitious, stable] do you value most in people? Please rank order them from one to four" (appendix A, question 15). "Ambitious" had the highest average rank order, and 51 of the 99 respondents who answered the question chose this quality as *most* valued.

ACTIVITY AND WORK

Few characteristics of the 100 Icelanders I interviewed impressed me as much as how much they worked. This was true both of their work on their jobs and their work in their homes. A large proportion of Icelanders build their own homes or do a large share of the work themselves. Given the choice of more leisure or more work, the Icelanders usually prefer more work. Among the 56 families that Björn Björnsson (1971, p. 115) interviewed, he noted an attitude "which counts every spare hour 'an hour wasted.'" A recent OECD economic survey (1978, p. 14) made the observation that the average number of hours worked in Iceland "are very high by comparison with other OECD countries." Such an attitude toward work is comprehensible in a society where life has been difficult, where no leisure class has ever developed, where manual labor has never been stigmatized, and where material aspirations are very high.

FREEDOM AND DEMOCRACY

Although democracy and freedom are analytically distinct (Robin Williams, Jr., 1970, pp. 479-84, 492-94), people tend to link them together. When they were asked what were the "two best things about living in Iceland" (appendix A, question 8), 37 percent of the sample mentioned that Iceland was a democratic and/or a free country, the most frequent by far of the 26 different "best things" volunteered by the respondents. Freedom and democracy are as much dominant values in Iceland as in any other Scandinavian or Anglo-American society.

NATIONALISM AND PATRIOTISM

It does not take very much experience with Icelanders to become aware that they are a vigorously patriotic and nationalistic people. This characteristic is sometimes disdained by foreigners who know the Icelanders well. Many Icelanders see themselves as a uniquely literate and poetic people, more knowledgeable about their history and more intelligent than other people. Some Icelanders, however, are able to make fun of this ethnocentrism.

TOLERANCE

As I have pointed out several times throughout this book, the Icelanders are an extraordinarily tolerant people. They manifest a tolerance in moral, religious, and intellectual matters that is pervasive and goes deep. The only exception is in politics, and it *is* a striking exception. Perhaps this tolerance is related to the strong communal nature of the Icelanders and their strong primordial sentiments, which are similar to the feelings people have toward kin. Also part of the explanation may be the fear Icelanders have of making enemies, a characteristic noted by Burton (1875, volume 1, p. 142) over a century ago. In a small country like Iceland, the person one offends today may be one's in-law or workmate tomorrow. Another factor is that Iceland is more a "shame culture" than a "guilt culture." "Guilt cultures" prevail in Western societies in which Christianity is more deeply rooted than in Iceland (Sigurður A. Magnússon, 1977, pp. 171-72). Icelanders do not want to confess their sins—they just do not want anybody to know about them. They do not have guilt feelings to project into others.

The conservative attitudes that the Icelanders express on abortion (appendix A, question 25) and on homosexuality (question 26) do not negate or even qualify the pervasive and deep-going tolerance asserted here. Of the interview sample, 52 of the 100 respondents opposed abortion in the early stages, 34 approved, and 14 had no opinion or qualified their answers. But there is no stigma to having an illegitimate child, and, in almost all cases, there is a mother, a sister, or a cousin who will foster an inconvenient child. Few Icelanders really comprehend the "modern reasons" for having an abortion. The conservative stand on homosexuality—only 49 of the 100 believed that homosexuals should be treated the "same as anyone else," 20 answered that they should not be, and 31 gave "I don't know" or qualified answers—results from the fact that giving rights to homosexuals was not at all a salient issue in Iceland in the early 1970s. The figures actually mean little. Many respondents expressed the belief that homosexuals need "a doctor" or "treatment," but none expressed any hostility toward them; however, many of the respondents expressed a lack of comprehension of, or distanced themselves, from the topic. It was a subject beyond the ken of most of the respondents.

EXPERIENCE

Sigurður A. Magnússon (1977, p. 162) observed that Icelanders have a strong craving for all kinds of experience; this craving finds an "outlet in travel and adventure, scholarly and artistic pursuits and all manner of 'licentious' living." He went on to observe that this is no modern phenomenon but "goes back to the dawn of Icelandic history." In most of the sagas, the major characters are always going abroad for one reason or another. Modern Icelanders, too, are enormously eager to travel outside of their country and do so when they can. In 1976, according to the official statistics (*Hagtíðindi*, 1977, p. 36), 60,000 Icelanders traveled abroad, a figure equal to 30 percent of the population. Of the 100 Icelanders I interviewed, 53 had been abroad at least once, and a large minority had been abroad a number of times (appendix A, question 7). Fourteen of the 100 volunteered as one of "the two worst things" about living in Iceland (question 9) Iceland's isolation, its distance from other lands.

EMPIRICISM

Like all of the Nordic peoples, the Icelanders are predominantly empirical—not ideological or theoretical or philosophical—in their approach to experience. They are more concerned with the immediately apprehended than with underlying structures or the unseen component of things. A major and pervasive exception to their otherwise empirical orientation to the world is their concern with psychic experiences of all sorts, a characteristic not much shared by their Scandinavian cousins.

MATERIALISM

The Icelanders, who have only become affluent since the 1950s, have few inhibitions about indulging their desire for consumer goods. Icelanders tend to live to the material maximum that their income affords. Considering that per capita income is not at the very highest level and that consumer goods, in general, are more expensive than in any other modern society, their expenditures on consumer goods— houses, automobiles, appliances, clothes—are strikingly high. Icelanders, for example, have more spacious houses and more automobiles than the more affluent Danes and Norwegians (Nordic Council, 1978, pp. 152, 212). Part of the explanation of this materialism is the high level of inflation that has been a constant accompaniment of advanced modernization. Indeed, materialism might be better treated as a consequence of living in an inflationary economy than as a value.

ICELANDIC AND AMERICAN VALUES

Icelandic values bear a certain "family resemblance" to American values, but this is not surprising since both are new societies, or frontier societies, as I pointed out in chapter 1. A comparison of Icelandic values to American values is revealing. Let us look at the systematic presentation put forth by Robin Williams, Jr. (1970, pp. 438-504). He discussed fifteen dominant American value orientations to which I, in turn, posed this question: to what extent are these also dominant Icelandic value orientations?[2] Several of the values are even more dominant in Icelandic culture than in American culture; there is a crude similarity between the two cultures' values in most cases; and only one of the values is clearly less dominant in Iceland. In table 8-2, the fifteen values being compared are listed together with my estimates of the comparative extent to which each may be considered a dominant Icelandic value. Here it should be noted that the concern is not with similarities in behavior but with the extent to which there is similarity in the patterned principles of the desirable.

I have already discussed a number of these values as dominant Icelandic values. In five of the fifteen cases, I would argue that the "American" value orientations are more dominant in Icelandic culture than in American culture. This is true of achievement, equality, and nationalism-patriotism. Also, the value of external conformity is probably stronger in Icelandic culture than in American culture, and it is related to the value of equality. As Toqueville noticed in America during the 1830s, pressures toward conformity are likely to be strong in egalitarian societies. While Icelanders are clearly less nationalistic and patriotic (or, rather, ethnocentric) than they were in the past, these traits are still more dominant in Icelandic culture than in American. Racism and related group-superiority themes are also stronger than in America; modern Icelanders are naively color conscious. They are sensitive to the presence of blacks, southern

Table 8-2. American Value Orientations Compared with
Icelandic Value Orientations

American Value	More Dominant in Icelandic Culture	About the Same	Less or Not Dominant in Icelandic Culture
Achievement and success	+		
Activity and work		+	
Moral orientation			+
Humanitarian mores		+	
Efficiency and practicality		+	
Progress		+	
Material comfort		+	
Equality	+		
Freedom		+	
External conformity	+		
Science and secular rationality		+	
Nationalism and patriotism	+		
Democracy		+	
Individual personality		+	
Racism and related group-superiority themes	+		

Source: American value orientations from Robin Williams, Jr., 1970, pp. 438-504.

Europeans, and even deeply tanned northern Europeans. The pressure exerted by the Icelanders in the past to keep black military personnel from serving at United States military installations in the country is only an official example of their almost innocent racial xenophobia. Icelanders also have the tendency, although this is abating, to regard themselves as culturally superior to other people. The ethnic cosmopolitanism that has so penetrated the cultures of the other Scandinavian countries and of the United States since the Second World War has affected Iceland to a lesser extent. The only dominant American value orientation that is *not* a dominant Icelandic value is moral orientation. Icelanders may be pragmatic, emotional, or rational in their approach to human behavior, but they do not tend to be idealistic or moralistic. As I have already suggested, this may be interpreted as a consequence of being a "shame culture," one in which no Puritan ethic or its equivalent has penetrated deeply.

A FINAL CONCLUSION

Out of my study of the Icelandic experience has come an awareness of how much cultural continuity manifests itself in all modern societies and how much contemporary social scientists have tended to underestimate the forces of folk cultures and of the persistence of elements of traditional cultures and social structures. However, these forces are sometimes recognized in the semirespectable concept of national character. Many of the cultural and structural differences, say, between France and Spain or between England and Scotland are manifestations of the inertia of old patterns. From at least early medieval times, many strands of cultural persistence have been evident among modern peoples; medievalists are most conscious of this continuity, while sociologists seem to neglect it. (See Morrill, 1967, pp. 1-18; Burns, 1948, pp. 9-16; and Heer, 1963.) A penchant for philosophical pessimism, for example, has characterized Germans from at least the twelfth century, just as philosophical empiricism has characterized the English for as long (Heer, 1963, pp. 278-91). A comparison between "the West" and "the East" makes the persistence of fundamentally different values even more obvious (see Northrop, 1946, especially pp. 312-74; and Hsu, 1970). Since antiquity the West has emphasized the unseen or the theoretical component of culture, whereas the East has emphasized the immediately apprehended or the empirical. The uniqueness, perhaps even the survival, of the Jews among Western peoples for two millennia is partly the result of the persistence of their messianism—their basic optimism about being able to make a better world, their intellectualism, and their moralistic-legalistic orientation toward behavior (van den Haag, 1969, pp. 38-46).

In the interpretation of the development of Western societies, the influences of folk cultures have been underestimated by modern social scientists in a way that was not characteristic of their nineteenth-century predecessors, who used evolutionary approaches to the study of society but so frequently overstated their case. Louis Hartz has speculated that the smoother development of democratic politics among the Germanic peoples needs to be partially attributed to certain protodemocratic elements in the Germanic folk cultures.[3] Indeed, these were pointed out by Tacitus in the first century A.D. The freedom of the English that Thomas Paine wrote about and the hoary belief of the Swedes in their tradition of liberty go back to times far before the political refinement of such ideas during the seventeenth and eighteenth centuries. Another manifestation of the persistence of tribal values and one that was recognized by some nineteenth-century students of society (and which is exemplified by Iceland) is the general failure of Latin-Christian conceptions of marriage and family to overcome very different Germanic institutions (Sumner, 1968, pp. 336-54).

Indeed, going to an even more general level, I might pose the question of whether the Protestant Reformation cannot be viewed as essentially a movement of Germanic values in opposition to Latin-Christian values carried by the Church of Rome. Rosalie Wax (1969, p. 117) suggested that an indigenous "super Protestant ethos" was well developed in twelfth- and thirteenth-century Scandinavians, with "their scorn of magic, general hard-mindedness, and their emphasis on implacable fate."

The anthropologist Robert Redfield (1955, 1956) wrote much on what he called sometimes "the great tradition" and "the little tradition," sometimes "high culture" and "folk culture" and sometimes "the learned tradition" and "the popular tradition." The former is the tradition of theology, philosophy, and literature—a tradition carefully and self-consciously cultivated and refined—the latter is the tradition of "the little people" and "is for the most part taken for granted and not submitted to much scrutiny or considered refinement and improvement" (1956, p. 70). But predominant in Iceland has been a refined folk tradition, perhaps unique in the world, a type that Redfield did not consider.

NOTES

Notes

CHAPTER 1

1. In the same way, M. I. Finley (1978) has attempted to write an anthropological account of ancient Greek society from a close reading of the *Iliad* and the *Odyssey*.

CHAPTER 2

1. A number of Latin American countries unilaterally extended their economic jurisdiction to 200 miles from their coasts during the 1940s after two proclamations by United States president Harry S. Truman in 1945 supported conservation and the utilization of the resources of the United States continental shelf and coastal fisheries. The 200-mile distance was set by Chile and Peru in 1947 because the richest fishing grounds extended to 200 miles off their coasts (See Hjertonsson, 1973). Yet, Iceland's extension of its fishery limits violated the traditional law of the sea or, rather, that version of the law that has long been accepted by the countries of northwestern Europe. The classic statement of this tradition is Hugo Grotius's account of maritime law in *Mare liberum* (1609), which holds that the high seas cannot be possessed and therefore must belong to all humankind. In the United Nations and other international bodies, Iceland supported the newly emerging "progressive law of the sea" as elaborated by the developing nations. Icelanders distinguished the "progressive" law from the "old colonial school of thought" descending from Grotius. The developing countries wanted to exploit the economic potential of their coastal seas and seabeds and feared competition from technically more advanced nations; Iceland maintained that control over its coastal seas was essential to the nation's survival.

2. In 1973, there were only 485 *glíma* participants registered among the 48,375 members of the Icelandic Federation of Sports Associations (Statistical Bureau of Iceland, 1976, p. 229).

3. There are other persistent Icelandic values, too, but I don't believe they belong to this configuration. For example, the belief in prescience, second sight, and other psychic phenomena has been characteristic of the Icelanders from the beginning.

4. Here I am thinking of the writings of the radical English Puritans.

CHAPTER 3

1. The Icelandic geologist Sigurður Thorarinsson first pointed this out to me. Ireland, until the time of the great famine of the 1840s, had a relatively benign demographic history compared with Iceland. See Connell, 1950.

2. Sturla Fridriksson, personal communication, 16 September 1974.

3. Closest are England and Wales and Finland during the nineteenth century. See population figures in B. R. Mitchell, 1975, pp. 19-27.

4. A census was taken in New France in 1666, but this involved only 3,215 persons and can hardly be regarded as a national census. See Canada, 1931, volume 1, p. 32.

5. When the distribution of ages by single years is compared with what might be expected by assuming complete accuracy in reporting, the following was obtained: 11.4 percent of the population was enumerated in the first year of life and at ages ending in 0, the expected—assuming complete accuracy—would be very close to 10 percent; 9.6 percent were enumerated at ages exactly divisible by 5, expected would be 10 percent; 40.0 percent were enumerated at other even-numbered ages, expected 40 percent; and 39.0 percent at odd-numbered ages not exactly divisible by 5, expected 40 percent. See Smith and Zopf, 1976, pp. 151-56.

6. Most of the statistics in this closing section are from official statistics, the sources of which have already been cited.

Chapter 4

1. Among well-known Icelandic clergymen who were sacked for their sexual activities were Magnús Ólafsson í Laufási (1573-1636), Magnús Jónsson á Kvennabrekku (1635-1684), and Jón Thorláksson (1744-1819).

2. Arngrímur Jónsson (1568-1648), called "the learned," seriously challenged the veracity of these accounts, but they are not wholly fabrications. See J. Benediktsson, 1943.

Chapter 5

1. But newspaper circulation in Denmark is less than two-thirds that of Iceland, 362 compared with 555 copies per 1,000 population per day for 1977. Denmark has, by far, the lowest newspaper circulation in the Scandinavian countries (Nordic Council, 1979, p. 296).

2. Three of those interviewed were to some degree mentally disorganized or slow-witted, but this did not seem to me to be a reason for excluding them from the sample.

3. I supplied all of the respondents with pencil and paper so that they could write down the literary names themselves. A number of the Icelandic writers have similar names and a few are known by two names; I wanted to make sure I got the names correctly. Sometimes I contributed my own knowledge about whether a particular foreign writer was living or dead. In a few instances, when neither the respondent nor I was sure, I asked for an additional name. If a writer was dead and the respondent put him among the living, I later gave credit, when needed, to the score for the deceased foreign writers—and the other way around. I spent much time coaxing out the names of foreign writers; sometimes, I fear, I even helped my struggling respondents with a name when they were close to it.

Chapter 6

1. Franklin D. Scott has suggested that it might have been more appropriate in Table 6-1 to use Norwegian rather than Swedish examples. Norwegian (particularly *landsmål*) is closer to Icelandic than Swedish; and, to a greater extent than Swedish, it reflects a similar effort to use words based on native roots rather than to adopt international words. For example, television becomes *fjernsyn* (but *televisjon* is also used), captain is *skipsfører* (but also *kaptein*), democracy is *folkestyre* (but also *demokrati*), and telephone is *telefon*, but to call someone is (idiomatically) to *slå på tråden* (thread).

2. And occasionally by *h* in Faroese; for example, Thursday is *hósdagur.*

3. The importance of isolation and internal contact for the historical stability of language is illustrated by the Inupik dialect of Eskimo and the Polynesian languages. Spoken Inupik is almost the same in northern Alaska as in Greenland even though the Eskimo groups have been separated for almost a millennium (Katzner, 1975, pp. 256-57). There remains a certain degree of mutual intelligibility among the speakers of the Polynesian languages of the South Pacific in spite of their having been separated for over 3,000 years (Katzner, 1975, p. 26).

4. Factors 2, 3, and 4 also help explain the high degree of linguistic retentiveness of Icelanders in Canada, appreciably greater than that of the Norwegians, Swedes, and Danes. See Haugen, p. 290.

5. The only exception to this pattern was the National Library, where the card catalog indexed Icelanders by their patronymics; however, in 1974, the National Library reverted to the traditional practice.

6. Note how archaic the names seem in the index to some history of early England, such as Whitelock, 1952, pp. 249-56.

Chapter 7

1. At least, none that I have read.

2. However, in his 1952 novel *Gerpla*, Laxness satirized the saga cycle. This book has been translated into English, with the title *The Happy Warriors* (1958).

Chapter 8

1. An exception to this egalitarian spirit in Iceland was the holding of slaves during the early period of the settlement. See Carl Williams, 1937.

2. I made this same comparison between Swedish and American values (1970, pp. 283-90) and came up with quite different results.

3. In a conversation with Hartz in the fall of 1971.

APPENDIXES

Appendix A

The Interview Schedule

Now, I want to ask you a number of different kinds of questions. Your answers and comments will be used in helping me understand Iceland and the Icelanders. Everything you say to me will, of course, be held in confidence.

1. How do you think things are in Iceland now compared with when you were a child? Would you say things are better, things are worse, or things are about the same? How?

2. What organizations (unions, political parties, et cetera) do you belong to?

3. Which of the peoples listed on this card do you believe are the most like Icelanders? Which least? Please rank the following six peoples from 1 to 6 in the order of their similarity to Icelanders.

> a. Americans
> b. British (English)
> c. Danes
> d. Faroese
> e. Irish
> f. Norwegians

4. What two living Icelanders do you most admire? (What two Icelanders do you most admire who are not politicians?)

5. What two deceased Icelanders do you most admire?

6. Which of the following statements on this card best expresses your belief in God? Please read all four before you answer.

> a. I do not believe in any God.
> b. I believe in God, though not necessarily
>   the Christian God.
> c. I believe in the Christian God.
> d. I don't know what I believe.

7. Have you ever left Iceland? Yes or no? If yes, please tell me all of the countries you have visited.

8. What are the two best things about living in Iceland, aside from the lovely weather, your family, and your friends?

9. What are the two worst things about living in Iceland, aside from the exceptions noted in the previous question?

10. Have you ever written anything that has been published in a newspaper, magazine, or book? If yes, what?

11. Are you related to any of the great Icelanders from the time of Egill Skalla-Grímsson to the present? If yes, whom?

213

12. Do you believe girls should be brought up about the same as boys in most ways, or do you believe girls should be brought up differently in most ways?

13. Do you believe that it may be possible for some people to communicate with people who are not present? Would you say yes, no, or maybe?

14. How about with people who have died? Would you say yes, no, or maybe?

15. Which of the qualities on this card do you value most in people? Please rank order them from 1 to 4.

> a. intelligent (*gáfur*)
> b. good-natured (*góðmennska*)
> c. ambitious (*metnaður*)
> d. stable (*stöðuglyndi*)

16. Have you read a book in the past month? Yes or no? If yes, how many?

17. Please tell me the names of the last two books you have read?

18. How many books, approximately, have you read in the past year?

19. How many books would you estimate to be in this house?

20. Aside from all their "politicking," do you believe that most of the leaders of the political parties have the well-being of the country at heart? Would you say yes or no?

21. What work did your father have at about age 35 or 40?

22. What work did your father's father have at about age 35 or 40?

23. What work do you do? What does your (husband, wife) do?

24. What formal education have you had?

25. Do you believe that any woman should be allowed to have an abortion if she wants it, assuming she is in the early stages of pregnancy?

26. Do you believe a homosexual should be treated the same as anyone else?

27. Do you believe Icelanders are successful when they go to other countries like America, Canada, Australia, Sweden, and Denmark?

28. Which of the countries on this card would you wish to move to, if you had to leave Iceland? Please rank these six countries from 1 to 6:

> a. America
> b. Canada
> c. Australia
> d. Sweden
> e. Denmark
> f. Norway

29. In which saga do each of the following characters appear most prominently?

> a. Njal of Bergthorsknoll
> b. Guðrún Ósvífursdóttir
> c. Grettir Ásmundsson
> d. Helga the Fair
> e. Gunnar of Hlíðarendi

30. Can you name five living Icelandic poets and novelists? Please write them down on this piece of paper.

31. Can you name five deceased Icelandic poets and novelists? Please write them down.

32. Can you name five living foreign poets and novelists? Please write them down.

33. Can you name five deceased foreign poets and novelists? Please write them down.

34. With what country do you associate each of the following playwrights?

> a. Holberg
> b. Shaw
> c. Ibsen
> d. Strindberg
> e. O'Neill

35. With what country do you associate each of the following deceased authors?

a. Austin
b. Balzac
c. Dickens
d. Faulkner
e. Goethe

f. Hemingway
g. London
h. Pasternack
i. Shakespeare
j. Tolstoy

Appendix B

The Interview Sample

Name	Year of Birth	Residence	Occupation
Agnar Kristjánsson	1939	Reykjavík	worker
Andrés Kr. Guðlaugsson	1932	Reykjavík	carpenter
Ásgeir G. Överby	1944	Ísafjörður	seaman
Ásmundur Ólafsson	1937	Reykjavík	grocery store employee, carpenter
Bárður Guðmundsson	1950	Ísafjörður	technical school student
Bergur Sæmundsson	1923	Hvolsvöllur	bus driver
Bjarni Helgason	1930	Hvolsvöllur	machinist
Brynjólfur Gíslason	1938	Stafholtstungnahreppur	clergyman
Dúi Sigurjónsson	1933	Reykjavík	carpenter
Eiríkur Steinthórsson	1948	Reykjavík	truck driver
Elvar Ingason	1941	Ísafjörður	house painter
Erlendur Svavarsson	1942	Reykjavík	salesman, musician, actor
Friðfinnur Friðfinnsson	1941	Reykjavík	carpenter
Garðar Rafn Ásgeirsson	1929	Stafholtstungnahreppur	farmer
Guðjón Einarsson	1929	Hvolsvöllur	businessman
Guðmundur Brynjólfsson	1919	Stafholtstungnahreppur	farmer
Guðmundur Guðmundsson	1943	Ísafjörður	steam shovel operator
Guðmundur Ragnarsson	1946	Reykjavík	employee, Retail Trade Association
Gunnar Guðmundsson	1947	Hvolsvöllur	law school student
Gunnstein Sigurðsson	1938	Reykjavík	steam shovel operator
Hálfdán Hauksson	1948	Ísafjörður	employed by Icelandair
Halldór Vilhelmsson	1938	Reykjavík	carpenter
Helgi Pálsson	1930	Reykjavík	machinist
Hermann Hákonarson	1950	Ísafjörður	ship builder
Ingimar Benediktsson	1915	Reykjavík	school janitor
Ingólfur Eggertsson	1927	Ísafjörður	carpenter
Ingvi Thór Thorkelsson	1939	Reykjavík	junior high school teacher
Jóhann Gunnarsson	1941	Reykjavík	plasterer
Jónas E. Tómasson	1928	Stafholtstungnahreppur	farmer
Karl Guðmundsson	1925	Reykjavík	truck driver
Karl Hólm Helgason	1930	Reykjavík	plasterer

216

Appendix B, cont.

Name	Year of Birth	Residence	Occupation
Kjartan R. Guðmundsson	1906	Reykjavík	physician
Kristján Axelsson	1945	Stafholtstungnahreppur	farmer
Kristófer Thorgeirsson	1929	Stafholtstungnahreppur	greenhouse worker
Leó Sveinsson	1910	Reykjavík	fireman and fire inspector
Ólafur J. Long	1926	Reykjavík	worker
Óskar Halldórsson	1930	Ísafjörður	seaman
Óskar Ingvarsson	1903	Reykjavík	taxi driver
Páll Thórðarson	1944	Stafholtstungnahreppur	lawyer
Pétur Kjartansson	1948	Stafholtstungnahreppur	law school student
Ragnar Thór Magnús	1943	Reykjavík	businessman
Sigurður H. Dagsson	1944	Reykjavík	gym teacher
Sigurður Guðgeirsson	1926	Reykjavík	typographer
Sigurður Thorsteinsson	1919	Stafholtstungnahreppur	farmer
Sigurgeir Sigurðórsson	1915	Reykjavík	boat owner
Smári Guðlaugsson	1925	Hvolsvöllur	businessman
Stígur Stígsson	1930	Ísafjörður	worker
Sveinbjörn Sveinbjörnsson	1924	Ísafjörður	secretary of ship-building company
Thór Karlsson	1947	Reykjavík	seaman
Thórður Gröndal	1931	Reykjavík	mechanical engineer, director of firm
Ágústa S. Gunnlaugsdóttir	1950	Reykjavík	clerk in police station
Anna Lára Axelsdóttir	1942	Reykjavík	housewife
Anna Gunnarsdóttir	1942	Reykjavík	chocolate factory worker
Ásta Björnsdóttir	1927	Reykjavík	cashier
Auðbjörg Díana Árnadóttir	1941	Stafholtstungnahreppur	housewife
Auður Guðjónsdóttir	1942	Hvolsvöllur	housewife
Birna F. Kristiansen	1931	Hvolsvöllur	school teacher
Edda Gunnarsdóttir	1948	Reykjavík	child care worker
Elín Guðmundsdóttir	1915	Stafholtstungnahreppur	housewife
Erla Kristjánsdóttir	1950	Stafholtstungnahreppur	housewife
Ester Bára Gustafsdóttir	1938	Reykjavík	fish factory worker
Fanný Bryndís Hjartardóttir	1910	Reykjavík	food maker
Geirthrúður Charlesdóttir	1932	Ísafjörður	housewife
Guðlaug Jónsdóttir	1920	Reykjavík	housewife
Guðlaug Jónsdóttir	1926	Reykjavík	housewife
Guðrún Aðalbjarnardóttir	1928	Hvolsvöllur	cleaning lady
Guðrún Árnadóttir	1927	Hvolsvöllur	telephone operator
Guðrún A. Nor dahl	1927	Reykjavík	housewife
Guðrún Óskarsdóttir	1947	Hvolsvöllur	housewife
Helga Brynjólfsdóttir	1937	Reykjavík	bank cashier
Helga Friðbjörnsdóttir	1937	Hvolsvöllur	housewife
Helga Hansen	1945	Hvolsvöllur	housewife
Helga Ísleifsdóttir	1941	Hvolsvöllur	housewife
Hrefna Smith	1944	Reykjavík	hairdresser
Iðunn Haraldsdóttir	1944	Ísafjörður	housewife
Ingibjörg Magnúsdóttir	1931	Reykjavík	housewife
Ingibjörg Sveinsdóttir	1917	Reykjavík	housewife

Appendix B, cont.

Name	Year of Birth	Residence	Occupation
Ingibjörg Thorgilsdóttir	1937	Hvolsvöllur	seamstress
Ingilief Auðunsdóttir	1905	Reykjavík	housewife
Jónína Ögmundsdóttir	1931	Reykjavík	postal worker
Kolbrún M. Norðdahl	1938	Reykjavík	housewife
Kristín H. Thórarinsdóttir	1926	Hvolsvöllur	telephone operator
Laufey Pétursdóttir	1906	Stafholtstungnahreppur	housewife
Margrét Finnbogadóttir	1943	Reykjavík	housewife
María Ólafsdóttir	1945	Reykjavík	housewife
Nanna Lovísa Ísleifsdóttir	1937	Reykjavík	worker in father's shop
Olöf Finnbogadóttir	1932	Ísafjörður	housewife
Olöf Jónsdóttir	1904	Ísafjörður	weaver
Rebekka Jónsdóttir	1920	Ísafjörður	housewife
Sigriður Thorvaldsdóttir	1938	Stafholtstungnahreppur	housewife
Sigrún Björnsdóttir	1909	Stafholtstungnahreppur	housewife
Sigrún B. Björnsdóttir	1950	Reykjavík	teachers' college student
Sigrún Thorláksdóttir	1945	Hvolsvöllur	waitress
Snjólaug Guðmundsdóttir	1945	Stafholtstungnahreppur	weaving teacher
Sóley Magnúsdóttir	1911	Hvolsvöllur	housewife
Sonja Einara Svansdóttir	1940	Reykjavík	housewife
Stella Árnadóttir	1938	Reykjavík	housewife
Thóra Steingrimsdóttir	1924	Reykjavík	office worker
Vigdís Kristjánsdóttir	1935	Stafholtstungnahreppur	farm manager
Vilborg G. Guðnadóttir	1950	Reykjavík	nursing school student

Note: The first 50 respondents listed are males and the second 50 are females.

BIBLIOGRAPHY

Bibliography

Adam of Bremen. (1959) *History of the Archbishops of Hamburg-Bremen*. Translated by Francis J. Tschan. New York: Columbia University Press.

Albertsson, Kristján. (1953) *Tungan í tímans straumi*. Reykjavik: Helgafell.

Allen, Robert Loring. (1959) "The Vulnerability of Iceland's Economy." *Finanzarchiv* 19 (3): 441-62.

Allwood, Martin S. (1957) *Eilert Sundt: A Pioneer in Sociology and Anthropology*. Oslo: Olaf Norlis.

Andersen, Hans G. (1976) "The Icelandic Fisheries Zone." In Jóhannes Nordal and Valdimar Kristinsson (eds.), *Iceland, 874-1974*, pp. 168-75. Reykjavík: Central Bank of Iceland.

Anderson, Johann. (1746) *Nachrichten von Island*. Hamburg: Verlegts Georg Christian Grund.

Andersson, Theodore. (1964) *The Problem of Icelandic Saga Origins: A Historical Survey*. New Haven, Conn.: Yale University Press.

——————. (1967) *The Icelandic Family Saga*. Cambridge, Mass.: Harvard University Press.

——————. (1970) "The Displacement of the Heroic Ideal in the Family Sagas." *Speculum* 45 (4): 575-93.

Arensberg, Conrad M., and Solon, T. Kimball. (1968) *Family and Community in Ireland*, 2nd ed. Cambridge, Mass.: Harvard University Press.

Arlotto, Anthony. (1972) *Introduction to Historical Linguistics*. Boston: Houghton Mifflin.

Árnason, Björn R. (1960) *Sterker stofnar*. Akureyri: Kvöldvökuútgáfan.

Árnason, Jón. (1866) *Icelandic Legends*. Translated by E. J. Powell and Eiríkr Magnússon. London: Longmans, Green. (An earlier collection was published under the same title in 1864 by Richard Bentley.)

Asgeirsson, Thorhallur. (1942) *Development of the Progressive Party in Iceland*. Unpublished master's thesis. Minneapolis: Department of Political Science, University of Minnesota.

Auden, W. H., and Louis MacNeice. (1967) *Letters from Iceland*. London: Faber and Faber. (Originally published 1937.)

Baring-Gould, Sabine. (1863) *Iceland: Its Scenes and Sagas*. London: Smith, Elder.

Barrow, John. (1835) *A Visit to Iceland*. London: John Murray.

Bayldon, George. (1870) *An Elementary Grammar of the Old Norse or Icelandic Language*. London: Williams and Norgate.

Beck, Richard. (1950) *History of Icelandic Poets, 1800-1940*, volume 34 of *Islandica*. Ithaca, N.Y.: Cornell University Press.

Beinteinsson, Sveinbjörn. (1966) *Rímnasafnið*. Reykjavík: Helgafell.

Benediktsson, Hreinn. (1959) "The Vowel System of Icelandic: A Survey of its History." *Word* 15: 282-312.

221

—————————. (1961-1962) "Icelandic Dialectology: Methods and Results." *Íslenzk Tunga* 3: 72-113.

—————————. (1962a) "Islansk sprog." In *Kulturhistorisk leksikon for nordisk middelalder*, volume 7, columns 486-93. Reykjavík: Bókaverzlun Ísafolder.

—————————. (1962b) "The Unstressed and the Non-syllabic Vowel of Old Icelandic." *Arkiv för nordisk filologi* 77:7—31.

—————————. (1964a) "Upptök íslenzks máls." In Halldór Halldórsson (ed.), *þættir um íslenzkt mál*, pp. 9-28. Reykjavík: Almenna bókafélagið.

—————————. (1964b) "Íslenzkt málad fornu og nýju." In Halldór Halldórsson (ed.), *þættir um íslenzkt mál*, pp. 29-64. Reykjavík: Almenna bókafelagið.

—————————. (1975) "The Icelandic Language." In Jóhannes Nordal and Valdimar Kristinsson (eds.), *Iceland 874-1974*. pp. 57-71. Reykjavík: Central Bank of Iceland.

Benediktsson, Jakob (ed.). (1943) *Two Treatises on Iceland from the Seventeenth Century*. Copenhagen: Ejnar Munksgaard.

—————————. (1964) "þættir úr sögu íslenzks orðaforða." In Halldór Halldórsson (ed.), *þættir um íslenzkt mál*, pp. 88-109. Reykjavík: Almenna bókafélagið.

—————————. (1969) "*Landnámabók*: Some remarks on its value as a historical source." *Saga-Book* (of the Viking Society for Northern Research) 17 (4): 275-92.

Benediktz, Benedikt S. (1964) "The Master Magician in Icelandic Folk-Legend." *Durham University Journal* 1964: 22-34.

—————————. (1969) *The Spread of Printing, Western Hemisphere: Iceland*. Amsterdam: Vangendt.

—————————, and Ólafur F. Hjartar. (1964) "Skrá um doktorsritgerðer íslendinga, prentaðar og óprentaðar, 1666-1963." In *Landsbókasafn Íslands Ársbók 1962-1963*, Reykjavík: National Library of Iceland.

Berg, Ulf. (1971) *Patterns of Radio Listening and Television Viewing in Iceland*. Stockholm: Sveriges Radio. (Mimeographed.)

Bergman, Gösta. (1947) *A Short History of the Swedish Language*. Stockholm: Swedish Institute.

Bjarnar, Vilhjálmur. (1965) "The Laki Eruption and the Famine of the Mist." In Carl F. Bayerschmidt and Erik J. Friis (eds.), *Scandinavian Studies, pp. 410-21*. Seattle: University of Washington Press.

Bjarnason, Björn. (1950) *Idróttir fornmanna á norðurlöndum*. Reykjavík: Bókfellsútgáfan H.F. (Originally published in 1908.)

Bjarnason, Dóra S. (1974) *A Study of the Intergenerational Difference in the Perception of Stratification in Urban Iceland*. Unpublished master's thesis. Keele, England: Department of Sociology, University of Keele.

—————————. (1977) "Socioeconomic Change in Iceland; Entrepreneurship a Key to Modernization in an Egalitarian Society." (Mimeographed.)

Bjarnason, O., et al. (1973) "The Blood Groups of Icelanders." *Annals of Human Genetics* 36: 425-54.

Bjarnason, Stefán. (1970) *Íslenzkir samtíðarmenn*. Reykjavík: Prentismiðjan Leifur H. F.

Björnsson, Björn. (1971) *The Lutheran Doctrine of Marriage in Modern Icelandic Society*. Oslo: Universitsforlaget.

Björnsson, Ólafur. (1964) *þjóðarbúskapur íslendinga*, 2nd ed. Reykjavík: Hlaðbúð.

Blaisdell, Foster W., Jr. (1959) *Preposition-Adverbs in Old Icelandic*, Berkeley: University of California Press.

Blöndal, Lárus H., and Vilmundur Jónsson. (1970) *Læknar á Íslandi*, 2 volumes. Reykjavík: Læknafélag Íslands.

Böðvarsson, Árni. (1964) "Viðhorf Íslendinga til móðurmálsins fyrr og siðar." In Halldór Halldórsson (ed.), þættir um íslenzkt mál, pp. 177-200. Reykjavík: Almenna bókafélagi .

Book of Settlements. Translated, with introduction and notes, by Hermann Pálsson and Paul Edwards. Winnipeg: University of Manitoba Press.

Boorstin, Daniel J. (1958) The Americans: The Colonial Experience. New York: Random House.

Boswell, James. (1893) Boswell's Life of Johnson. Edited and with an introduction by Mowbray Morris. New York: Thomas Y. Crowell.

Boucher, Alan E. (1949) Iceland: Some Impressions. Reykjavík: Prentfell H. F.

Broddason, Thorbjörn. (1970) Children and Television in Iceland. Unpublished dissertation. Lund, Sweden: Department of Sociology, Lund University.

——————. (1972) "Um dreifingu bóka á Íslandi og í Svíþjóð." Skírnir 142: 5-28.

——————. (1974) "On the Myth of Social Equality in Iceland." (Mimeographed.)

Brøndsted, Johannes. (1965) The Vikings, 2nd ed., translated by Kalle Skov. Harmondsworth, England: Penguin.

Browne, J. Ross. (1863) "A Californian in Iceland." Harper's Magazine 26 (January, February, and March issues): 145 ff., 289 ff., 448 ff.

——————. (1867) The Land of Thor. New York: Harper.

Browne, Lina Fergusson (ed.). (1969) J. Ross Browne: His Letters, Journals and Writings. Albuquerque: University of New Mexico Press.

Bryce, James. (1872) "Impressions of Iceland." In Memories of Travel (1923), pp. 1-43. New York: Macmillan.

——————. (1901) "Primitive Iceland." In Studies in History and Jurisprudence, pp. 263-300. New York: Oxford University Press.

——————. (1916) Preface in Jon Steffanson, Denmark and Sweden with Iceland and Finland, pp. ix-xii. London: T. Fisher Unwin.

Burns, C. Delisle. (1948) The First Europe. London: George Allen and Unwin.

Burton, Richard F. (1875) Ultima Thule, or A Summer in Iceland, 2 volumes. London: William P. Nimmo.

Byock, Jesse. (1978) Wealth and Power among the Saga Age Chieftains: A Reevaluation of Social Interdependence in the Old Icelandic Commonwealth. Unpublished doctoral dissertation. Cambridge, Mass.: Harvard University Press.

Canada. (1934) Census of Canada, 1931, volume 1. Ottawa: Statistics Canada.

Chadwick, H. Munro. (1926) The Heroic Age. Cambridge: Cambridge University Press. (Originally published in 1912.)

Chamberlin, William Charles. (1947) Economic Development of Iceland through World War II. New York: Columbia University Press.

Chambers, Robert. (1856) Tracings of Iceland & the Faröe Islands. London and Edinburgh: W. & R. Chambers.

Chapman, Kenneth G. (1962) Icelandic-Norwegian Linguistic Relationships. Oslo: Universitetsforlaget.

Cipolla, Carlo M. (1969) Literacy and Development in the West. Harmondsworth, England: Pelican.

Cleasby, Richard, Gudbrand Vigfusson, and William A. Craigie. (1957) An Icelandic-English Dictionary, 2nd ed. Oxford: Clarendon Press. (First published in 1874.)

Connell, K. H. (1950) The Population of Ireland. Oxford: Oxford University Press.

Conybeare, C.A. Vansittart. (1877) The Place of Iceland in the History of European Institutions. Oxford and London: James Parker.

Craigie, William A. (1896) *Scandinavian Folk-Lore*. London: Alexander Gardner.
————. (1913) *The Icelandic Sagas*. Cambridge: Cambridge University Press.
————. (1937) *The Art of Poetry*. Oxford: Clarendon Press.
————. (1957) Preface in Richard Cleasby, Gudbrand Vigfusson, and William A. Craigie, *An Icelandic-English Dictionary*, 2nd ed., pp. iii-vii. Oxford: Clarendon Press.
Dahlstedt, Karl-Hampus. (1958) "Isländsk dialektgeografi: några synpunkter." *Scripta Islandica* 9:5-33.
Dahrendorf, Ralf. (1967) *Society and Democracy in Germany*. Garden City, N. Y.: Doubleday.
Davidson, H. R. Ellis. (1964) *Gods and Myths of Northern Europe*. Harmondsworth, England: Penguin.
Davis, Kingsley. (1939a) "The Forms of Illegitimacy." *Social Forces* 18 (1): 77-89.
————. (1939b) "Illegitimacy and the Social Structure. *American Journal of Sociology* 45 (2): 215-33.
Davis, Morris. (1963) *Iceland Extends Its Fisheries Limits*. Oslo: Universitetsforlaget.
Denmark. (1966) *Befolkningsudvikling og sunhedsforhold*. Copenhagen: Det Statistiske Departement.
Dillon, Arthur. (1840) *A Winter in Iceland and Lappland*. London: Henry Colburn.
Drake, Michael. (1969) *Population and Society in Norway, 1735-1865*. Cambridge: Cambridge University Press.
Driskill, Joseph D. (1971) "Icelandic Illegitimacy: Some Insights." Unpublished paper. Nashville, Tenn.: Department of Sociology, Vanderbilt University.
Dublin, Louis I., Alfred J. Lotka, and Mortimer Spiegelman. (1949) *Length of Life*, rev. ed. New York: Ronald Press.
Duckett, Eleanor Shipley. (1956) *Alfred the Great*. Chicago: University of Chicago Press.
Dufferin, Lord. (1910) *Letters from High Latitudes*. London: Oxford University Press. (First published in 1856.)
Edmond, Charles. (1857) *Voyage dans les mers du nord*. Paris: Michel Lévy Frères.
Egil's Saga. (1960) Translated by Gwyn Jones. Syracuse, N. Y.: Syracuse University Press.
Einarsson, Indriði. (no date) "Yfirlit yfir mannfjölda fædda og dána o. fl. á 19 öldinni." Stockholm: National Central Bureau of Statistics. Offprint number 3/662.
Einarsson, Sigurbjörn. (1965) "The Chruch in Iceland, 2: The Church's Life and Structure." In Leslie Stannard (ed.), *Scandinavian Churches*, pp. 111-17. London: Farber and Farber.
————. (1967) "The Church in Iceland." *Iceland Review* 5 (4): 16-22.
Einarsson, Stefán. (1948) *History of Icelandic Prose Writers, 1800-1940*, volumes 32-33 of *Islandica*. Ithaca, N. Y.: Cornell University Press.
————. (1957) *A History of Icelandic Literature*. Baltimore: Johns Hopkins University Press.
Eldjárn, Kristján. (1957) *Ancient Icelandic Art*. Munich: Hanns Reich Verlag.
Espólín, Jón. (1821) *Íslands árbækur í sögu-formi*, volume I. Copenhagen: Íslenska bókmenntafélags.
Evans, H. Meurig, and W. O. Thomas. (1953) *The New Welsh Dictionary*. Llandebie, Wales: Llyfrau'r Dryw.
Eyrbyggja Saga. (1959) Translated by Paul Schach and Lee M. Hollander. Lincoln: University of Nebraska Press.
Finley, M. I. (1967) "The Silent Women of Rome." In *Aspects of Antiquity*, pp. 129-42. New York: Viking.
————. (1978) *The World of Odysseus*, rev. ed. New York: Viking.
Finnbogason, Guðmundur. (1933) *Íslendingar*, Reykjavík: Bókadeild menningarstóðs.
————. (1943) "The Icelanders." Lecture to the Anglo-American Society of Reykjavík. Reykjavík: National Library of Iceland.

—————. (1969) *Land og þjóð*. Reykjavík: Menningarsjóðs og þjóðvinafélagsins. (Originally published in 1921.)

Finnsson, Hannes. (1970) *Mannfækkun af hallærum á Íslandi*. Reykjavík: Almenna bókafélagið. (First published in 1796.)

Fiske, Willard. (1905) *Chess in Iceland and in Icelandic Literature*. Florence: Florentine Tyopgraphical Society.

Foote, Peter G., and David M. Wilson. (1970) *The Viking Achievement*. London: Sidgwick & Jackson.

Forbes, Charles S. (1860) *Iceland: Its Volcanoes, Geysers, and Glaciers*. London: John Murray.

Fraser, Stewart E., and Bragi S. Jósepsson. (1968) *Education in Iceland: An Historical and Contemporary Study*. Nashville, Tenn.: Peabody International Center, George Peabody College for Teachers. (Mimeographed.)

Fridriksson, Sturla. (1969) "The Effects of Sea Ice on Flora, Fauna, and Agriculture." *Jökull* 19: 146-57.

—————. (1971) "Origin of the Icelanders and Trends in the Icelandic Population." Reykjavík: The Genetical Committee, University of Iceland. (Mimeographed.)

—————. (1972) "Grass and Grass Utilization in Iceland." *Ecology* 53 (5): 785-96.

Frímannsson, Gunnar. (1971) *Bruk av beroendeframkallande medel i Reykjavík*. Mimeographed research report. Uppsala: Department of Sociology, Uppsala University.

Gaimard, Paul. (1839-1852) *Voyage en Island et au Groënland éxecuté pendant les années 1835 et 1836*, 13 volumes. Paris: Arthus Bertrand.

Gallup, George. (1964) *The Miracle Ahead*. New York: Harper & Row.

Geipel, John. (1971) *The Viking Legacy*. Newton Abbot, England: David and Charles.

Gille, Halvor. (1949-1950) "The Demographic History of the Northern European Countries in the Eighteenth Century." *Population Studies* 3: 3-65.

Gíslason, Benedikt. (1950) *Íslenzki bóndinn*. Reykjavík: Bókaútgáfan nordri.

Gíslason, Gylfi Th. (1966) "Problems of Icelandic Culture." *American Scandinavian Review* 54 (3): 241-48.

—————. (1973) *The Problem of Being an Icelander*. Translated by Pétur Kidson Karlsson. Reykjavík: Almenna bókafélagið.

Gíslason, Magnús. (1977) *Kvällsvaka: en isländsk kulturtradition belyst genom studier i bondebefolkningens vardagsliv och miljö under senare hälften av 1800-talet och början av 1900-talet*. Uppsala: Studia Ethnologica Upsaliensia 2.

Gjerset, Knut. (1925) *History of Iceland*. New York: Macmillan.

Goode, William J. (1960) "Illegitimacy in the Carribean." *American Sociological Review* 25 (1): 21-30.

—————. (1961) "Illegitimacy, Anomie, and Cultural Penetration." *American Sociological Review* 26 (6): 910-25.

—————. (1963) *World Revolution and Family Patterns*. New York: Free Press of Glencoe.

Gordon, E. V. (1957) *An Introduction to Old Norse*, 2nd ed. Revised by A. R. Taylor. Oxford: Clarendon Press.

Griffiths, John C. (1969) *Modern Iceland*. London: Pall Mall Press.

Grímsson, Ólafur R. (1970) *Political Power in Iceland Prior to the Period of Class Politics, 1845-1918*. Unpublished doctoral dissertation. Manchester: Faculty of Economic and Social Studies, University of Manchester.

Grímsson, Sigurður (ed.). (1946) *Gloggt er gests augað: úrval ferðasagna um Ísland*. Reykjavík: Menningar- og fræðslusamband.

Groenke, Ulrich. (1966) "On Standard, Substandard, and Slang in Icelandic." *Scandinavian Studies* 38 (3): 217-30.

Gröndal, Benedikt. (1967) "A Poetic Parliament." *Iceland Review* 5 (1): 17-20.

—————. (1971) *Iceland from Neutrality to NATO Membership*. Oslo: Universitetsforlaget.

Guðjónsson, Pétur. (1967) "The Habits of Icelanders: A Survey." *65°* 1: 20-24, 34.

Guðmundsson, Barði. (1967) *The Origin of the Icelanders*. Translated, with an introduction, by Lee M. Hollander. Lincoln: University of Nebraska Press.

Guðmundsson, Gils. (1950) *Öldin okkar*. Reykjavík: Forlagið Iðunn.

Guðmundsson, Helgi. (1972) *The Pronominal Dual in Icelandic*. Reykjavík: Institute of Nordic Studies.

Guðmundsson, Ivar. (1978) "Iceland." *Scandinavian Review* 66 (4): 77.

Guðmundsson, Valtýr. (1902) *Islands kultur ved aarhundredskiftet 1900*. Copenhagen: Ernst Bojesen.

Guðnason, Jón, and Pétur Haraldsson. (1965, 1967) *Íslenzkir samtíðarmenn*, 2 volumes. Reykjavík: Bókaútgáfan samtíðarmenn.

Gunnlaug Serpent-Tongue, Saga of. (1938). In Sigurður Nordal and Guðni Jónsson (eds.), *Borgfirðinga sögur*, pp. 51-107. Reykjavík: Hið íslenzka fornritafélag. (Icelandic title is *Gunnlaugs saga ormstungu*.)

Gustafsson, Bernt. (1965) "Det religiösa livet." In Edmund Dahlström (ed.), *Svensk samhällstruktur i sociologisk belysning*, 3rd ed., pp. 313-47 Stockholm: Svenska bokförlaget.

Hajnal, John. (1965) "European Marriage Patterns in Perspective." In D. V. Glass and D. E. C. Eversley (eds.), *Population in History*, pp. 101-43. London: Edward Arnold.

Hallberg, Peter. (1962) *The Icelandic Saga*. Translated by Paul Schach. Lincoln: University of Nebraska Press.

Halldórsson, Halldór. (1962) "Kring språkliga nybildningar i nutida isländska." *Scripta Islandica* 13: 3-24.

—————. (1964) "Nýgervingar í fornmáli og frá síðari öldum." In Halldór Halldórsson (ed.), *þættir um íslenzkt mál*, pp. 110-57. Reykjavík: Almenna bókafélagið.

Hallgrímsson, Hallgrímur. (1925) *Íslensk alþýðumentun á 18. öld*. Reykjavík: Prentasmiðjan Acta.

Hannesson, Gunnar. (1925) *Körpermasse und Körperproportionen der Isländer*. Reykjavík: Árbok háskóla Íslands.

Hannesson, Jóhann S. (1964) "The American Impact in Iceland." In Lars Åhnebrink (ed.), *Amerika och Norden*, pp. 59-64. Stockholm: Almqvist & Wiksell.

Hansen, Sigurð. (1858) "Um mannaheiti á Íslandi." *Skýrslur um Landshagi á Íslandi* 4: 503-72. Copenhagen: Hinu íslenzka bókmenntafélagi.

Haraldsson, Erlendur. (1977) "National Survey of Psychical Experiences and Attitudes towards the Paranormal in Iceland." In J. D. Morris, W. G. Roll, and R. l. Morris (eds.), *Research in Parapsychology 1976*, pp. 182-86. Metuchen, N. J.: Scarecrow Press.

—————. (1978) *Þessa heims og annars*. Reykjavík: Bókaforlagið Saga.

—————, and Ian Stevenson. (1974) "An Experiment with the Icelandic Medium Hafstein Björnsson." *Journal of the American Society for Psychical Research* 68 (2): 192-202.

Hardy, Thomas. (1954) *Tess af D'Uberville-ættini*. 2nd ed. Translated by Snæbjörn Jónsson. Reykjavík: Prentsmiðjan Hólar.

Hargreaves-Mawdsley, W. M. (1968) *Dictionary of European Writers*. London: J. M. Dent.

Hartz, Louis. (1955) *The Liberal Tradition in America*. New York: Harcourt, Brace & World.

—————. (1964) *The Founding of New Societies*. New York: Harcourt, Brace & World.

Haugen, Einar. (1966) *Language Conflict and Language Planning*. Cambridge, Mass.: Harvard University Press.

—————. (1969) *The Norwegian Language in America*, 2nd ed. Bloomington: Indiana University Press.

——————. (1975) "Pronominal Address in Icelandic: From you-two to you-all." *Language in Society* 4: 323-39.
——————. (1976) *The Scandinavian Languages*. Cambridge, Mass.: Harvard University Press.
——————, and T. L. Markey. (1972) *The Scandinavian Languages: Fifty Years of Linguistic Research, 1918-1968*. The Hague: Mouton.
Heer, Friedrich. (1963) *The Medieval World*. New York: Mentor.
Helgason, Jón. (1931) "Islandsk litteratur under 1500—talets senare hälft." *Island: bilder från gammal och ny tid*, pp. 15-35. Uppsala: Skrifter utgivna av Samfundet Sverige-Island.
——————. (1931) "Från Oddur Gottskálksson til Fjölnir. Tre hundra års isländsk språkutveckling." *Island: bilder från gammal och ny tid*, pp. 36-50. Uppsala: Skrifter utgivna av Samfundet Sverige-Island.
Helgason, Tómas. (1964) *Epidemiology of Mental Disorders in Iceland*. Copenhagen: Munksgaard.
Henderson, Ebenezer. (1818) *Iceland; or the Journal of a Residence in that Island during the Years 1814 and 1815*, 2 volumes. Edinburgh: Oliphant, Waugh, and Innis.
Henriksen, Edvard (ed.). (1959) *Scandinavia Past and Present: Five Modern Democracies*, 3 volumes. Odense, Denmark: Andelsboktrykkeriet.
Hermannsson, Halldór. (1919) *Modern Icelandic*, volume 12 of *Islandica*. Ithaca, N.Y.: Cornell University Press.
——————. (1925) *Eggert Ólafsson*, volume 16 of *Islandica*. Ithaca, N. Y.: Cornell University Press.
——————. (1928) *Sir Joseph Banks and Iceland*, volume 18 of *Islandica*. Ithaca, N. Y.: Cornell University Press.
——————. (1932) *Saemund Sigfússon and the Oddaverjar*, volume 22 of *Islandica*. Ithaca, N.Y.: Cornell University Press.
Heusler, Andreas. (1911) *Das Strafrecht der Isländersagas*. Leipzig: Verlag von Duncker & Humbolt.
——————. (1946) "Íslenzk þjoðareinkenni." In Sigurður Grímsson (ed.), *Glöggt er gests augað*, pp. 321-29. Reykjavík: Menningar- og fræðslusamband alþýðu (Originally published in German in 1896.)
Hilen, Andrew. (1947) *Longfellow and Scandinavia*. New Haven, Conn.: Yale University Press.
Hjaltalín, Jón A. (1867) *On the Civilization of the First Icelandic Colonists, with a Short Account of Their Manners and Customs*. Reykjavík: National Library of Iceland.
——————. (1872) "Rights of Women among the Old Scandinavians." *Journal of Jurisprudence* 16 (190): 505-26.
Hjartar, Ólafur F. (1968) "Íslenzk bókager 1887-1966." In *Landsbókasafn Íslands Árbók 1967*, pp. 137-41. Reykjavík: National Library of Iceland.
Hjertonsson, Karin. (1973) *The New Law of the Sea*. Stockholm: P. A. Norstedt.
Hjörleifsson, Einar, et al. (1915) *Íslenzk mannanöfn: lög, nefndarálit og nafnaskrár* Reykjavík: Gutenberg.
Hoare, Dorothy M. (1937) *The Works of Morris and Yeats in Relation to Early Saga Literature*. Cambridge: Cambridge University Press.
Hofstadter, Richard. (1971) *America at 1750*. New York: Alfred A. Knopf.
Holland, Henry. (1872) *Recollections of Past Life*. London: Longmans, Green.
Holmsen, Andreas, and Magnus Jensen. (1949) *Norges historie: fra de eldste tider til 1660*. Oslo: Gyldendal.
Homans, George Casper. (1942) *English Villagers of the Thirteenth Century*. Cambridge, Mass.: Harvard University Press.
Hood, John C. F. (1946) *Icelandic Church Saga*. London: Society for Promoting Christian Knowledge.
Hooker, W. J. (1813) *Journal of a Tour in Iceland in the Summer of 1809*, 2 volumes. London: Longman, Hurst, Rees, Orme, and Brown.

228   Bibliography

Horrebow, Niels. (1758) *The Natural History of Iceland*. London: A. Linde in Catherine Street. (Original published in Danish in 1752.)

Hsu, Francis L. K. (1970) *Americans and Chinese*. Garden City, N.Y.: Doubleday.

Huntington, Ellsworth. (1924) *The Character of Races*. New York: Scribner's.

Huntington, Samuel P. (1966) "Political Modernization: America vs. Europe." *World Politics* 18 (3): 378-414. (Reprinted in Rheinhard Bendix [ed.]. (1968) *State and Society*, pp. 170-200. Boston: Little Brown.)

Ibn, Fadhlan. (1948) "Observations on the Manners and Customs of the Northmen Encamped on the Volga." In Carleton S. Coon (ed.), *A Reader in General Anthropology*, pp. 410-16. New York: Henry Holt.

"Iceland Is. . . ." (1968) *Iceland Review* 6 (2): 35-43.

Ireland. (1968) *Census of Population of Ireland 1966*, volume 2. Dublin: Central Statistics Office.

Jack, Robert. (1957) *Artic Living: The Story of Grimsey*. London: Hodder & Stoughton.

Jacobsen, Grethe. (1978) *The Position of Women in Scandinavia during the Viking Period*. Unpublished master's thesis. Madison: Department of History, University of Wisconsin.

James, Patricia (ed.). (1966) *The Travel Diaries of Thomas Robert Malthus*. Cambridge: Cambridge University Press.

Janzén, Assar. (1947) "De fornvästnordiska personnamen." In *Personnavne: Nordisk kultur*, volume 7, pp. 22-86. Stockholm: Bonniers.

Jensdóttir, Sólrún. (1975-1976) "Books Owned by Ordinary People in Iceland 1750-1830." *Saga-Book* (of the Viking Society for Northern Research.) 19 (2-3): 264-92.

Jespersen, Otto. (1938) *Growth and Structure of the English Language*, 9th ed. Garden City, N.Y.: Doubleday.

Jóhannesson, Alexander. (1953) "Om det islandske sprog." *Scripta Islandica* 4: 5-14.

Jóhannesson, Jón. (1974) *A History of the Old Icelandic Commonwealth*. Translated by Haraldur Bessason. Winnipeg: University of Manitoba Press. (Published originally in Icelandic in 1956.)

——————, Magnús Finnbogason, and Kristján Eldjárn (eds.). (1946) *Sturlunga Saga*, 2 volumes. Reykjavík: Sturlunguútgáfan.

Jóhannesson, Thorkell. (1950) *Saga Íslendinga: tímabilið 1770-1830, upplýsingaröld*. Reykjavík: *Menntamálaráð og þjóðvinafélag*.

Johnsen, Oscar Albert. (1936) "Norges folk i middelalderen." In *Nordisk kultur: befolkning i middelalderen*, volume 2, pp. 58-105. Copenhagen: J. H. Schultz.

Johnson, Paul. (1972) *The Offshore Islanders*. London: Weidenfeld and Nicolson.

Johnson, Sveinbjorn. (1930) *Pioneers of Freedom*. Boston: Stratford.

Jonasson, Jónas. (1961). *Íslenzkir þjóðhættir*. Reykjavík: Ísafoldarprentsmiðja. (Originally published in 1934.)

Jónasson, Matthías. (1956) *Greinarþroski og greinarpróf*. Reykjavík: Menntamálaraðuneytinu.

Jones, Gwyn. (1964) *The Norse Atlantic Saga*. London: Oxford University Press.

——————. (1968) *A History of the Vikings*. London: Oxford University Press.

Jones, Oscar F. (1964a) "Icelandic Neologisms in *ó*." *Word* 20 (1):18-27.

——————. (1964b) "Some Icelandic Götumál Expressions." *Scandinavian Studies* 36 (1): 59-64.

Jónsson, Agnar Kl. (1963) *Logfræðingtal 1736-1963*. Reykjavík: Ísafoldarprentsmiðja.

Jónsson, Guðni. (1948) *Annálar og nafnaskrá*. Reykjavík: Íslendingasagnaútgáfan.

——————. (1968) *Nafnaskrá*, volume 13 of *Islendinga sögur*. Reykjavík: Íslendingasagnaútgáfan.

Jónsson, Jón Adalsteinn. (1964) "Íslenzkar mállýzkur." In Halldór Halldórsson (ed.), *þættir um íslenzkt mál*, pp. 65-87. Reykjavík: Almenna bókafélagið.

Jónsson, Jónas. (1955) *Saga Íslendinga: tímabilið 1830-1874, Fjölnismenn og Jón Sigurðsson*. Reykjavík: Menntamálaráð og þjóðvinafélag.

Jónsson, Klemens. (1930) *Fjögur hundruð ára saga prentlistárinnar á Íslandi*. Reykjavík: Felagsprentsmiðjan.

Jónsson, Magnús. (1957-1958) *Saga Íslendinga: tímabilið 1871-1903, landhöfðingjatímabilið*, 2 volumes, Reykjavík: Menntamálaráð og þjóðvinafélag.

Jósefsson, Jóhannes. (1908) *Icelandic Wrestling*. Akureyri: Thórh. Bjarnarson.

Jósepsson, Bragi S. (1968) "Icelandic Culture and Education: An Annotated Bibliography." Bowling Green, Ky.: Department of Sociology, Western Kentucky University. (Mimeographed.)

——————. (1970) *Educational Systems: A Comparative Study of Educational Legislation in Scandinavia*. Bowling Green, Ky.: Department of Sociology and Anthropology, Western Kentucky University. (Mimeographed.)

Katzner, Kenneth. (1975) *The Languages of the World*. New York: Funk and Wagnalls.

Kendrick, T. D. (1930) *A History of the Vikings*. London: Methuen. (Reprinted in 1968 by Frank Cass.)

Ker, W. P. (1904) *The Dark Ages*. Edinburgh and London: William Blackwood.

——————. (1906) *Sturla the Historian*. Oxford: Clarendon Press.

——————. (1908) "Iceland and the Humanities." *Saga-Book of the Viking Club*. Reykjavík: National Library of Iceland.

——————. (1957) *Epic and Romance: Essays on Medieval Literature*, 2nd rev. ed. New York: Dover. (Originally published in 1908.)

Klinckowström, Axel. (1911) *Bland vulcaner och fågelberg*, 2 volumes, Stockholm: P. A. Norstedt.

Kluckhohn, Florence R., and Fred Strodbeck. (1961) *Variations in Value Orientations*. Evanston, Ill.: Row, Petersen.

Kneeland, Samuel. (1876) *An American in Iceland*. Boston: Lockwood, Brooks. (Also published as: *Travels in Iceland*. (1875) New York: A. L. Burt.)

Landnámabók, volume 2. (1968) Reykjavík: Hið íslenzka fornritafélag.

Lárusson, Björn. (1967) *The Old Icelandic Land Registers*. Lund, Sweden: C.W.K. Gleerup.

Lárusson, Magnús Már. (1965) "The Church in Iceland, 1: A Historical Sketch." In Leslie Stannard (ed.), *Scandinavian Churches*, pp. 104-10. London: Farber and Farber.

Lárusson, Ólafur. (1936) "Island." In *Nordisk kultur: befolkning i oldtiden*, volume 1, pp. 121-37. Copenhagen: J. H. Schultz.

——————. (1960) *Nöfn íslendinga árið 1703*. Reykjavík: Hið íslenzka bókmenntafélag.

Laslett, Peter. (1965) *The World We Have Lost*. New York: Scribner's.

Laxdaela Saga. (1969) Translated by Magnus Magnusson and Hermann Pálsson. Harmondsworth, England: Penguin.

Laxness, Halldór. (1958) *The Happy Warriors*. Translated by Katherine John. London: Methuen. (Originally published in 1952.)

——————. (1966) *The Fish Can Sing*. Translated by Magnus Magnusson. London: Methuen. (Originally published in 1957.)

——————. (1969) *World Light*. Translated by Magnus Magnusson. Madison: University of Wisconsin Press. (Originally published 1937-1940.)

Leaf, Horace. (1949) *Iceland: Yesterday and Today*. London: George Allen & Unwin.

Leith, Disney (trans.). (1895) *Stories of the Bishops of Iceland*. London: J. Masters.

Lenski, Gerhard, and Jean Lenski. (1978) *Human Societies*, 3rd ed. New York: McGraw-Hill.

Liestøl, Knut. (1930) *The Origin of the Icelandic Family Sagas*. Oslo: H. Aschehoug.

Lind, E. H. (1905) *Norsk-Isländska dopnamn ock fingerade namn från medeltiden*. Uppsala, Sweden: A. B. Lundeqvistska.

Lindal, Sigurður (ed.). (1974, 1975) *Saga Íslands I, II*. Reykjavík: Hið íslenzka bókmenntafélag Sögufélagið.

Lindroth, Hjalmar. (1937) *Iceland: A Land of Contrasts*. Translated from the Swedish by Adolph B. Bensen. Princeton, N. J.: Princeton University Press. (Originally published in 1930.)

Lipset, Seymour M. (1963) *The First New Nation: The United States in Comparative and Historical Perspective.* New York: Basic Books.

Lock, William George. (1882) *Guide to Iceland.* Charleston, England: Published by the author.

McGill, Alexander. (1921) *The Independence of Iceland: A Parallel for Ireland.* Glasgow: P. J. O'Callaghan.

MacKenzie, George Steuart. (1811) *Travels in the Island of Iceland during the Summer of the Year 1810.* Edinburgh: Archibald Constable.

McKeown, Thomas. (1976) *The Modern Rise of Population.* London: Edward Arnold.

McNeill, William H. (1963) *The Rise of the West.* Chicago: University of Chicago Press.

Magnús, Gunnar M. (1939) *Saga alþýðufræðslunnar á Íslandi.* Reykjavík: Samband Íslenzkra Barnakennara.

Magnússon, Ásgeir Blöndal. (1964) "Um geymd íslenzkra orða." In Halldór Halldórsson (ed.), *þættir um íslenzkt mál,* pp. 158-76. Reykjavík: Almenna bókafélagið.

Magnússon, Björn. (1957) *Gudfræðingatal 1847-1957.* Reykjavík: H. F. Leiftur.

Magnússon, Jón. (1967) *Píslarsaga.* Reykjavík: Almenna bókafélagið.

Magnússon, Magnús. (1968) "Iceland Is . . . . " *Iceland Review* 6 (2): 35-43.

Magnússon, Sigurður A. (1969) "Isländsk skönlitteratur 1965-67." In *Ny litteratur i norden 1965-67.* pp. 55-77. Stockholm: Rabén & Sjögren.

—————. (1970) "The Modern Icelandic Novel: From Isolation to Political Awareness." *Mosaic* 4 (2): 133-43.

—————. (1977) *Northern Sphinx: Iceland and the Icelanders from the Settlement to the Present.* Montreal: McGill-Queen's University Press.

Malinowski, Bronislaw. (1930) "Parenthood, the Basis of Social Structure." In V. F. Calverton and Samuel D. Schmalhausen (eds.), *The New Generation,* pp. 113-68. New York: Macaulay. (Reprinted in B. Malinowski. [1962] *Sex, Culture, and Myth,* pp. 42-88. New York: Harcourt, Brace & World.)

Mallet, M. (1898) *Northern Antiquities.* Translated from the French by Bishop Percy; revised and "considerably enlarged" by I. A. Blackwell in 1847. London: George Bell. (Originally published in 1770.)

Margolin, David. (1975) "Literate Bilingualism in the North Atlantic: The Linguistic Development of the Faroe Islands and Greenland." Unpublished special paper. Cambridge, Mass.: Department of Anthropology, Harvard University.

Marmier, Xavier. (1855) *Lèttres sur l'Islande et poésies,* 4th ed. Paris: Arthus Bertrand. (Originally published in 1837.)

Merrill, Robert T. (1964) "Notes on Icelandic Kinship Terminology." *American Anthropologist* 66 (4, part 1): 867-72.

Metcalfe, Frederick. (1861) *The Oxonian in Iceland.* London: Longman, Green, Longman, and Roberts.

Miles, Pliny. (1854) *Norðurfari, Rambles in Iceland.* London: Longman, Brown, Green, and Longmans.

Ministry for Foreign Affairs. (1975) *The Fishery Limits off Iceland: 200 Nautical Miles.* Reykjavík: Setberg.

Mitchell, B. R. (1975) *European Historical Statistics.* London: Macmillan.

Mitchell, P. M. (1965) "The Scandinavian Literary Engagement." In Carl F. Bayerschmidt and Erik J. Friis (eds.), *Scandinavian Studies,* pp. 331-43. Seattle: University of Washington Press.

—————. (1978) *Halldór Hermannsson,* volume 41 of *Islandica.* Ithaca, N.Y.: Cornell University Press.

Modéer, Ivar. (1957) "Ur det isländska allmogespråkets skattkammare." *Scripta Islandica* 8: 21-25.

Morgan, Lewis H. (1871) *Systems of Consanguinity and Affinity of the Human Family.* Washington, D. C.: Smithsonian Institution Contributions to Knowledge, volume 17.

Morison, Samuel Eliot. (1971) *The European Discovery of America: The Northern Voyages A.D. 500-1600.* New York: Oxford University Press.

Morrill, John B. (1967) *The Medieval Imprint.* New York: Basic Books.

Morris, William. (1911) *Journals of Travel in Iceland, 1871, 1873,* 2 volumes. London: Longmans, Green.

Myrdal, Alva. (1945) *Nation and Family.* London: Routledge & Kegan Paul.

"Namngjeving." (1968) In *Kulturhistorisk leksikon for nordisk middlealder,* volume 12, pp. 206-12. Reykjavík: Bókaverzlun Ísafoldar.

Nawrath, Alfred, Sugurður Thorarinsson, Halldór Laxness. (1959) *Iceland: Impressions of a Heroic Landscape.* Bern: Kummerly & Frey.

Netherlands, Central Bureau of Statistics. (1970) *Statistisch zakboek '70.* The Hague: Centraal Bureau voor de Statistiek.

Nicoll, James. (1841) *An Historical and Descriptive Account of Iceland, Greenland, and the Faröe Islands.* Edinburgh: Oliver and Boyd.

Njal's Saga. (1960) Translated by Magnus Magnusson and Hermann Pálsson. Harmondsworth, England: Penguin.

Njarðvik, Njörður. (1973) *Island i forntid.* Stockholm: Wahlström & Widstrand.

Nordal, Jóhannes. (1953) *Changes in Icelandic Social Structure Since the End of the Eighteenth Century, With Particular Reference to Trends in Social Mobility.* Unpublished doctoral dissertation. London: London School of Economics.

——————, and Valdimar Kristinsson (eds.). (1975) *Iceland, 874-1974.* Reykjavík: Central Bank of Iceland.

Nordal, Sigurður. (1924) *Islenzk lestrarbók, 1400-1900.* Reykjavík: Sigfúsar Eymundssonar.

——————. (1942) *Íslenzk menning.* Reykjavík: Mál og menning.

——————. (1954a) "Tid och kalvskinn." *Scripta Islandica* 5: 5-18.

——————. (1954b) Introduction in Snorri Sturluson, *The Prose Edda,* translated by Jean I. Young. Berkeley: University of California Press.

——————. (1957) *The Historical Element in the Icelandic Family Sagas.* Fifteenth W. P. Ker Memorial Lecture delivered at the University of Glasgow, 1954. Glasgow: Jackson, Son & Company.

——————. (1958) *Hrafnkels Saga Freysgoða.* Translated from the Icelandic by R. George Thomas. Cardiff: University of Wales Press. (Originally published in 1940.)

——————. (1970) *Íslenzk lestrarbók, 1750-1930.* Reykjavík: Bókaútgáfa Guðjóns O. Guðjónssonar.

——————. Guðrun P. Helgadóttir, and Jón Jóhannesson. (1953) *Sýnisbók: Íslenzka bókmennta til miðrar átjándu alder.* Reykjavík: Bókaverzlun Sigfúsar Eymundssonar H.F.

Nordic Council. (Published annually) *Yearbook of Nordic Statistics.* Stockholm: Nordic Council and Nordic Secretariat.

Northrop, F. S. C. (1946) *The Meeting of East and West.* New York: Macmillan.

Norway, Central Bureau of Statistics. (1969) *Historisk statistikk.* Oslo: Statistisk Sentralbyrå.

——————. (1971) *Vital Statistics and Migration Statistics, 1970.* Oslo: Statistic Sentralbyrå.

Nuechterlein, Donald E. (1961) *Iceland: Reluctant Ally.* Ithaca, N.Y.: Cornell University Press.

——————. (1969) "Small States in Alliances: Iceland, Thailand, Australia." *Orbis* 13 (2): 600-23.

Odhe, Thorsten. (1939) *Samvinnan á Íslandi.* Translated from Swedish into Icelandic by Jón Sigurðson frá Ystafelli. Reykjavík: Samband ísl. samvinnufélaga.

——————. (1960) *Iceland: The Cooperative Island.* Chicago: Cooperative League of the United States of America.

O'Faolain, Julia, and Lauro Martines (eds.). (1973) *Not in God's Image.* New York: Harper & Row.

Ólafsson, Eggert, and Bjarni Pálsson. (1943) *Ferðabók*, 2 volumes, Reykjavík: Ísafoldaprent-smiðja. (Originally published in Danish in 1772.)

Ólafsson, Jón. (1923, 1932) *The Life of Jón Ólafsson*, 2 volumes. Edited and translated by Bertha S. Phillpotts. London: Hakluyt Society.

Ólason, Páll Eggert. (1942) *Saga Íslendinga: seytjánda öld, höfuðþættir*. Reykjavík: Mennta-málaráð og þjóðvinafélag.

―――――. (1944) *Sextánda öld*. Reykjavík: Menntamálaráð og þjóðvinafélag.

―――――. (1945-1946) *Jón Sigurðsson, foringinn mikli*, 2 volumes. Reykjavík: Isafolda-prentsmiðja H.F.

―――――. (1948-1952) *Íslenzkar æviskrár: frá landnámstímum til ársloka 1940*, 5 vol-umes. Reykjavík: Hið íslenzka bókmenntafélag.

―――――, and Thorkell Jóhannesson. (1943) *Saga Íslendinga: tímabilið 1701-1770*. Reykjavík: Menntamálaráð og þjóðvinafélag.

OECD. (1978) *OECD Economic Survey: Iceland*. Paris: Organization for Economic Cooper-ation and Development.

Otterbjörk, Roland. (1963) "Moderna isländska förnamn." *Scripta Islandica* 14: 27-41.

Paijkull, C. W. (1866) *En sommar på Island*. Stockholm: Bonniers.

Pálsson, Einar. (1968) "Spoken Icelandic." 65^0 2 (2): 18-20, 26.

Pálsson, Hermann. (1960) Islenzk mannanöfn. Reykjavík: Heimskringla.

Pedersen, Holger. (1931) *The Discovery of Language: Linguistic Science in the 19th Century*. Translated from the Danish by John Webster Spargo. Cambridge, Mass.: Harvard Uni-versity Press.

"Personnavn." (1968) In *Kulturhistorisk leksikon for nordisk middelalder*, volume 12, col-umns 198-234. Reykjavík: Bókaverzlun Ísafolder.

"Perspectives in Culture: A Roundtable Discussion." (1973) *Atlantica & Iceland Review* 11 (2): 24-36.

Pfeiffer, Ida. (1852) *A Journey to Iceland and Travels in Sweden and Norway*. Translated from the German by Charlotte Fenimore Cooper. London: Richard Bentley (Origi-ally published in 1847.)

Phillpotts, Bertha S. (1931) *Edda and Saga*. London: Home University Library.

Prioux-Marchal, France. (1974) "Le Mariage en Suède." *Population* 29 (4-5): 825-60.

Purkis, John. (1962) *The Icelandic Jaunt: A Study of the Expeditions Made by Morris to Iceland in 1871 and 1873*. Surrey, England: William Morris Society.

Redfield, Robert. (1955) *The Little Community*. Chicago: University of Chicago Press.

―――――. (1956) *Peasant Society and Culture*. Chicago: University of Chicago Press.

Rich, George W. (1976) "Changing Icelandic Kinship." *Ethnology* 15 (1): 1-19.

―――――. (1978) "The Domestic Cycle in Modern Iceland." *Journal of Marriage and the Family* 40 (1): 173-83.

Rokkan, Stein. (1967) "Geography, Religion, and Social Class: Cross-cutting Cleavages in Norwegian Politics." In Seymour M. Lipset and Stein Rokkan (eds.), *Party Systems and Voter Alignments, pp. 367-444. New York*: Free Press.

Rudorff, Raymond. (1970) *The Myth of France*. London: Hamish Hamilton.

Sallé, M. Michel. (1968) *La vie economique et politique en Islande*. Unpublished doctoral dissertation. Paris: Foundation Nationale des Sciences Politiques, Cycle Supérieur d'Etudes Politiques.

Scherman, Katherine. (1976) *Daughter of Fire: A Portrait of Iceland*. Boston: Little, Brown.

Schram, Gunnar G. (1970) *Logfræðihandbókin*, 2nd ed. Reykjavík: Bókaútgáfan Örn og Örlygur H.F.

Seaton, Ethel. (1935) *Literary Relations of England and Scandinavia in the Seventeenth Century*. Oxford: Clarendon Press.

Selby, Alice. (1974) "Icelandic Journey." *Saga-Book* (of the Viking Society for Northern Research) 19 (1).

Siegel, Sidney. (1956) *Nonparametric Statistics*. New York: McGraw-Hill.

Sigurðsson, Jón, and Helgi Hjörvar. (1930) *Alþingismannatal 1845-1930*. Reykjavík: Skriftstofa alþingis gaf ut.

Simonson, William, and Gilbert Geis. (1956) "Courtship Patterns of Norwegian and American University Students." Marriage and Family Living 18:334-38.

Simpson, Jacqueline (ed.). (1965) *The Northmen Talk*. Madison: University of Wisconsin Press.

—————. (1972) *Icelandic Folktales and Legends*. London: B. T. Batsford.

Smith, T. Lynn, and Paul E. Zopf, Jr. (1976) *Demography: Principles and Methods*. Port Washington, N.Y.: Alfred.

Statistical Bureau of Iceland. (Published monthly) *Hagtíðindi*. Reykjavík: Hagstofa Íslands.

—————. (1930-1931) *Árbók hagstofu Íslands*. Reykjavík: Hagstofa Íslands.

—————. (1933) *Mannfjöldaskýrslur, árin 1926-1930*. Reykjavík: Hagstofa Íslands.

—————. (1960) Manntalið 1703. Reykjavík: Hagstofa Íslands.

—————. (1967) *Statistical Abstract of Iceland*. Reykjavík: Hagstofa Íslands.

—————. (1969) *Manntal á Islandi 1. Desember 1960*. Reykjavík: Hagstofa Íslands.

—————. (1970) *Skrár yfir fyrirtæki á Íslandi 1969*. Reykjavík: Hagstofa Íslands.

—————. (1975a) *Mannfjöldaskýrslur, árin 1961-1970*. Reykjavík: Hagstofa Íslands.

—————. (1975b) *Manntal 1729: í þremur sýslum*. Reykjavík: Hagstofa Íslands.

—————. (1976) *Statistical Abstract of Iceland*. Reykjavík: Hagstofa Íslands.

—————. (1978) *Alþingiskosningar, árið 1978*. Reykjavík: Hagstofa Íslands.

Stefansson, Jon. (1902) "Iceland: Its History and Inhabitants." Paper read before the Victoria Institute (Philosophical Society of Great Britain) on April 21. Reykjavík: National Library of Iceland.

—————. (1916) *Denmark and Sweden with Iceland and Finland*. London: T. Fisher Unwin.

Stefánsson, Sigurður. (1963) *Jón Thorláksson*. Reykjavík: Almenna bókafélagið.

Stefansson, Vilhjalmur. (1939) *Iceland: The First American Republic*. New York: Doubleday, Doran.

Steffensen, Jón. (1967-1968) "Aspects of Life in Iceland in the Heathen Period." *Saga-Book* (of the Viking Society for Northern Research) 17 (2-3): 178-205.

—————. (1968) "Population: Island." In *Kulturhistorisk leksikon for nordisk middelalder*, volume 8, columns 390-92. Reykjavík: Bókaverzlun Ísafolder.

Steingrímsson, Jón. (1956) *Prosten Jón Steingrimssons självbiografi*. Translated from Icelandic into Swedish by Vimar Ahlström. Lund, Sweden: Carl Blom. (Written 1784-1791.)

Stephensen, Magnús. (1808) *Island i det Attende Aarhundrede*. Copenhagen: Gylendal. (Originally published in Icelandic in 1806.)

Sturlunga Saga. (1946) 2 volumes. Edited by Jón Jóhannesson, Magnús Finnbogason, and Kristján Eldjárn. Reykjavík: Sturlunguútgafan.

Sturluson, Snorri. (1967) *Heimskringla: History of the Kings of Norway*. Translated by Lee M. Hollander. Austin: University of Texas Press.

Sumner, William Graham. (1968) *Folkways*. New York: Mentor. (Originally published in 1906.)

Sundbärg, Gustav. (1970) *Bevölkerungsstatistik Schwedens 1750-1900*. Stockholm: National Central Bureau of Statistics. (Originally published in 1907; reprinted in 1923 and 1970.)

Sveinsson, Einar Ol. (1944) "Lestrarkunnátta Íslendinga í fornöld." *Skírnir* 118- 173-97.

—————. (1953) *The Age of the Sturlungs: Icelandic Civilization in the Thirteenth Century*. Translated by Jóhann S. Hannesson, volume 36 of *Islandica*. Ithaca, N.Y.: Cornell University Press.

—————. (1956) "Läs- och skrivkunnighet på Island under fristatstiden." *Scripta Islandica* 7: 5-20.

—————. (1959) "Celtic Elements in Icelandic Tradition." Paper read at the International Congress of Celtic Studies, Dublin. Reykjavík: National Library of Iceland.

—————. (1971) *Njal's Saga: A Literary Masterpiece*. Edited and translated by Paul Schach. Lincoln: University of Nebraska Press.

Sweden, National Central Bureau of Statistics. (1969) *Historisk statistik för Sverige*, part 1. Stockholm: National Central Bureau of Statistics.

—————. (1974) *Befolkningsförandringar 1973*, part 3. Stockholm: National Central Bureau of Statistics.

Tacitus. (1948) *Germania*. Translated by S. A. Handford. Harmondsworth, England: Penguin.

Taylor, Bayard. (1874) *Egypt and Iceland in the Year 1874*. New York: G. P. Putnam's.

Taylor, Charles Lewis, and Michael C. Hudson. (1972) *World Handbook of Political and Social Indicators*, 2nd ed. New Haven, Conn.: Yale University Press.

Taylor, Paul B., and W. H. Auden (translators). (1970) *The Elder Edda: A Selection*. New York: Vintage Books.

Thompson, Claiborne. (1973) "Moral Values in the Icelandic Sagas: Recent Reevaluations." Unpublished paper. Ann Arbor: Department of Germanic Languages, University of Michigan.

Thompson, Laura. (1969) *The Secret of Culture*. New York: Random House.

Thorarinsson, Sigurður. (1944) "Tefrokronologiska studier på Island." *Geografiska Annaler*, pp. 1-217.

—————. (1956) *The Thousand Year Struggle against Ice and Fire*. Reykjavík: Bókaútgáfa Menningarsjóðs.

—————. (1958) "Iceland in the Saga Period: Some Geographical Aspects." Third Viking Congress reprint. Reykjavík: National Library of Iceland.

—————. (1961) "Population Changes in Iceland." *Geographical Review* 51 (4): 519-33.

—————. (1967) *The Eruptions of Hekla in Historical Times*. Reykjavík: H. F. Leiftur.

Thórðarson, Matthías. (1946) *Litið til Baka, Endurminningar*, volume 1. Copenhagen: Carl Bryrup.

Thoroddsen, Jón. (1890) *Lad and Lass*. Translated by Arthur M. Reeves. London: Sampson Low, Marston, Searle, and Rivington. (Originally published in 1850.)

Thoroddsen, Thorvaldur. (1958-1960) *Ferðabók*, 4 volumes. Reykjavík: Snæbjörn Jónsson.

Thorsteinsson, Björn. (1966) *Ny íslandssaga*. Reykjavík: Heimskringla.

Thorsteinsson, Thorstein. (1915) *Islenzk mannanöfn samkvæmt manntalinu 1. des. 1910*. Reykjavík: Hagskýrslur Islands 5.

—————. (1961) *Islenzk mannanöfn: nafngjafir þriggja áratuga 1921-1950*. Reykjavík: Bókaútgafa menningarsjóðs.

Tomasson, Richard F. (1970) *Sweden: Prototype of Modern Society*. New York: Random House.

—————. (1972) "Iceland on the Brain." *American-Scandinavian Review* 60 (4): 380-91.

—————. (1975a) "The Literacy of the Icelanders." *Scandinavian Studies* 47 (1): 66-93.

—————. (1975b) "Iceland as 'The First New Nation.' " In *Scandinavian Political Studies*, volume 10, pp. 33-51. Oslo: Universitetsforlaget.

—————. (1975c) "The Continuity of Icelandic Names and Naming Patterns." *Names* 23 (4): 281-89.

—————. (1976a) "Premarital Sexual Permissiveness and Illegitimacy in the Nordic Countries." *Comparative Studies in Society and History* 18 (2): 252-70.

—————. (1976b) "Iceland's Survival and the Law of the Sea." *Current History* 70 (4): 155-58, 181-82.

—————. (1977) "A Millennium of Misery: The Demography of the Icelanders." *Population Studies* 31 (3): 405-27.

Torgersen, Johann. (1968) "Population: Norge." In *Kulturhistorisk leksikon for nordisk middelalder*, volume 8, columns 388-90. Reykjavík: Bókaverzlun Ísafolder.

Toynbee, Arnold J. (1962) *A Study of History*, volume 2. New York: Oxford University Press. (Originally published in 1934.)

Trevor-Roper, H. R. (1969) *The European Witch-Craze of the 16th and 17th Centuries*. Harmondsworth, England: Penguin.

Trial, George T. (1945) *History of Education in Iceland*. Cambridge: W. Heffer.

Trollope, Anthony. (1878) *How the "Mastiffs" Went to Iceland*. London: Virtve & Company.

Tryggvason, Baldvin. (1970) *The Mass Media in Iceland*. A lecture to commemorate the 40th anniversary of the Iceland State Broadcasting System. (Mimeographed.)

Turner, Victor W. (1971) "An Anthropological Approach to the Icelandic Saga." In T. O. Beidelman (ed.), *The Translation of Culture*, pp. 349-74. London: Travistock.

Turville-Petre, G. (1951) *The Heroic Age of Scandinavia*. London: Hutchinson's University Library.

—————. (1953) *Origins of Icelandic Literature*. Oxford: Clarendon Press.

—————. (1964) *Myth and Religion of the North*. London: Weidenfeld and Nicolson.

—————. (1972) "Dreams in Icelandic Tradition." In *Nine Norse Studies*, pp. 30-51. London: Viking Society for Northern Research, University College. (Also appeared in *Folklore* 1958 (69): 93-111.)

Undset, Sigrid. (1937) *Kristin Lavransdatter*. Translated by Charles Archer and J. S. Scott. New York: Alfred A. Knopf.

United Nations. (1953) *The Determinants and Consequences of Population Trends*. New York: United Nations.

—————. (1978) *Statistical Yearbook 1977*. New York: United Nations.

Utterström, Gustaf. (1955) "Climatic Fluctuations and Population Problems in Early Modern History." *Scandinavian Economic History Review* 3 (1): 3-47.

—————. (1965) "Two Essays on Population in Eighteenth Century Sweden." In D. V. Glass and D. E. C. Eversley (eds.), *Population in History*, pp. 523-48. London: Edward Arnold.

van den Haag, Ernest. (1969) *The Jewish Mystique*. New York: Dell.

van den Toorn, M. C. (1955) *Ethics and Morals in Icelandic Saga Literature*. Assen, Holland: van Gorcum.

von Troil, Uno. (1780) *Letters on Iceland*, 2nd ed. ("Corrected and improved.") London: J. Robson, W. Richardson, and N. Conant. (Originally published in Sweden in 1777.)

Walters, Thorstina. (1953) *Modern Sagas: The Story of the Icelanders in North America*. Fargo: North Dakota Institute for Regional Studies.

Watt, Ian. (1957) *The Rise of the Novel*. Berkeley: University of California Press.

Wax, Rosalie H. (1969) *Magic, Fate, and History*. Lawrence, Kans.: Coronado Press.

Wessén, Elias. (1965) *De nordiska språken*, 7th ed. Stockholm: Almqvist & Wiksell.

West, John F. (1972) *Faroe: The Emergence of a Nation*. London: C. Hurst.

Whitelock, Dorothy. (1952) *The Beginnings of English Society*. Baltimore: Penguin.

Wikman, K. Robert V. (1937) *Die Einleitung der Ehe. Eine vergleichende ethnosoziologische Undersuchung über die Vorstufe der Ehe in den Sitten des schwedishen Volkstums*. Åbo, Finland: Acta Academiae Aboensis.

Williams, Carl O. (1937) *Thraldom in Ancient Iceland*. Chicago: University of Chicago Press.

Williams, Robin, Jr. (1970) *American Society*, 3rd ed. New York: Alfred A. Knopf.

Withycombe, E. G. (1950) *The Oxford Dictionary of English Names*, 2nd ed. Oxford: Clarendon Press.

Ziegler, Philip. (1969) *The Black Death*. Harmondsworth, England: Penguin.

INDEX

Index

239